MEDIA
ANALYSIS
TECHNIQUES

The China Connection

For Kaye Chon and my colleagues at the School of Hotel and Tourism Management at Hong Kong Polytechnic University, for Zheng Yue and Dean Dong Tiance and my colleagues and students at Jinan University in Guangzhou, and for Junchao Wang and my colleagues and students at Tsinghua University in Beijing. Thanks, so much, to my students for doing such good work and to my former colleagues for your wonderful friendship and hospitality.

MEDIA
ANALYSIS
TECHNIQUES

Fifth Edition

ARTHUR ASA BERGER
San Francisco State University

Los Angeles | London | New Delhi
Singapore | Washington DC

Los Angeles | London | New Delhi
Singapore | Washington DC

FOR INFORMATION:

SAGE Publications, Inc.
2455 Teller Road
Thousand Oaks, California 91320
E-mail: order@sagepub.com

SAGE Publications Ltd.
1 Oliver's Yard
55 City Road
London, EC1Y 1SP
United Kingdom

SAGE Publications India Pvt. Ltd.
B 1/I 1 Mohan Cooperative Industrial Area
Mathura Road, New Delhi 110 044
India

SAGE Publications Asia-Pacific Pte. Ltd.
3 Church Street
#10-04 Samsung Hub
Singapore 049483

Acquisitions Editor: Matt Byrnie
Editorial Assistant: Gabrielle Piccininni
Production Editor: Stephanie Palermini
Copy Editor: Mark Bast
Typesetter: Hurix Systems Pvt. Ltd
Proofreader: Christine Dahlin
Indexer: Arthur Asa Berger
Cover Designer: Candice Harman
Marketing Manager: Liz Thornton

Printed in the United States of America

Library of Congress Cataloging-in-Publication Data

Berger, Arthur Asa, 1933-

  Media analysis techniques / Arthur Asa Berger,
San Francisco State University. — Fifth Edition.

    pages cm
  Includes bibliographical references and index.

  ISBN 978-1-4522-6135-5 (pbk. : alk. paper) —
  ISBN 978-1-4833-1231-6 (web pdf)

  1. Mass media—Methodology. 2. Mass media criticism.
I. Title.

  P91.B43 2013
  302.23'01—dc23

                                        2013025666

This book is printed on acid-free paper.

13 14 15 16 17 10 9 8 7 6 5 4 3 2 1

Brief Contents

Detailed Contents

4 Sociological Analysis   99

Preface to the Fifth Edition

The first edition of this book was published in 1982, long before many of the readers of this edition were born. So it has been around, in various rebirths and reincarnations, for more than 30 years. I learned over the course of my career as a writer that a book is never finished. There are always new things I find to write about, new enhancements of discussions to make, and new topics to explore, so I've spent 30 years updating and revising this book.

The reason this book has lasted so long is because it teaches you techniques of analysis so you can make your own interpretations of pop culture, media, and almost anything else that interests you. Once you learn the methodologies I discuss in the first four chapters of the book, and see how I've applied them in the second section of the book, you'll be able to use them to analyze and interpret any film, television program, print advertisement, video, commercial, or any other aspect of the media and culture that strikes your attention. In academic jargon, we call these works "texts."

Let me say something about why I wrote this book. In 1976, a young student wrote a letter to me, after having read my book *Pop Culture*. Let me quote part of her letter:

> While wandering through the stacks of Central Library, looking for a book for my freshman composition class, my eyes fell upon your book, *Pop Culture*. I took it out and read it the same night. . . . Popular culture inundates us; it *is* us. What have we to strive for except numerous credit cards, a two-car garage, and white teeth. . . . You brought out many things which are always on my mind, always disturbing me. . . . However hard I try to remain aware of popular culture, and criticize it continuously, I am nevertheless sucked in. There is no way not to be drawn into the flow of it. Please write back your ideas on how to study this society in terms of popular culture.

Six years later, in 1982, my answer to this young student's request appeared as my book *Media Analysis Techniques*.

A PEDAGOGICAL PERSPECTIVE ON MEDIA ANALYSIS

I wrote this book to help change the way professors teach courses on popular culture and media criticism and the way students learn to analyze texts and other aspects of mass-mediated culture. I wanted to empower students to make their own critiques of our mass-mediated culture rather than learning what professors, critics, philosophers, and other writers had written about media and the texts carried by the media. The distinction between media and the texts they carry is important. For example, when someone says, "I think I'll watch some television," that person really means he or she is going to watch a particular program. Some television viewers active with their remote controls actually watch a mélange of various shows—in a sense, they might be said to be watching television rather than particular programs. But this is not the way most people watch television, and the fad of skimming television has died out in recent years.

Teaching methods of media analysis has another virtue. Because new kinds of programs and other forms of popular culture are constantly being invented, students who learn the methods of analysis taught in this book can use these concepts to analyze new programs and entertainments as they appear.

And so, in the first part of the book, on techniques of interpretation, I introduce readers to basic concepts in semiotic theory, psychoanalytic theory, Marxist theory, and sociological theory. In the second part of the book, I show students how to apply the theories they learned to various texts.

In order to help my readers learn how to apply the methodologies I discuss, I've developed a number of learning exercises and games found at the end of the book. It's one thing to learn a methodology; it's another thing to learn how to apply the methodology and its concepts to texts and other aspects of mass-mediated culture. There is also a glossary that offers definitions of the most important concepts used in the book.

A MESSAGE TO STUDENTS READING THIS BOOK

Media criticism and analysis is not based on personal opinions about a film, television show, video game, or whatever. You are entitled to your taste, but if you wish to convince others your opinions are worth considering, you have to support them. This book helps you do that; it provides you with what I consider to be the four most important methods of analyzing and interpreting mass-mediated culture. The more you know, the more you see, and after reading this book, you'll have learned a number of concepts that will help you interpret texts and better understand the impact of media on society.

Students sometimes ask me why they should study media analysis when they could be taking "practical" studio or production courses. I explain to them that criticism and creativity are two sides of the same coin. Creative people (directors, artists, musicians, writers, performers, and so on) must be analytic about what they do; they need to understand why their work succeeds when it does and how to avoid repeating their mistakes.

If you are a creative artist and don't know what you're doing, everything you do is, in effect, an accident. That's why artists study art history and film students study film history and film theory. It's the theory that drives the practice—in the arts and in industry as well. A number of my former students have told me that when they got a job, to their surprise, they discovered that the most useful courses they took were media criticism, media aesthetics, and media and communication research methods. Anyone can be taught how to operate a camera (or any other device involved in production). It's what you do with that camera that counts.

In *Media Analysis Techniques*, Fifth edition, I discuss a variety of interesting and provocative texts, such as the cult classic *The Prisoner* (1967–1968), which many of you have probably never heard of. I chose certain episodes from this series because they offer good examples for analysis. If you've never seen the series, you can view many important episodes of *The Prisoner* for free at www.amctv.com/originals/the-prisoner. The series is also available on DVD. A newer version of *The Prisoner* was broadcast in 2009 but was not successful. When I taught media criticism, I would teach my students a methodology, such as semiotics, and then show them an episode of *The Prisoner*. Then I would ask them to write a semiotic analysis of the episode they had just seen. I chose a different episode of *The Prisoner* for each of the four methodologies discussed in this book, but other films, television shows, or other kinds of texts could be used as well.

Television shows and other popular culture texts come and go rather quickly, so if, for example, I picked a television show popular in 2010, it might not be around in 2014. The fact that media texts are born and die so fast affected my choice of topics in the applications section of the book. I chose topics that will be around for a long time, such as the classic film *Murder on the Orient Express*. You can read Agatha Christie's mystery novel, compare it with the film, and now compare the film and the book with a PBS *Masterpiece Theater* television production of the story that takes considerable liberties with the novel. I also have chapters on all-news shows, football, magazine advertisements, video games, and social media, which are an important part of our media diet.

WHAT'S NEW IN THIS EDITION?

I have updated statistics on media and related matters and enhanced my discussions of numerous topics throughout the book. Also new are discussions on the following topics:

- Roland Barthes on semiotics
- The semiotics of branding
- Ideology and the mass media
- The Frankfurt School
- Culture codes and their impact on individuals and societies
- Myths and their use in analyzing texts and other aspects of culture
- Ways the Oedipus complex can be applied to media: James Bond, *Star Wars*
- Postmodernism
- Psychoanalytic interpretation of mysteries
- Herbert Gans on taste cultures

I've also added many new drawings and images to enhance the visual attractiveness of this book. I hope you will find this new edition interesting, entertaining, and useful and that it will help you become a more discriminating user and critic of media. It also will help you better understand the role the media play in your life and in the society in which you live. This book has been translated into Italian, Chinese, Korean, and Spanish.

CODA

I used to tell my students at the beginning of my courses in media criticism, "You'll find that this course will change your lives." The students invariably laughed. But quite a few of my students told me, when I happened to bump into them after they had finished the course, that the methodologies they learned from *Media Analysis Techniques* had affected the way they looked at media and numerous other aspects of their everyday lives. Let me offer an example.

A few years ago I was doing some shopping in a grocery store when a woman of about 40 approached me, smiling. "Dr. Berger," she said. "Don't you remember me? I took your seminar in semiotics 20 years ago." When I got a chance to look at her I recalled having had her as a student, but I didn't remember what course she took from me. Then she said something very interesting: "That semiotics you taught us . . . *it's still with me.*" That's an important point. Once you learn these methodologies, they will stay with you and will have an impact on the way you live.

Acknowledgments

I would like to thank everyone who has helped me with this book since it was first published in 1982. This includes all the editors, editorial assistants, copy editors, art directors, cover designers, and production editors who helped produce the book and the professors who reviewed different editions of it. I had the pleasure of working with my former editor, Margaret Seawell, and my production editor, Astrid Virding, on several editions of *Media Analysis Techniques*; Stephanie Palermini is the production editor for this edition of the book. I also worked with her on the third edition of *Media and Communication Research Methods*.

For this fifth edition, I want to thank my editor, Matt Byrnie; his assistant, Gabrielle Piccininni; and the following reviewers who offered numerous and very helpful suggestions:

Daniel Lepard (Saint Mary's College of California)

Michael Savoie (Valdosta State University)

Dorian Davis (Marymount Manhattan College)

Karen Burke (Southern Connecticut University)

Ann Andaloro (Morehead State University)

I'm also grateful to the professors who have adopted *Media Analysis Techniques* over the years and to the students who have read it and e-mailed me their reactions to the book. My chapter on semiotic analysis appeared in an earlier form in *Understanding Television: Essays on Television as a Social and Cultural Force,* edited by Richard P. Adler. The first edition of *Media Analysis Techniques* was translated into Italian, and the first three editions of the book have been translated into Chinese.

P A R T   I

Techniques of Interpretation

C.S. Peirce

Semiology is the term used for the science of signs explicated by Swiss linguist Ferdinand de Saussure. A different science of signs, semiotics, was first elaborated by American philosopher Charles Sanders Peirce. *Semiotics* is the term now generally used to refer to both systems. Both are concerned with how meaning is generated in texts (films, television programs, and other works of art). In this chapter, after a discussion of the most essential semiotic concepts and some related concerns, semiotic concepts are applied to an episode of a television program. Codes, formulas, and the "language" of television are then addressed.

CHAPTER 1

Semiotic Analysis

I face this assignment—explaining semiotics (also known as semiology) and showing how it can be applied to television and popular culture to those who know little or nothing about the subject—with a certain apprehension. I'm not sure whether semiotics is a subject, a movement, a philosophy, or a cultlike religion. I do know that there is a large and rapidly expanding literature on the subject and that many of the writings of semioticians are difficult to understand and highly technical. You might be interested to know there are more than 12,000 books on semiotics and semiology listed on Amazon.com, and Google lists 827,000 results for semiotics and 3,400,000 for semiology (as of November 8, 2012). We find, then, that there is a considerable amount of interest in this subject.

So my mission, if not impossible, is quite challenging: Not only am I to explain the fundamental notions or elements of semiotics, but I am also to apply them to television and popular culture in general. It is a large undertaking, but I think it can be done. The price I must pay involves a certain amount of simplification and narrowness of focus. I am going to explain the basic principles of semiotics and discuss some sample applications. I hope that after reading this chapter and the annotated bibliography provided, those interested in semiotics will probe more deeply at their own convenience.

A BRIEF HISTORY OF THE SUBJECT

Although interest in signs and the way they communicate has a long history (medieval philosophers, John Locke, and others have shown interest), modern semiotic analysis can be said to have begun with two men: Swiss linguist Ferdinand de Saussure (1857–1913) and American philosopher Charles Sanders Peirce (1839–1914). (Peirce called his system *semiotics*, and that has become the dominant term used for the science of signs. Saussure's *semiology* differs from Peirce's semiotics in some respects, but as both are concerned with signs, I will treat the two as more or less the same in this chapter.)

Saussure's book *A Course in General Linguistics*, first published posthumously in 1915, suggests the possibility of semiotic analysis. It deals with many of the concepts applied to signs and explicated in this chapter. Saussure (1915/1966) wrote, "The linguistic sign unites not a thing and a name, but a concept and a sound-image. . . . I call the combination of a concept and a sound-image a *sign*, but in current usage the term generally designates only a sound-image" (pp. 66–67). His division of the sign into two components, the signifier (or "sound-image") and the signified (or "concept"), and his suggestion that the relationship between signifier and signified is arbitrary, were of crucial importance for the development of semiotics. Peirce, on the other hand, focused on three aspects of signs: their iconic, indexical, and symbolic dimensions (see Table 1.1).

3

Table 1.1	Three Aspects of Signs		
	Icon	*Index*	*Symbol*
Signified by	Resemblance	Causal connection	Convention
Examples	Pictures, statues	Fire–smoke	Flags
Process	Can see	Can figure out	Must learn

From these two points of departure a movement was born, and semiotic analysis spread all over the globe. Important work was done in Prague and Russia early in the 20th century, and semiotics is now well established in France and Italy (where Roland Barthes, Umberto Eco, and many others have done important theoretical as well as applied work). There are also outposts of progress in England, the United States, and many other countries.

Semiotics has been applied, with interesting results, to film, theater, medicine, architecture, zoology, and a host of other areas that involve or are concerned with communication and the transfer of information. In fact, some semioticians, perhaps carried away, suggest that *everything* can be analyzed semiotically; they see semiotics as the queen of the interpretive sciences, the key that unlocks the meanings of all things great and small.

Peirce argued that interpreters have to supply part of the meanings of signs. He wrote that a sign "is something which stands to somebody for something in some respect or capacity" (qtd. in Zeman, 1977, p. 24). This is different from Saussure's ideas about how signs function. Peirce considered semiotics important because, as he put it, "This universe is perfused with signs, if it is not composed exclusively of signs" (qtd. in Sebeok, 1977, p. v). Whatever we do can be seen as a message or, as Peirce would put it, a sign. If everything in the universe is a sign, semiotics becomes extremely important, if not all-important (a view semioticians support wholeheartedly).

Whether this is the case is questionable, but without doubt, all kinds of people have used semiotics in interesting ways. Semiotics has only recently been taken seriously in the United States, however, and it is still not widely used or taught here. There are several reasons for this. First, Americans tend to be pragmatic and down-to-earth; we do not generally find abstruse, theoretical, and formalistic methodologies congenial. Also, a kind of international cultural lag exists; it takes a while for movements important in the European intellectual scene to become accepted, let alone popular, in the United States. It was the French who "discovered" Faulkner and film (as a significant art form), and, although Peirce did important work on semiotics in the United States, Americans had to wait for semiotic analysis to evolve and mature in Europe before it caught their attention.

THE PROBLEM OF MEANING

In what follows, you are going to be learning a new language and concepts that will enable you to look at films, television programs, fashion, foods—almost anything—in ways somewhat different from the manner you may be used to. The basic concern of this discussion is *how meaning is generated and conveyed*, with particular emphasis on television programs (referred to here as *texts*).

But how is meaning generated? The essential breakthrough of semiotics is that it takes linguistics as a model and applies linguistic concepts to other phenomena—texts—and not just to language itself. In fact, semioticians treat texts like languages, in that relationships (rather than things per se) are all-important. To quote Jonathan Culler (1976),

> The notion that linguistics might be useful in studying other cultural phenomena is based on two fundamental insights: first, that social and cultural phenomena are not simply material objects or events but objects or events with meaning, and hence signs; and second, that they do not have essences but are defined by a network of relations. (p. 4)

Signs and relations—these are two of the key notions of semiotic analysis. A text such as *Star Trek* can be thought of as a system of signs, and the meaning in the program stems from the signs and from the system that ties the signs together. This system is generally not obvious and must be elicited from the text.

SOCIAL ASPECTS OF SEMIOTICS: THE INDIVIDUAL AND SOCIETY

Semiotics can help answer this question: What is the relation between individuals and society? Some people believe that only individuals exist and that society is an abstraction. In his book *Ferdinand de Saussure* (revised edition), Jonathan Culler (1986) quotes British philosopher Jeremy Bentham, who wrote, "Society is a fictitious body, the sum of the several members who compose it" (p. 85). Culler made an interesting point about the social dimensions of semiotics. He writes (1986),

> The assumption that society is the result of individuals, each acting in accordance with self-interest, is the very basis of utilitarianism. . . . Saussure, Durkheim, and Freud seem to have recognized that this view gets things the wrong way around. For human beings, society is a primary reality, not just the sum of individual activities . . . and if one wishes to study human behavior, one must grant that there is a social reality. . . . In short, linguistics and psychoanalytic psychology are possible only when one takes the meanings which are attached to and differentiate objects and actions in society as a primary reality. (p. 87)

Because meanings are socially produced, society has to teach individuals what signs mean. Ironically, the idea that there are only individuals and that society is an abstraction is something people learn as a result of growing up in a society. Saussure, Freud, and Durkheim argue that "behavior is made possible by collective social systems individuals have assimilated, consciously or unconsciously" (Culler, 1986, p. 87). We are unaware of the extent to which culture shapes our feelings, actions, and even our identities. Meaning, then, is always social.

SAUSSURE ON THE SCIENCE OF SEMIOLOGY

In semiotic analysis, an arbitrary and temporary separation is made between content and form, and attention is focused on the system of signs that makes up a text. Thus a meal, to stray from television for a moment, is not seen as steak, salad, baked potato, and apple pie but rather as a sign system conveying meanings related to matters such as status, taste, sophistication, and nationality.

Perhaps it would be useful to quote one of the founding fathers of semiotics, Ferdinand de Saussure (1915/1966):

> Language is a system of signs that express ideas, and is therefore comparable to a system of writing, the alphabet of deaf-mutes, symbolic rites, polite formulas, military signals, etc. But it is the most important of all these systems.
>
> *A science that studies the life of signs within society* is conceivable; it would be a part of social psychology and consequently of general psychology; I shall call it *semiology* (from Greek *sêmeîon* "sign"). Semiology would show what constitutes signs, what laws govern them. Since the science does not yet exist, no one can say what it would be; but it has a right to existence, a place staked out in advance. (p. 16, italics in original)

This is the charter statement of semiotics, a statement that opens the study of media to us, for not only can we study symbolic rites and military signals, but we can also study commercials, soap operas, situation comedies, and almost anything else as "sign systems."

Saussure offered another crucial insight relevant here: that concepts have meaning because of relations, and the basic relationship is oppositional. "In language there are only differences," according to Saussure (1915/1966, p. 120). Thus, *rich* doesn't mean anything unless there is *poor*; *happy* unless there is *sad*. "Concepts are purely differential and defined not by their positive content but negatively by their relations with the other terms of the system" (p. 117). It is not "content" that determines meaning, but "relations." The "most precise characteristic" of these concepts "is in being what the others are not" (p. 117). Saussure adds, "Signs function, then, not through their intrinsic value but through their relative position" (p. 118). We can see this readily enough in language, but it also holds for texts. Nothing has meaning in itself!

One thing we must remember when thinking about oppositions is that the opposing concepts must be related in some way. There is always some topic (not always mentioned) that connects them. For example, *rich/WEALTH/poor* or *happy/MENTAL STATE/sad*. I wrote an article a number of years ago in which I discussed blue jeans and what I called the "denimization" phenomenon and contrasted it with wearing fancy clothes (see Table 1.2).

If you believe a pair of terms are oppositional but can find no subject to which both terms relate, there is probably something wrong with the pairing of those terms.

So where are we now? I have suggested that semiotic analysis is concerned with meaning in texts and that meaning stems from relationships—in particular, the relationship among signs. But what, exactly, is a sign?

Table 1.2	Topics and Oppositions of Denim	
Denim	**Relationship**	**Fancy Clothes**
Cheap	COST	Expensive
Rough	TEXTURE	Smooth
Mass produced	FABRICATION	Handmade
Department stores	WHERE PURCHASED	Boutiques

SIGNS

A sign, according to Saussure (1915/1966), is a combination of a concept and a sound-image, a combination that cannot be separated. But because Saussure does not find these terms quite satisfactory, he modifies them slightly:

> I propose to retain the word sign [*signe*] to designate the whole and to replace concept and sound-image respectively by *signified* [*signifié*] and *signifier* [*signifiant*]; the last two terms have the advantage of indicating the opposition that separates them from each other and from the whole of which they are parts. (p. 67)

The relationship between the signifier and signified—and this is crucial—is arbitrary, unmotivated, and unnatural. There is no logical connection between a word and a concept or a signifier and signified, a point that makes finding meaning in texts problematic.

Saussure uses trees as an example. He offers a diagram of the sign in general (see Figure 1.1) and then of the symbol for *tree* (see Figure 1.2). The difference between a sign and a symbol, Saussure suggests, is that a symbol has a signifier that is never wholly arbitrary:

> One characteristic of the symbol is that it is never wholly arbitrary; it is not empty, for there is a rudiment of a natural bond between the signifier and signified. The symbol of justice, a pair of scales, could not be replaced by just another symbol, such as a chariot. (p. 68)

We can now start looking at texts differently and can start thinking about signifiers. How do signifiers generate meaning? And how is it that we know these meanings? If the relationship between signifier and signified is arbitrary, the meanings that signifiers hold must be learned somehow, which implies certain structured associations, or codes, we pick up that help us interpret signs. (I will deal with this subject in more detail shortly.)

Let's look at the television program *Star Trek* in terms of its signifiers and what is signified. Anyone who has seen the program knows that it is a space adventure/science fiction series. We know this because we are told so at the beginning of each episode, when the captain's voice-over describes the mission of the starship *Enterprise*—to explore new worlds and seek out new civilizations, "to boldly go

Figure 1.1   Saussure's Diagram of a Sign

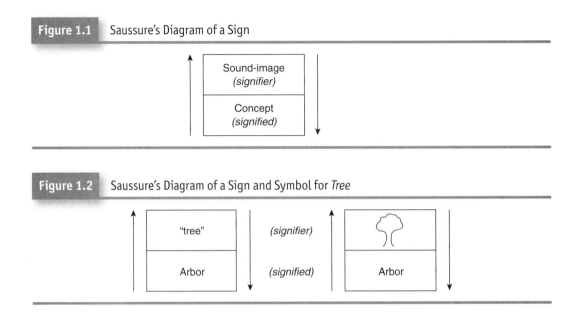

Figure 1.2   Saussure's Diagram of a Sign and Symbol for *Tree*

where no man has gone before." We can say that science fiction adventure is the general "signified" and that a number of "signifiers" show this, including spaceships, futuristic uniforms, ray guns, advanced computer technology, extraterrestrials with strange powers (such as Mr. Spock, whose pointy ears signify he is only partly human), and magic or science.

It is precisely because the program is so rich in signifiers that legions of "Trekkies" are able to hold conventions, wear costumes, sell "phasers," and so on. When you have appropriated the signifiers, you have captured, so to speak, the signified. This, I might point out, is how many commercials work. People purchase the "right" products and assume (or hope) these products will signify a certain social class, status, lifestyle, or what have you.

All of this is based on associations we learn and then carry around with us. Anyone who communicates uses associations between signifiers and signifieds all the time. Because in real life the relationships are arbitrary and change rapidly, one must be on one's toes all the time. Signifiers can become dated and change their significance all too quickly. In a sense, then, we are all practicing semioticians who pay a great deal of attention to signs—signifiers and signifieds—even though we may never have heard these terms before.

Many of us have followed the adventures of a detective who is (like all classic detectives) a first-class semiotician—although we were unaware of this because we didn't know about the existence of semiotics. I am talking about Sherlock Holmes. Inevitably, in a Sherlock Holmes mystery story, some situation arises that puzzles everyone, which Holmes then "solves." He does this by reading signs that others have ignored or have believed to be trivial or inconsequential. In one story, "The Blue Carbuncle," Watson finds Holmes examining a hat that had been brought to him by a policeman. Watson describes the hat: It is old, its lining is discolored, and it is cracked, very dusty, and spotted in places. Holmes asks Watson what he can deduce from the hat about its wearer. Watson examines the hat and says that he can deduce nothing. Holmes then proceeds to describe, in remarkable detail, what the man who owns the hat is like: He is highly intellectual, has had a decline in fortune, his wife no longer loves him, he is sedentary, and he probably doesn't have gas in his house. Watson exclaims, "You are certainly joking, Holmes." Holmes then shows Watson how he reached his conclusions. He examined the hat, noticed certain things about it (signifiers), and proceeded from there (described the implied signifieds).

Figure 1.3 shows that signs are made of signifiers and signifieds.

Table 1.3 offers a list of signifiers found in "The Blue Carbuncle" and suggests their signifieds. Holmes, we see, is an excellent semiotician.

SHERLOCK HOLMES
Consulting Detective

Holmes explains Watson's mistake: "You fail . . . to reason from what you see. You are too timid in drawing your inferences" (Mysterynet.com, n.d.). Watson had said that he saw nothing in the hat. What he did was fail to recognize the signifiers he found for what they were. Such failure is common in readers of detective novels, who pass over vital information and don't recognize it for what it is. Some semioticians, on the other hand, are not timid enough in drawing their inferences, but that is another matter. The meanings in signs, and in texts (which can be viewed as collections of signs), are not always (or even often) evident; they have to be elicited. And too many people are like Watson, I would suggest—not bold enough in drawing inferences.

Figure 1.3 Sign: A Combination of Signifier and Signified

SIGN	
signifier Sound-image	*signified* Concept

Table 1.3 Sherlock Holmes's Examination of Signifiers

Signifiers	Signifieds
Cubic capacity of hat (large brain)	Man is intellectual.
Good-quality hat, but 3 years old	Man hasn't a new hat, suggesting decline in fortune.
Hat not brushed in weeks	Man's wife no longer loves him.
Dust on hat is brown house dust	Man seldom goes out.
Wax stains from candles on hat	No gas in house.

FORMS OF SIGNS

Signs, we must recognize, take a number of forms. Words, of course, are their most familiar form—they stand for things, ideas, concepts, and so on. But signs have a number of other forms we might consider.

Signs and Advertising

We think of signs, most commonly, as connected with advertising—as some kind of display, perhaps with words and images, announcing where businesses are located and the nature of the businesses. All kinds of media are used in the creation of advertising signs: Carved wood, neon and other lighting, molded plastic, paint, and other materials form words and images. We see advertising signs in the windows of supermarkets, announcing "specials." We see signs on restaurants, on stores—wherever there is some kind of commercial activity going on. The nature of such signs—their design and the materials they are made of—generally indicates whether the establishments on which they appear are upscale or down-market.

Many corporations use symbols and icons as a means of establishing some kind of "corporate identity" because it is easy to remember a symbol or icon. The design of a firm's symbols and icons—through the use of color and form and often specific words or numbers—helps give people a sense of what the corporation is like.

Semiotics is of great interest to marketers, who use it in an effort to understand the way consumers think and what goes on in their minds when they contemplate purchasing a product or service.

Branding has now become a major way in which companies get people to purchase their products. Rob Walker (2008) deals with the role of brands in his book *Buying In: What We Buy and Who We Are*. He supports the notion that new generations "see through" advertising. He writes,

> *Everybody* sees right through traditional advertising. You'd have to be an idiot not to recognize that you're being pitched to when watching a thirty-second commercial.
>
> But recognition is not the same as immunity. And what's striking about contemporary youth is not that they are somehow "brand-proof" but that they take for granted the idea that a brand is as good a piece of raw identity as anything else. These are consumers, in fact, who are most amenable to using brands to fashion meaning for themselves—to define themselves, to announce who they are and what they stand for. What this argues, in effect,

is that it is the semiotic significance of brands that is important for young people, and others, who purchase these products—it is their sign value, as revealed by logos in many cases, that is crucial (p. 111, italics in original).

Brands

Brands play an important role in the way people fashion their identities. The advertisement for Prada shown here has a model wearing enormous dark sunglasses that give her a mysterious quality. Her brilliant red lips attract our attention and give the product a kind of sexual allure. People use sunglasses like those from Prada not only to protect themselves from the glare of the sun but also to project a certain kind of image.

In his book *Understanding Media Semiotics*, Marcel Danesi (2002) discusses branding in some detail. He writes,

> Brand names, clearly, do much more than just identify a product. . . . They are constructed to create connotative signification systems for the product. At a practical informational level, naming a product has, of course, a denotative function; i.e. it allows consumers to identify what product they desire to purchase (or not). But at a connotative level, the product's name generates images that go well beyond this simple identifier function. Consider Armani shoes as a specific case-in-point. Denotatively, the name allows us to identify the shoes. . . . However, this is not all it does. The use of the manufacturer's name, rather than some invented name or expression, assigns an aura of craftsmanship and superior quality to the product. The shoes are perceived to be the "work" of an artist (the manufacturer). They constitute, in effect, a "work of shoe art," so to speak, not just an assembly line product for everyone to wear. (pp. 185–186)

I would suggest that many people use brands to create and consolidate their identities and give them a sense of security about their status. Brands are all about differentiation: from other brands and from people who wear other brands or no-name generic products. From my essay "The Branded Self," (2011a) I suggest that, to a certain extent, we are our brands:

> From a semiotic perspective, brands are signifiers that we use to help define ourselves to others and, to a certain degree, without being too reductionistic, we can say that we *are* the brands we assemble to forge a public identity. . . . Brands, from a Peircean perspective, are icons that function as status symbols, among other things.

The fact that our valuations of brands change and our sense of style is open to fashion currents suggests that identities based on brands are open to constant revision and change, which brings the question of postmodernism into the discussion.

The notion that our identities or selves are, in some way, temporary constructions is a central notion in postmodern theory and discussed later in the book.

Material Culture

Objects and artifacts—the things that make up what is known as *material culture*—also serve as signs and can convey a great deal of information. When we "read" people, either in real life or in mass-mediated texts such as advertisements, commercials, and films, we pay a great deal of attention to things like their hairstyles; the brands of sunglasses, clothing, accessories, and shoes they wear; and their body ornaments. All of these objects are signs meant to convey certain notions about what these people are like. In addition, where people are located tells us a great deal about them. If they are in a room, we scrutinize the furniture and other objects in the room, the color of the walls, and any paintings or drawings on the walls.

Some anthropologists study people's garbage to gain information about their lifestyles. Frequently what these "garbologists" find in people's garbage contradicts statements the people themselves have made to these researchers about their tastes and lifestyles.

Objects and Identity

I once conducted an interesting exercise in a semiotics seminar I was teaching. I asked students to go home and find a simple object they believed reflected their character and personality. They were to put that object in an unmarked brown paper bag, write a note about what the object reflected about themselves, and put the note in the bag as well. The first object I pulled out of a brown bag was a large seashell. I asked my students to tell me what they believed the object signified. They said things like "sterility," "death," and "emptiness." Then I took out the slip of paper the student submitted and read what she thought it signified: "beautiful," "simple," "elegant," and "natural." The moral: People don't always correctly interpret the messages you send them, or, to make the point stronger, people *seldom* interpret the messages you send them (by your facial expression, body language, clothes, hairstyle, and whatever) correctly.

Activities and Performances

Thanks to the work of semioticians and psychologists, we now pay a great deal of attention to body language, gestures, facial expressions, and the ways people use their voices. These are all signs we use to "read" people—that is, to attempt to gain some insights into their truthfulness, temperaments, personalities, and values.

Actors, we must remember, are people who pretend to have certain feelings and beliefs, which they "reveal" to audiences by the way they say things and also by their use of facial expression and body language, among other things. Poker players also are concerned with signs. They look for "tells" (body movements and facial expressions) displayed by their opponents that telegraph information about the strength of their hands or intentions to act. The problem poker players face is that sometimes their opponents bluff, or "lie," to them.

Music and Sound Effects

Music and sound effects are used to generate certain responses in audiences—based, in large part, on culturally acknowledged associations between given sounds and certain emotions. A musical phrase or a sound is a signifier, and the emotion it generates is the signified; as is true for all signs, the relation between the signifier and signified is arbitrary and based on convention.

Music and sound effects play an important role in generating a sense of realism in films and television shows. The musical selections and sounds used function as cues that indicate to audiences what they should feel about what they are watching.

SIGNS AND TRUTH

Umberto Eco (1976), a distinguished Italian semiotician, has suggested that (as noted earlier) if signs can be used to tell the truth, they can also be used to lie:

> Semiotics is concerned with everything that can be taken as a sign. A sign is everything which can be taken as significantly substituting for something else. This something else does not necessarily have to exist or to actually be somewhere at the moment in which a sign stands for it. Thus semiotics is in principle the discipline studying everything which can be used in order to lie. If something cannot be used to tell a lie, conversely it cannot be used to tell the truth; it cannot be used "to tell" at all. I think that the definition of a "theory of the lie" should be taken as a pretty comprehensive program for a general semiotics. (p. 7)

Table 1.4 presents some of the ways in which we can (and do) lie—or, to be kinder, mislead others—with signs.

UM BERTO   ECO

Table 1.4	Semiotics as Everyday Signs of Lying
Area	**Misleading Signs**
Wigs	Bald people have hair or people hide their true hair color
Elevator shoes	Short people made taller
Dyed hair	Brunettes become blondes, blondes become redheads, and so on
Implants	Women with small breasts seem to have big ones
Impostors	People pretend to be doctors, lawyers, or whatever
Impersonation	People pretend to be different people, steal "identities"
Malingering	People pretend to be ill
Theater	People pretend to have feelings, beliefs, and the like
Food	Imitation crab, shrimp, lobster, and so on
Words	White lies told so as not to hurt people

We live in a world full of signs that can be used to lie and mislead, and many of us spend a good deal of effort trying to determine whether or not we are being conned. Much of this lying with signs is relatively harmless (e.g., blondes who are naturally brunettes), but in some cases (e.g., the truck driver who pretends to be a doctor) it can be very dangerous. Eco's point is an important one: If signs can be used to communicate, they can be used to communicate lies.

FACIAL EXPRESSIONS AS SIGNS

Psychologist Paul Ekman has done important work on facial expressions. I first encountered his work at an international conference on semiotics. He argues that it is possible to discern when people are lying from examining their facial expressions and detecting extremely minute changes in the way certain facial muscles are activated or not activated. Ekman's research led him to delineate eight universal facial expressions: anger, determination, disgust, fear, neutral, pouting, sadness, and surprise. In a report to the National Science Foundation, he writes the following with Terrence J. Sejnowski (Ekman & Sejnowski, 1992):

Facial expressions provide information about affective state, including both emotions such as fear, anger, enjoyment, surprise, sadness, disgust, and more enduring moods such as euphoria, dysphoria, or irritableness;

cognitive activity such as perplexity, concentration, or boredom;

temperament and personality, including such traits as hostility, sociability, or shyness;

truthfulness, including the leakage of concealed emotions and clues as to when the information provided in words about plans or actions is false;

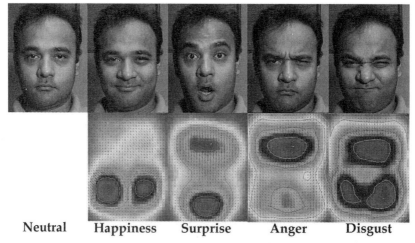

Neutral   Happiness   Surprise   Anger   Disgust

Source: Courtesy of Irfan Essa.

psychopathology, including not only diagnostic information relevant to depression, mania, schizophrenia, and other less severe disorders, but also information relevant to monitoring responses to treatment.

What is remarkable is that the authors suggest it is possible to develop automated systems to monitor facial expressions, which could revolutionize fields such as law, communications, medicine, and education. Faces, they argue, are "windows" into our emotional states, which play an important part in our social lives. The images on page 14 show five of the universal facial expressions and the amount of energy needed to go from neutral to each of the other four. Faces may be windows, but we often find it difficult to see through those windows and determine what a given facial representation actually means.
 Many people find it difficult to distinguish one facial expression from another.

HYPERREALITY

Jean Baudrillard, a postmodernist social theorist (I'll have more to say about postmodernism later in the book), argues that reality has been replaced by what he calls *hyperreality*, which suggests that the sign is now more important than what it stands for. Peter Brooker has this to say in *Cultural Theory: A Glossary* (1999):

Hyperreality. A term associated with the effects of MASS PRODUCTION and REPRODUCTION and suggesting that an object, event, experience so reproduced replaces or is preferred to its original: that the copy is "more real than real." In the writings of the French social philosopher and commentator on POSTMODERNISM, Jean Baudrillard (1929–) and Umberto Eco (1932–), hyperreality is associated especially with cultural tendencies and a prevailing sensibility in contemporary American society.

In Baudrillard's discussion, hyperreality is synonymous with the most developed form of SIMULATION: the autonomous simulacra which is free from all reference to the real. (pp. 121–122)

According to this theory, then, simulations (such as Disneyland) become, ultimately, more important and more real for people than the reality they were designed to imitate. Indeed, Baudrillard has even suggested that Disneyland is now the ultimate reality and the United States an imitation of it! As he wrote in "The Precision of Simulacra" (in *Simulacra and Simulation*):

Everywhere in Disneyland the objective profile of America, down to the morphology of individuals and of the crowd is drawn. All its values are exalted by the miniature and the comic strip. . . . Disneyland exists in order to hide that it is the "real" country, all of the "real" America that *is* Disneyland. . . . Disneyland is presented as imaginary in order to make us believe that the rest is real, whereas all of Los Angeles and the America that surrounds it are no longer real, but belong to the hyperreal order and to the order of simulation. (European Graduate School, n.d.)

Baudrillard spells out how Disney's iconic creations have shaped our consciousness and our perceptions of reality. And, now, Disney owns Marvel Comics and the Star Wars film franchise.

LANGUAGE AND SPEAKING

Earlier, I suggested that texts (such as films, television programs, and commercials) are like languages and that the rules of linguistics can be applied to them. What a language does is enable the communication of information, feelings, ideas, and the like by establishing systems and rules that people learn. And just as there is grammar for writing and speaking, there are grammars for various kinds of texts—and for different media.

Saussure makes a distinction that is useful here—between *language* and *speaking*. Language is a social institution, made up of systematized rules and conventions, that enables us to speak (or, more broadly, to communicate). Each person speaks in his or her own manner, but this speaking is based on the language and rules everyone learns. A television program such as *Star Trek*—and I must point out that most of what I'm discussing here involves narratives—can be viewed as speech intelligible to its audience because the audience knows the language. That is, we know the signs and what they signify; we know the conventions of the genre, or what is acceptable and unacceptable. We know the codes!

Sometimes there is confusion, and the code applied by the creator of a program isn't the code used by members of the audience. In such cases there is bad communication. What makes things complicated is that, generally speaking, people are not consciously aware of the rules and codes and cannot articulate them, although they respond to them. An example of this kind of mix-up is a scene in a film or TV program that is meant to be sad but occasions laughter in audience members.

It is obvious, then, that people are "speaking" all the time, even when they aren't saying anything verbally. Hairstyles, eyeglasses, clothes, facial expressions, posture, gestures, and many other things communicate or "speak" (that is, signify continually) to those sensitive to such things and mindful of signs and signifiers. Maya Pines (1982) has offered this explanation of semiotics:

Everything we do sends messages about us in a variety of codes, semiologists contend. We are also on the receiving end of innumerable messages encoded in music, gestures, foods, rituals, books, movies, or advertisements. Yet we seldom realize that we have received such messages, and would have trouble explaining the rules under which they operate. (p. G1)

What semiotics does, Pines adds, is teach us how to decipher these rules and "bring them to consciousness." I have described the messages we give and receive as similar to speech. Speech always implies, as Saussure (1915/1966) tells us, an established system, although this system is also evolving continually.

Let me offer a brief summary of what we have covered thus far concerning semiotics:

1. Semiotics is concerned with how *meaning* is created and conveyed in texts and, in particular, in narratives (or stories).

2. The focus of semiotics is the *signs* found in texts. Signs are understood to be combinations of *signifiers* and *signifieds*.
3. Because nothing has meaning in itself, the *relationships* among signs are crucial. An analogy can be made with words and grammar: It is the ways in which words are combined that determine what they mean. *Language* is a social institution that tells how words are to be used; *speaking* is an individual act based on language.
4. *Texts* can be viewed as similar to speech and as implying grammars or languages that make the texts meaningful. Codes and conventions make the signs in a narrative understandable and also shape the actions.

CONNOTATION AND DENOTATION

The word *connotation* comes from the Latin *connotare*, "to mark along with," and refers to the cultural meanings that become attached to words (and other forms of communication). A word's connotations involve the symbolic, historic, and emotional matters connected to it. In his book *Mythologies*, Roland Barthes (1972), a distinguished French semiotician, addresses the cultural connotations of many aspects of French daily life, such as steak and *frites*, detergents, Citroen automobiles, and wrestling. In the preface he writes,

> This book has a double theoretical framework: on the one hand an ideological critique bearing on the language of so-called mass culture; on the other, a first attempt to analyzing semiologically the mechanics of this language. I had just read Saussure and as a result acquired the conviction that by treating "collective representations" as sign-systems, one might hope to go further than the pious show of unmasking them and account *in detail* for the mystification which transforms petit-bourgeois culture into a universal nature. (p. 9, italics in original)

The first chapter in the book deals with wrestling. Barthes (1972) explains that what interests him about wrestling is that it is a spectacle of excess in which "a light without shadow generates an emotion

Roland Barthes

without reserve" (p. 15) that is similar to Greek drama and bullfights. Wrestling, he adds, is a spectacle, not a sport, and is an externalized image of torture.

He offers, in his discussion of wrestling, a description of a French wrestler, Thauvin, whose body suggests many things to the French public:

> Each sign in wrestling is therefore endowed with an absolute clarity, since one must always understand everything on the spot. As soon as the adversaries are in the ring, the public is overwhelmed with the obviousness of the roles. As in the theatre, each physical type expresses to excess the part which has been assigned to the contestant. Thauvin, a fifty-year-old with an obese and sagging body, whose type of asexual hideousness always inspires feminine nicknames, displays in his flesh the characters of baseness, for his part is to represent what, in the classical concept of the *salaud*, the "bastard" (the key-concept of any wrestling match), appears as organically repugnant. (pp. 16–17)

Barthes mentions that the French call Thauvin *la barbaque*, which means "stinking meat." Thauvin's very body, then, is a sign that generates any number of strong feelings on the part of French viewers of professional wrestling. We could say the same, as well, for the many villains and heroes in American professional wrestling. Barthes's purpose, he says, is to take the world of "what-goes-without-saying" (1972, p. 11) and show this world's connotations and, by extension, its ideological foundations.

Denotation, on the other hand, refers to the literal or explicit meanings of words and other phenomena. For example, *Barbie Doll* denotes a toy doll, first marketed in 1959, that was originally 11.5 inches high, had measurements of 5.25 inches at the bust, 3 inches at the waist, and 4.25 inches at the hips. The connotations of *Barbie Doll*, in contrast, are the subject of some controversy. Some scholars have suggested that the arrival of the Barbie Doll signified the end of motherhood as a dominant role for women and the importance of consumer culture, because Barbie is a consumer who spends her time buying clothes and having relationships with Ken and other dolls. The Barbie Doll doesn't prepare little girls for the traditional role of motherhood in the way other kinds of dolls do—allowing them to imitate their mothers in caring for their "children." Table 1.5 presents a comparison of connotation and denotation.

A great deal of media analysis involves discovering the connotations of objects and symbolic phenomena and of the actions and dialogue of the characters in texts—that is, the meanings these may have for audiences—and tying these meanings to social, cultural, ideological, and other concerns.

Table 1.5 Comparison of Connotation and Denotation

Connotation	Denotation
Figurative	Literal
Signified(s)	Signifier(s)
Inferred	Obvious
Suggests meanings	Describes
Realm of myth	Realm of existence

THE SYNCHRONIC AND THE DIACHRONIC

The distinction between the synchronic and the diachronic is yet another legacy from Saussure. As he uses the terms, *synchronic* means analytic and *diachronic* means historical, so a synchronic study of a text looks at the relationships among its elements, and a diachronic study looks at the way the narrative evolves. Another way of putting this is that in conducting a synchronic analysis of a text, one looks for the pattern of paired oppositions buried in the text (the paradigmatic structure), whereas in doing diachronic analysis, one focuses on the chain of events (the syntagmatic structure) that forms the narrative.

Saussure (1915/1966) makes a distinction between static (synchronic) linguistics and evolutionary (diachronic) linguistics:

> All sciences would profit by indicating more precisely the coordinates along which their subject matter is aligned. Everywhere distinctions should be made . . . between (1) *the axis of simultaneity* . . . which stands for the relations of coexisting things and from which the intervention of time is excluded; and (2) *the axis of successions* . . . , on which only one thing can be considered at a time but upon which are located all the things on the first axis together with their changes. (pp. 79–80, italics in original)

To explain the differences between these two perspectives, Saussure suggests the reader imagine a plant. If one makes a longitudinal cut in the stem of a plant, one sees the fibers that make up the plant, but if one makes a cross-sectional cut, one can see the plant's fibers in relationship to each other.

Table 1.6 contrasts synchronic analysis and diachronic analysis. For example, a researcher might focus on how video games evolved (thus using a diachronic perspective) or might compare the most important video games being played at a particular moment (thus using a synchronic perspective). Or the researcher could first use a diachronic perspective, to establish context, and then do a synchronic analysis, focusing on some important games. Claude Lévi-Strauss and Vladimir Propp are mentioned in this table as exemplars of these two styles of analysis. I will explain the ideas these two theorists developed in the sections that follow.

Table 1.6   Comparison of Synchronic Analysis and Diachronic Analysis

Synchronic Analysis	Diachronic Analysis
Simultaneity	Succession
Static	Evolutionary
Instant	Historical perspective
Relations in a system	Relations in time
Focus on analysis	Focus on development
Paradigmatic	Syntagmatic
Claude Lévi-Strauss	Vladimir Propp

SYNTAGMATIC ANALYSIS

A syntagm is a chain, and in syntagmatic analysis, a text is examined as a sequence of events that forms some kind of narrative. In this section I discuss the ideas of Vladimir Propp, a Russian folklorist who wrote a pioneering book in 1928 titled *Morphology of the Folktale.* Morphology is the study of forms—that is, the components of something and their relationships to each other and to the whole.

Propp (1928/1968), whose work involved a group of fairy tales, has described his method as follows:

The Prisoner

We are undertaking a comparison of the themes of these tales. For the sake of comparison we shall separate the component parts of fairy tales by special methods; and then, we shall make a comparison of the tales according to their components. The result will be a morphology (i.e., a description of the tale according to its component parts and the relationship of these components to each other and to the whole). (p. 19)

Propp refers to the essential or basic narrative unit in his study as a "function":

Function is understood as an act of a character, defined from the point of view of its significance for the course of the action. (p. 21)

Propp's observations may be briefly formulated in the following manner:

1. Functions of characters serve as stable, constant elements in a tale, independent of how and by whom they are fulfilled. They constitute the fundamental components of a tale.
2. The number of functions known to the fairy tale is limited.
3. The sequence of functions is always identical.
4. All fairy tales are of one type in regard to their structure. (pp. 21–23)

Propp's work has great significance for this discussion, for we can adopt and adapt his ideas to films, television stories, comics, and all kinds of other narratives. Whether or not Propp was correct in all of his assertions is not of great importance for our purposes. His concept of functions can be applied to all kinds of texts with interesting results.

For each of his functions, Propp gives a summary of its essence, an abbreviated definition, and a conventional sign or designation. Some of the functions are rather complicated and have numerous subcategories, all of which fulfill the same task. Propp's (1928/1968) description of his first function is quoted here so that you can see what a simple one looks like and how he develops each (the numbers in parentheses refer to specific fairy tales Propp studied):

I. ONE OF THE MEMBERS OF A FAMILY ABSENTS HIMSELF FROM HOME. (Definition: *absentation.* Designation: β.)

1. *The person absenting himself can be a member of the older generation* (b_1). Parents leave for work (113). "The prince had to go on a distant journey, leaving his wife to the care of strangers" (265). "Once, he (a merchant) went away to foreign lands" (17). Usual forms of absentation: going to work, to the forest, to trade, to war, "on business."
2. *An intensified form of absentation is represented by the death of parents* (b_2).
3. *Sometimes members of the younger generation absent themselves* (b_3). They go visiting (101), fishing (108), for a walk (137), out to gather berries (244). (p. 26)

This is one of the briefer descriptions Propp provides for his functions; for instance, Function 9 (about a villain doing harm or injury to a member of a family) has 19 subcategories.

Even though you do not know all the subcategories of each function, you can still use Propp's 31 functions to conduct syntagmatic analyses of selected texts (Table 1.7 displays a simplified and slightly modified list of these functions and gives a brief description of each). What will become obvious to you as you use these functions is the extent to which a lot of contemporary stories contain many of Propp's functions. His definition of the hero as "that character who either directly suffers from the action of the villain . . . or who agrees to liquidate the misfortune or lack of another person" is also worth considering (p. 50). Heroes also, Propp tells us, are supplied with magical agents or helpers that they make use of in difficult situations.

Table 1.7 Propp's Functions

α	*Initial situation*	Introduced are members of a family or the hero.
β	*Absentation*	One of the members of the family absents himself from home.
γ	*Interdiction*	An interdiction is addressed to the hero.
δ	*Violation*	An interdiction is violated.
ε	*Reconnaissance*	The villain makes an attempt at reconnaissance.
η	*Delivery*	The villain receives information about his victim.
ζ	*Trickery*	The villain attempts to deceive his victim.
θ	*Complicity*	The victim submits to deception, unwittingly helps his enemy.
A	*Villainy*	The villain causes harm or injury to a member of a family.
A	*Lack*	One member of a family lacks something or wants something.
B	*Mediation*	Misfortune is made known, hero is dispatched.
C	*Counteraction*	Seekers agree to decide on counteraction.
↑	*Departure*	The hero leaves home.
D	*1st function of donor*	Hero is tested, receives magical agent or helper.
E	*Hero's reaction*	Hero reacts to actions of the future donor.

(Continued)

Table 1.7	(Continued)	
F	*Receipt of magic agent*	Hero acquires the use of a magical agent.
G	*Spatial transference*	Hero is led to object of search.
H	*Struggle*	Hero and villain join in direct combat.
J	*Branding*	Hero is branded.
I	*Victory*	Villain is defeated.
K	*Liquidation*	Initial misfortune or lack is liquidated.
↓	*Return*	The hero returns.
Pr	*Pursuit*	A chase: The hero is pursued.
Rs	*Rescue*	Hero is rescued from pursuit.
O	*Unrecognized arrival*	The hero, unrecognized, arrives home or in another country.
L	*Unfounded claims*	A false hero presents unfounded claims.
M	*Difficult task*	A difficult task is proposed to the hero.
N	*Solution*	The task is resolved.
Q	*Recognition*	The hero is recognized.
Ex	*Exposure*	The false hero or villain is exposed.
T	*Transfiguration*	The hero is given a new appearance.
U	*Punishment*	The villain is punished.
W	*Wedding*	The hero is married and ascends the throne.

There are seven dramatis personae in Propp's scheme:

1	*Villain*	Fights with hero.
2	*Donor*	Provides hero with magical agent.
3	*Helper*	Aids hero in solving difficult tasks.
4	*Princess* *Her father*	Sought-after person. Assigns difficult tasks.
5	*Dispatcher*	Sends hero on his mission.
6	*Hero*	Searches for something or fights with villain.
7	*False hero*	Claims to be hero but is unmasked.

Propp's functions can be applied to an episode of the television program *The Prisoner* to show how Propp's work can help uncover the morphology of a narrative text. *The Prisoner* is a remarkable existential television series first broadcast a number of years ago and today is regarded by many as a classic.

It is about a man who, having resigned from some mysterious (apparently espionage) organization, has been abducted and is being held against his will in "the Village," a strange resortlike place on an island, where everyone is called by a number rather than by name. The hero is locked into battles with various adversaries, each called Number Two, in the 17 episodes of the series. At the end of the series, the prisoner (Number Six) escapes from the Village, which he destroys, and returns to his apartment in London. Episodes of *The Prisoner* can be viewed at www.amctv.com/originals/the-prisoner.

The first episode of *The Prisoner* is titled "Arrival." It opens with a scene in which the hero, unnamed, is shown resigning. He is in an office with some officials; he pounds the table and leaves. He returns to his apartment and begins to pack, but as he does, he is gassed and passes out. He awakes in the Village, a totalitarian society where everyone has numbers instead of names; he is told that he is Number Six. The prisoner is pitted against Number Two, who wishes to find out why Six resigned. Six tries to escape by running along the seashore but is captured by a huge and terrifying rubber sphere, Rover, that is kept beneath the sea and is controlled by Number Two. Six is sent to the Village hospital, where he finds himself sharing a room with an old friend, also a spy. While Six is being examined by a doctor, there is a commotion outside the exam room. Six rushes back to his room and is told that his friend has committed suicide. After Six is released from the hospital, he notices a woman acting strangely at his friend's burial procession. Six talks with the woman, who tells him she was the friend's lover and that they were planning to escape from the island. She has a watch with a special device that will enable Six to evade Rover and steal a heli-

copter. Six takes the watch and "escapes" via the helicopter, but shortly after he has left the island he discovers the helicopter is rigged and controlled by Number Two. The episode ends with the helicopter returning to the Village and the spy friend, who had supposedly committed suicide, telling Number Two that Six is an unusual person who will need special treatment.

VLADIMIR   PROPP

Although *The Prisoner* is not a fairy tale per se, it contains many of the same elements as a fairy tale. Many contemporary narrative texts are modified and updated fairy tales that, to a considerable degree, resemble the tales Propp has described. Table 1.8 lists a few of the Proppian functions that can be applied to events in "Arrival." This analysis could be extended and made more detailed through the use of some of Propp's subcategories, but I only want to suggest the possibilities of this kind of analysis here.

Table 1.8   Proppian Functions in "Arrival" Episode of *The Prisoner*

Propp's Function	Symbol	Event
Initial situation	α	Hero shown resigning.
Interdiction violated	δ	(implicit) Spies can't resign.
Villain causes injury	A	Hero abducted to the Village.
Receipt of a magical agent	F	Woman gives Six watch with device.
False hero exposed	Ex	Friend shown with Two.

There are two important things to be learned from syntagmatic analysis. First, narratives, regardless of kind or genre, are composed of certain functions (or elements) essential for the creation of a story. Propp's work leads us, then, to an understanding of the nature of formulas. Second, the order in which events take place in a narrative is of great importance. There is a logic to narrative texts, and the arrangement of elements in a story can greatly affect our perception of what anything "means." That, in fact, is the purpose served by editing.[1]

Let me offer a quotation that uses Proppian analysis to make a point about James Bond novels. In Tony Bennett and Janet Woollacott's *Bond and Beyond: The Political Career of a Popular Hero* (1987) they write about Umberto Eco's analysis of the Bond phenomenon:

> Just as Vladimir Propp argued that "all fairytales are of one type in regard to their structure," so Eco argues that, at the level of plot, the Bond novels are structurally uniform. Indeed, he further contends that the "Bond formula" is merely a variant of the archetypal structure of the traditional fairy tale. According to Propp, the basic plot elements of the fairytale consists of functions performed by its central protagonists—the hero, the villain, the princess—in developing the course of action within the story. Likewise, Eco argues that the main characters of the Bond novels are motivated by the functions assigned to them, functions which he likens to a series of moves required by the rules of the game. (p. 70)

This would suggest that some of the appeal of the Bond novels and films is due to their being modernized and updated fairy tales, and thus they play a role in our psyches similar to that of conventional fairy tales. I have more to say about James Bond in my chapter on psychoanalytic theory.

PARADIGMATIC ANALYSIS

The paradigmatic analysis of a text involves a search for a hidden pattern of oppositions buried in it that generate meaning. As Alan Dundes writes in his introduction to Propp's *Morphology of the Folktale* (1928/1968), the paradigmatic form of structural analysis

> seeks to describe the pattern (usually based upon an a priori binary principle of opposition) which allegedly underlies the folkloristic text. This pattern is not the same as the sequential structure at all. Rather, the elements are taken out of the "given" order and are regrouped in one or more analytic schema. (p. xi)

We search for binary or polar oppositions because meaning is based on the establishment of relationships, and the most important kind of relationship in the production of meaning in language is that of opposition.

We return here to Saussure's (1915/1966) notion that "in language there are only differences" (p. 129). Or, as Jonathan Culler (1976) puts it, "Structuralists have generally followed Jakobson and taken the binary opposition as a fundamental operation of the human mind basic to the production of meaning" (p. 15). Thus some kind of systematic and interrelated sets of oppositions can be elicited in all texts, whether they are narrative or not. Many people are not conscious of these oppositions—and sometimes they are only implied—but without differences, there is no meaning.

Some people argue that the oppositions and other structures semioticians elicit from texts are not really there. These critics assert that semioticians do not *discover* systems of relationships but, instead, *invent* them. This controversy is sometimes known as the "hocus-pocus" versus the "God's truth" problem. I believe the oppositions semioticians find in texts are actually there; not only that, but they *have* to be there. Finding meaning without discerning polar oppositions is like listening to the sound of one hand clapping.

Given that I've used *The Prisoner* in an earlier example, let me offer a paradigmatic analysis of "Arrival." The most important opposition found in this episode is between freedom and control, and I use these two concepts as heading the list of oppositions displayed in Table 1.9, which shows the ideational structure on which the narrative is hung.

Claude Lévi-Strauss, a distinguished French anthropologist, has suggested that a syntagmatic analysis of a text reveals the text's manifest meaning and that a paradigmatic analysis reveals the text's latent meaning. The manifest structure of a text consists of what happens in it, whereas the latent structure consists of what the text is about. Or, to put it another way, when we use a paradigmatic approach, we are not so much concerned with what characters *do* as with what they *mean*.

Lévi-Strauss studied the ways narratives are organized or structured and how their organization generates meaning. He has done a great deal of work (much of it highly controversial) on myths, kinship systems, and related matters. According to Lévi-Strauss (1967), myths are composed of fundamental or minimal units, or "mythemes," that combine in certain ways to give messages. Mythemes can be expressed in short sentences that describe important relationships. For example, in the case of the Oedipus myth, Lévi-Strauss offers mythemes such as "Oedipus kills his father, Laius," "Oedipus marries his mother," and "Oedipus immolates the Sphinx." These mythemes and their rules of combination (what Lévi-Strauss calls "bundles," or relations) are the stuff of which myths are made. Myths are

Table 1.9   Polar Oppositions in "Arrival"

Freedom	Control
Number Six	Number Two
The individual	The organization
Willpower	Force
Escape	Entrapment
Trust	Deception

important not only because they function as charters for the groups that tell and believe them but also because they are the keys to the ways in which the human mind works.

What is most significant about myths is the stories they tell, not their style. Thus the structured relationships among the characters and what these relationships ultimately mean should be the focus, not the way a story is told. Myths, Lévi-Strauss asserts, give coded messages from cultures to individuals, and the task of the analyst is to discover these masked or hidden messages by "cracking the code." In the final analysis, this involves eliciting the paradigmatic structure of a text.[2]

In making a paradigmatic analysis of a text, an analyst should take care to avoid certain possible errors. First, the analyst must be sure to elicit true oppositions (as opposed to mere negations). For example, I would suggest that *poor* is the opposite of *rich* and should be used instead of something such as *unrich* or *nonrich*. Second, the analyst should be sure that the oppositions elicited are tied to characters and events in the text.

If I had offered a more detailed synopsis of "Arrival," I would have been able to undertake more detailed syntagmatic and paradigmatic analyses of this story, and my lists of Proppian functions and polar oppositions (Tables 1.8 and 1.9) would have been longer. I might add that it is useful for the analyst to explicate the terms in his or her list of oppositions and to explain why each pair is included.

INTERTEXTUALITY

Intertextuality is a term about which there is a good deal of controversy. For purposes of this discussion, it refers to the use in texts (consciously or unconsciously) of material from other previously created texts. Parody, or the humorous imitation of a text, is a good example of the conscious reuse of material from a text. In order for parody to be effective, audience members must be familiar with the original text, so that they can appreciate the ways in which it is being ridiculed. There are also parodies of *style* (e.g., contests are held in which entrants compete to produce the most ridiculous imitation of Hemingway's writing style) and parodies of *genre*, which play upon the basic plot structures of formulaic kinds of texts, such as soap operas and westerns.

Woody Allen (1978) offers a superb parody of course descriptions in his "Spring Bulletin":

> *Philosophy I:* Everyone from Plato to Camus is read. The following topics are covered: Ethics: The categorical imperative and six ways to make it work for you. Aesthetics: Is art the mirror of life, or what? . . . Epistemology: Is knowledge knowable? If not, how do we know this? The Absurd: Why existence is considered silly, particularly for men who wear brown and white shoes. Manyness and oneness are studied as they relate to otherness. (Students achieving oneness will move ahead to twoness.) (p. 44)

The humor here relies on our being able to compare Allen's parody with typical college catalog course descriptions. Here, Allen spoofs both the genre and the style of writing found in catalogs.

Another kind of conscious intertextuality takes place when screenwriters or film directors create scenes recognizable as "quotations" from other films. Avant-garde filmmakers and other artists often consciously "quote" from the works of other artists—they patch together bits and pieces from well-known (or not so well-known) works and create new works. Thus, as Marcel Danesi points out in

Understanding Media Semiotics (2002), the film *Blade Runner* contains many allusions to biblical themes, such as the search for a creator. Another example of intertextuality is the Leonard Bernstein/Stephen Sondheim musical *West Side Story*, which is based on Shakespeare's *Romeo and Juliet*. Some television critics have suggested that the short-lived 2003 television show *Skin* was yet another modernized version of *Romeo and Juliet*.

One of the most famous television commercials ever made, for the Macintosh computer in 1984, contains an important use of intertextuality. In this commercial, directed by Ridley Scott, there is a scene in which a blonde woman, carrying a sledgehammer, races into a large auditorium, pursued by helmeted police. In the auditorium are the inmates from the totalitarian institution in which the action is taking place. They are gazing at a huge screen in which someone is talking to them, but what he is saying is gibberish. The woman tosses her sledgehammer at the screen and it explodes. With that, we are to assume, the power of the people who control the institution is destroyed. This episode can be seen as a retelling of the David and Goliath story in the Old Testament, and the power of the commercial is tied to its connection to this story. Those interested in seeing this commercial can find it on YouTube.

Unconscious intertextuality involves textual materials of many kinds (plots, themes, kinds of characters, and so on) that become common currency, pervading cultures and finding their way into new texts without the creators' knowledge. Some literary theorists argue, in fact, that all creative work is, ultimately, intertextual. That is, all texts are related to other texts, to varying degrees.

DIALOGICAL THEORY

Russian semiotician Mikhail Bakhtin has suggested that language is "dialogic," by which he means that when we speak, what we say is tied both to things that have been said before and to utterances we expect to be made in the future. As he explains in his book *The Dialogic Imagination: Four Essays* (1981),

> The word in living conversation is directly, blatantly, oriented toward a future answer-word: it provokes an answer, anticipates it and structures itself on the answer's direction. Forming itself in an atmosphere of the already spoken, the word is at the same time determined by that which has not yet been said but which is needed and in fact anticipated by the answering word. Such is the situation in any living dialogue. (p. 280)

Mikhail Bakhtin

If we take this notion and move it from speech to texts, we gain some insight into intertextuality. Bakhtin discusses the relationships among texts, including what he calls the matter of "quotation" (which we now call intertextuality) in the Middle Ages:

The role of the other's word was enormous at that time; there were quotations that were openly and reverently emphasized as such, or that were half-hidden, completely hidden, half-conscious, unconscious, correct, intentionally distorted, deliberately reinterpreted and so forth. The boundary lines between someone else's speech and one's own speech were flexible, ambiguous, often deliberately distorted and confused. Certain types of texts were constructed like mosaics out of the texts of others. . . . One of the best authorities on medieval parody . . . states outright that the history of medieval literature and its Latin literature in particular "is the history of appropriation, re-working and imitation of someone else's property"—or as we would say, of another's language, another's style, another's word. (p. 69)

The "appropriation" of the work of others that took place in the Middle Ages is similar to what happens today. This is because, in part, many inhabitants of the Western world share a common cultural heritage that informs the work of artists and is reflected in texts even when there is no conscious decision made to quote from other texts or sources.

METAPHOR AND METONYMY

Metaphor and metonymy are two important ways of transmitting meaning. In metaphor, a relationship between two things is suggested through the use of *analogy*. Thus we might say, "My love is a red rose." One of the most common metaphoric forms is the simile, in which *like* or *as* is used and a comparison is suggested. For example, "He's as sharp as a razor" or "She's as good as an angel."

Sometimes we incorporate metaphors and similes into the verbs we use. Consider the following examples:

The ship *cut* through the waves. (The ship is like a knife.)

The ship *danced* through the waves. (The ship is like a dancer.)

The ship *raced* through the waves. (The ship is like a race car.)

The ship *pranced* through the waves. (The ship is like a horse.)

The ship *plowed* through the waves. (The ship is like a plow.)

In these examples, the ship takes on different identities. These verbs convey information different from that in the statement "The ship sailed through the waves."

In metonymy, a relationship is suggested that is based on *association*, which implies the existence of codes in people's minds that enable them to make the proper connections. As James Monaco (1977) notes,

A metonymy is a figure of speech in which an associated detail or notion is used to invoke an idea or represent an object. Etymologically, the word means "substitute naming" (from the Greek *meta*, involving transfer, and *onoma*, name). Thus in literature we can speak of the king (and the idea of kingship) as "the crown." (p. 135)

Table 1.10	Metaphor and Metonymy Contrasted

Metaphor	Metonymy
Meta (transfer, beyond)–*phor* (to bear)	*Meta* (transfer)–*onoma* (name)
Chaplin eats shoelaces like spaghetti.	Rover kills one of the villagers on command of Number Two.
Simile: important subcategory in which comparison is made using *like* or *as.*	*Synecdoche:* important subcategory in which a part stands for the whole or the whole for a part.
"No man is an island."	Red suggests passion.
Costume of Spider-Man.	Uncle Sam "stands for" the United States.
Long, thin objects can be seen as penises.	Bowler hat implies Englishman; cowboy hat implies the American West.

A common form of metonymy is a synecdoche, in which a part stands for the whole or vice versa.

A good example of metaphor in film is the famous scene in Chaplin's *The Gold Rush* in which he cooks his boots and eats the shoelaces as if they were spaghetti. A good example of metonymy is found in *The Prisoner* in the form of the monstrous balloon Rover, which symbolizes the oppressive regime that runs the Village. Table 1.10 compares and contrasts metaphor and metonymy.

Generally speaking, metaphor and metonymy are often mixed together, and sometimes a given object might have both metaphoric and metonymic significance. The distinction is important, because it enables us to see more clearly how objects and images (as well as language) generate meaning. And, in the case of metonymy, it becomes obvious that people carry *codes* around in their heads—highly complex patterns of associations that enable them to interpret metonymic communication correctly. Just as you can't tell the players without a program, you can't understand the meaning of most things without knowing the codes.

CODES

Codes are highly complex patterns of associations that all members of a given society and culture learn. These codes, or "secret structures" in people's minds, affect the ways individuals interpret the signs and symbols they find in the media and the ways they live. From this perspective, cultures are codification systems that play an important (although often unperceived) role in people's lives. To be socialized and to be a member of a culture means, in essence, to be taught a number of codes, most of which are quite specific to a person's social class, geographic location, ethnic group, and so on, although these subcodings may exist within a more general code—"American character," for example.

We all recognize that in order for people to be able to drive safely on the highways, a code is needed. This code is a collection of rules that tells drivers what they should and should not do in all conceivable situations. In like manner, we are all taught (often informally) other codes that tell us what to do in various situations and what certain things "mean." Obviously, we carry these rules and understandings about life over to our exposure to media productions, or to *mass-mediated culture*.

It is quite possible, then, for misunderstandings to arise between those who create television programs and those who view them. Umberto Eco (1972) has even suggested that "aberrant decoding . . . is the rule in the mass media" (p. 106). This is because different people bring different codes to given messages and thus interpret the messages in different ways. As Eco puts it,

> Codes and subcodes are applied to the message [read "text"] in the light of a general framework of cultural references, which constitutes the receiver's patrimony of knowledge: his ideological, ethical, religious standpoints, his psychological attitudes, his tastes, his value systems, etc. (p. 115)

Eco offers some examples that suggest how such aberrant decodings might have taken place in the past: foreigners in strange cultures who do not know the codes or people who interpret messages in terms of their own codes rather than the codes in which the messages were originally cast. This was, Eco notes, before the development of mass media, when aberrant decodings were the exception, not the rule. With the development of mass media, however, the situation changed radically, and aberrant decoding became the norm. According to Eco, this is because of the wide gap between those who create and generate the material carried by the media and those who receive this material.

The transmitters of messages, because of their social class, educational level, political ideologies, worldviews, ethos, and so on, do not share the same codes as their audiences, who differ from the message transmitters in some or even most of the above respects and who interpret the messages they receive from their own perspectives. The work of British sociolinguist Basil Bernstein (1977) illustrates how this might be possible. His research led him to conclude that in Britain, children learn either of two linguistic codes, the "elaborated" code or the "restricted" code, and that the code a child learns plays a major role in his or her future development and adult life. Table 1.11 illustrates the differences between these two codes.

Table 1.11	Elaborated and Restricted Codes
Elaborated Code	**Restricted Code**
Middle classes	Working classes
Grammatically complex	Grammatically simple
Varied vocabulary	Uniform vocabulary
Complex sentence structure	Short, repetitious sentence structure
Careful use of adjectives and adverbs	Little use of adjectives and adverbs
High-level conceptualization	Low-level conceptualization
Logical	Emotional
Use of qualifications	Little use of qualifications
Users aware of code	Users unaware of code

The code a child learns becomes the matrix through which his or her thought is filtered; thus the two codes lead to very different value systems, belief systems, attitudes about the world, and so on. Bernstein's work enables us to see how language shapes us and demonstrates the enormous problems we face in trying to resocialize the hard-core poor and other disadvantaged persons in society.

It has been said that the United States and Great Britain are two nations separated by a common language. In the same manner, the different classes in Britain, with their different codes, seem to be separated. When we move from language to the mass media, where in addition there are aesthetic codes, iconic codes, and more disparate audience members, we can see that it is quite remarkable that the media can communicate with any degree of effectiveness.

CULTURE CODES

I would suggest that what we think of as "culture" can also be understood as a collection of codes we learn when we grow up in a society that tell us how to think, how to behave, what to eat and when to eat it, and all kinds of other things. As I explain in the first chapter of my book *Culture Codes* (2012),

> In this book I suggest that cultures can be thought of as collections of codes that shape our behavior.

> Codes that we are aware of we call "rules" or "laws," but codes that we do not recognize but which shape our thinking and behavior in many areas I call *culture codes*. . . . We know that genetic codes play a major role in shaping our physical bodies and in many illnesses that we are plagued with. In the same light, *culture codes* play a major role in our thoughts and behaviors, even though we generally are not aware of the existence of these codes. (p. 7)

Let me offer an example. In the fall of 2012 I spent a month in Argentina lecturing on semiotics and media analysis. People in Argentina, as someone there explained to me, eat four meals a day: breakfast in the morning, lunch anywhere from noon to 2:00 p.m. or so, a snack around 5:00 p.m., and dinner around 10:00 p.m. but sometime as late as midnight. A professor in Buenos Aires told me that he and his wife often go to the movies at 10:00 p.m. and then have dinner at midnight, after the film. This is considerably different from when people in the United States eat dinner, usually from 5:00 to 7:00 p.m., though later for dinner parties. One culture code that people in the United States and Argentina agree on is that steak should be broiled or grilled and never boiled. In the United States, we typically have our salads before we eat our steaks, while in France and many other countries, salads are eaten after the main course.

In my book I discuss, in some detail, many of the following topics:

- Characteristics of codes: coherence, covertness, clarity, concreteness, continuity, comprehensiveness, and so on
- Manifestations of codes: personality (in psychology), social roles (in social psychology), institutions (in sociology), ideologies (in political science), rituals (in anthropology)

- Problems: creation of codes, modification of codes, conflicts among codes, countercodes, codes and rules
- Codes in popular culture: formulas in spy stories, detective stories, westerns, science fiction adventures, pop music, fanzines, girlie fiction, horror stories, gothic novels, advertisements, sitcoms, and so on
- Ritual: mealtimes, drinking in bars, gift giving, dating, television watching, supermarket shopping, behavior in elevators, sports contests, lovemaking, dressing, and so on[3]

Codes are difficult to see because of their characteristics—they are all-pervasive, specific, and clear-cut, which makes them almost invisible. They inform almost every aspect of our existence (I've listed some of their manifestations) and provide a useful concept for the analyst of the popular arts and media; for not only do genres such as the western and the sitcom follow codes (commonly known as formulas), so do the media in general.

SEMIOTICS OF THE TELEVISION MEDIUM

I have, to this point, been concerned with the ways semiotic analysis can be used to explicate programs carried on television, with a specific focus on the television narrative. Table 1.12 reveals how media forms carry genres of the popular arts. Each medium, because of its nature, imposes certain limitations on whatever popular art forms or genres it carries. Because of the small screen and the nature of the television image, for instance, television is not the ideal medium for presenting huge battle scenes.

Table 1.12 Semiotics in the Media and Other Popular Art Forms

Media	Popular Art Forms in Media
Radio	Soap operas
Television	Advertisements/commercials
Films	Westerns
Comics	Police dramas
CDs	Variety shows
Posters	Musicals
Newspapers	Talk shows
Magazines	News
Telephones	Spy stories
Books	Documentaries
Billboards	Love stories

Television is a "close-up" medium, better suited to revealing character than to capturing action.

In applying semiotics to television, then, it makes sense for us to concern ourselves with aspects of the medium that *function as* signs, as distinguished from *carrying* signs. What is interesting about television, from this point of view, are the kinds of camera shots employed in the medium. Table 1.13 lists some of the most important kinds of shots, which function as signifiers, and what is usually signified by each shot. The Chanel advertisement featuring an extreme close-up of a woman's lips is an example of how advertising focuses on sexually exciting parts of women to sell products. The woman's lips are slightly open, a convention used to suggest sexual excitement. And there is nothing else in the advertisement except the name of the company, Chanel, which gives the brand an association with sexuality and arousal.

Table 1.14 illustrates how camera work and editing techniques can be examined in the same way.

Table 1.13   How Camera Shots Function as Signifiers

Signifier (Shot)	Definition	Signified (Meaning)
Close-up	Face only	Intimacy
Medium shot	Most of body	Personal relationship
Long shot	Setting and characters	Context, scope, public distance
Full shot	Full body of person	Social relationship

Table 1.14   How Elements of Cinematography Function as Signifiers

Signifier	Definition	Signified
Pan down	Camera looks down	Power, authority
Pan up	Camera looks up	Smallness, weakness
Dolly in	Camera moves in	Observation, focus
Fade in	Image appears on blank screen	Beginning
Fade out	Image on screen goes blank	Ending
Cut	Switch from one image to another	Simultaneity, excitement
Wipe	Image wiped off screen	Imposed conclusion

These tables represent a kind of television grammar as far as shots, camera work, and editing techniques are concerned. We all learn the meanings of these phenomena as we watch television, and they help us understand what is going on in particular programs.

There are other matters that might be considered here also, such as lighting techniques and the use of color, sound effects, and music. All of these are signifiers that help us interpret what we see (and hear) on television. Television is a highly complex medium that uses verbal language, images, and sound to generate impressions and ideas in people. It is the task of the television semiotician to determine, first, how this is possible and, second, how this is accomplished.

SOME CRITICISMS OF SEMIOTIC ANALYSIS

You will notice that I have said very little up to this point about aesthetic judgments. This leads us to one of the major criticisms of semiotic analysis, namely, that in its concern for the relationship of elements and production of meaning in a text, it ignores the quality of the work itself. That is, semiotics is not really concerned with art but rather with meaning and modes of cognition (the codes needed to understand a text). It might be compared to judging a meal by the quality of the ingredients without any concern for how the food was cooked or what it tasted like.

In certain cases, the text is subjugated by the critic. It exists as nothing but (or perhaps little more than) an excuse for a virtuoso performance by the semiotician, who grabs the spotlight away from the work itself. But this is a problem of all forms of interpretation. Most works of art sit at the top of a huge mountain of criticism that analyzes and explicates them, sometimes at greater length than the original works themselves.

Another problem with semiotic analysis, especially of televised texts, is that a strong theoretical foundation is lacking to facilitate work in this area. Most of the work done in semiotics in recent years has been concerned with film, not television. Without a strong and well-articulated body of theoretical criticism, work in the applied semiotic analysis of television texts must remain tentative.

Nevertheless, a great deal is possible, and if you can avoid extremism in your analyses of signifying systems in texts, you can produce critical readings of considerable value and utility. You have enough theory to get started, and applied semiotic analyses are likely to lead to advances in critical theory.

A CHECKLIST FOR SEMIOTIC ANALYSIS OF TELEVISION

The following are questions you should address in undertaking a semiotic analysis of a television program. I have concentrated on narratives in this chapter, but much of what I have discussed is applicable to all kinds of programs.

- Isolate and analyze the important signs in your text.
  - What are the important signifiers, and what do they signify?
  - What is the system that gives these signs meaning?
  - What codes can be found?
  - What ideological and sociological matters are involved?

- What is the paradigmatic structure of the text?
  - What is the central opposition in the text?
  - What paired opposites fit under the various categories?
  - Do these oppositions have any psychological or social import?

- What is the syntagmatic structure of the text?
  - Which of Propp's functions can be applied to the text?
  - How does the sequential arrangement of elements affect meaning?
  - Are there formulaic aspects that have shaped the text?

- How does the medium of television affect the text?
  - What kinds of shots, camera angles, and editing techniques are used?
  - How are lighting, color, music, and sound used to give meaning to signs?

- What contributions have theorists made that can be applied?
  - What have theorists in semiotics written that can be adapted to your analysis of television?
  - What have media theorists written that can be applied to semiotic analysis?

I hope this chapter has given you a sense of the semiotic approach and enabled you to apply this fascinating—and powerful—analytic tool. You can apply semiotics to television, film, comics, advertisements, architecture, diseases, artifacts, objects, formulas, conventions, organizations, friends, enemies, and just about anything else in which communication is important—and in which there is signification.

For those interested in pursuing semiotics at an advanced level, the University of Tartu in Estonia (the home institution of Jurij Lotman) now offers a two-year MA degree, in English, and other institutions such as the University of Indiana and University of Toronto also offer advanced study.

STUDY QUESTIONS AND TOPICS FOR DISCUSSION

1. Contrast the work of Peirce and Saussure on the nature of signs.
2. Discuss the following concepts: synchronic/diachronic, syntagmatic/paradigmatic, language/speaking, metaphor/metonymy, elaborated/restricted codes.
3. Explain, in detail, Propp's theory. Discuss his ideas about "functions" in narrative texts. Make a syntagmatic analysis of a national news program on television. What problems did you face? What did your analysis reveal?
4. What significance does binary opposition have? What does it mean to say that concepts are "purely differential"?
5. What are codes? Why are they important? Are there any cultural and behavioral codes you follow?
6. Discuss the assertions in this chapter concerning how camera shots in television and film function as signs.
7. What are the differences between elaborated and restricted codes?
8. What criticisms can be made of semiotic analysis?

ANNOTATED BIBLIOGRAPHY

Bakhtin, Mikhail M. (1981). *The dialogic imagination: Four essays* (M. Holquist, Ed.; C. Emerson & M. Holquist, Trans.). Austin: University of Texas Press. This volume consists of four essays on literary theory, with a focus on the novel. After years of obscurity, Bakhtin has been "discovered," and his ideas have become extremely influential, especially his notions of "dialogism," discussed in this chapter, and of "carnival," discussed in his book on Rabelais.

Barthes, Roland. (1970). *Writing degree zero and elements of semiology* (A. Lavers & C. Smith, Trans.). Boston: Beacon. Barthes addresses the basic concepts used in semiotic analysis and makes reference to some of the work he has done on food, fashion, furniture, and automobiles.

Barthes, Roland. (1972). *Mythologies.* New York: Hill & Wang. This volume is a collection of short essays on everyday-life topics, such as wrestling, soap powders, margarine, and steak and chips and includes a long essay on semiotic aspects of myth. This is a fascinating book and one of the most interesting examples of applied semiotic analysis available.

Berger, Arthur Asa. (1997). *Bloom's morning: Coffee, comforters, and the hidden meaning of everyday life.* Boulder, CO: Westview. This book takes an everyman named Bloom (after the hero of Joyce's *Ulysses*) and analyzes the semiotic significance of every object he uses and everything he does from the moment he is awakened by his radio alarm clock to the time he has breakfast. The 35 short essays on Bloom's morning are preceded by a discussion of everyday life, and the book ends with a chapter titled "Myth, Culture, and Everyday Life." The book is illustrated with more than 35 drawings by the author.

Berger, Arthur Asa. (1997). *Seeing is believing: An introduction to visual communication* (4th ed.). New York: McGraw-Hill. This book functions as a primer to help readers become visually literate. Subjects covered include basic elements of visual communication; photography, film, television, comics, and cartoons; typography; and new technologies related to visual communication.

Berger, Arthur Asa. (1998). *Signs in contemporary culture: An introduction to semiotics* (2nd ed.). Salem, WI: Sheffield. This book is intended for people who have no familiarity with semiotic thought. It offers an exploration of the basic concepts of semiotic theory, along with applications of these concepts to aspects of contemporary society. Each chapter contains both discussion and application of a semiotic concept.

Berger, Arthur Asa. (2010). *The object of affection: Semiotics and consumer culture.* New York: Palgrave Macmillan. This book deals with material culture and the role it plays in consumer culture and the way people use brands to try to fashion their identities. The second part of the book deals with a number of culturally significant objects, such as McDonald's burgers, vodka, teddy bears, and computers.

Berger, Arthur Asa. (2012). *Culture codes.* Mill Valley, CA: Marin Arts Press. This book suggests that what we describe as "culture" can be seen as a collection of different codes that shape our thinking and behavior. It deals with the way we cook steak, think about playboys, interpret jokes, and the ritual involved in smoking cigarettes.

Bignell, Jonathan. (2002). *Media semiotics: An introduction* (2nd ed.). Manchester, England: Manchester University Press. Bignell offers chapters such as "Signs and Myths," "Advertisements," "Magazines," "Newspapers," "Television News," "Television Realisms," "Television Fictions," "Cinema," and "Interactive Media" in an approachable exposition of the importance of semiotics to media studies.

Chandler, Daniel. (2002). *Semiotics: The basics.* London: Routledge. An accessible introduction to semiotic theory that deals with signs, codes, and the theories of the major semioticians.

Coward, Rosalind, & Ellis, John. (1977). *Language and materialism: Developments in semiology and the theory of the subject.* London: Routledge & Kegan Paul. This is an important theoretical work that deals with semiotics and its relation to Marxism, the work of the French post-Freudian Lacan, and other topics.

Culler, Jonathan. (1976). *Structuralist poetics: Structuralism, linguistics and the study of literature.* Ithaca, NY: Cornell University Press. Culler provides an excellent discussion of the basic principles of semiotic analysis and its application to literature. Another book by Culler, *Ferdinand de Saussure* (in the Penguin Modern Masters series), is also highly recommended.

Danesi, Marcel. (2002). *Understanding media semiotics.* London: Arnold. Danesi, who is the director of the Program on Semiotics and Communication Theory at the University of Toronto, uses insights from semiotic theory to deal with topics such as print and audio media, film, television, the computer, the Internet, and advertising.

Eco, Umberto. (1976). *A theory of semiotics.* Bloomington: Indiana University Press. This book contains an important theoretical analysis of semiotics that deals with its range of applications; it is an advanced text for readers with a good background in the subject. See also Eco's *The Role of the Reader: Explorations in the Semiotics of Texts* (Indiana University Press, 1979).

Fiske, John, & Hartley, John. (1978). *Reading television.* London: Methuen. This is one of the most useful applications of semiotic theory to television to be found. The authors devote a good deal of attention to codes and to specific texts.

Goldman, Robert, & Papson, Stephen. (1996). *Sign wars: The cluttered landscapes of advertising.* New York: Guilford. Using semiotics and other methods of cultural criticism, the authors "decode" advertising in general and particular commercials and ad campaigns specifically. They also discuss, from a critical perspective, advertising's role in U.S. culture and society.

Gottdiener, Mark. (1995). *Postmodern semiotics: Material culture and the forms of postmodern life.* Oxford, UK: Basil Blackwell. Gottdiener is a sociologist who uses semiotic analysis (among other things) to analyze shopping malls, Disneyland, and postmodern architecture. The first part of the book is devoted to theoretical concerns (and is complicated and very sophisticated); the second part addresses cultural studies and sociosemiotics.

Guiraud, Pierre. (1975). *Semiology.* London: Routledge & Kegan Paul. This is a very brief but interesting explication of semiotic principles, originally published in the French "Que sais-je?" series. It focuses on the functions of media, signification, and codes.

Hall, Stuart. (Ed.). (1997). *Representation: Cultural representations and signifying practices.* London: Sage. This book, edited by Stuart Hall, contains his two long essays "The Work of Representation" and "The Spectacle of the 'Other'" as well as essays by other authors, including Sean Nixon's "Exhibiting Masculinity" and Christine Gledhill's "Genre to Gender: The Case of Soap Opera."

Johansen, Jorgen Dines, & Larsen, Svend Erik. (2002). *Signs in use: An introduction to semiotics* (Dinda L. Gorlee & John Irons, Trans.). London: Routledge. This book deals with a number of core concepts in semiotics such as codes, signs, discourse, narration, and material culture.

Leach, Edmund. (1970). *Claude Lévi-Strauss.* New York: Viking. This book represents one of the more successful attempts to make Lévi-Strauss's work understandable to the general reader. It includes some biographical material as well as chapters on myth, kinship, and symbolism.

Lévi-Strauss, Claude. (1967). *Structural anthropology.* Garden City, NY: Doubleday. This volume is a collection of essays on language, kinship, social organization, magic, religion, and art by this distinguished French anthropologist, an original mind and a great literary stylist.

Lotman, Jurij (Yuri) M. (1976). *Semiotics of cinema* (Mark E. Suino, Trans.). Ann Arbor, MI: Michigan Slavic Contributions. This book is an application of semiotics to cinema that deals with narration, montage, plot, acting, and other related topics. Lotman is identified with the Tartu school of Russian semiotics and applies its principles to art and culture. Another of Lotman's books, *The Structure of the Artistic Text*, has also been published by Michigan Slavic Contributions (located at the University of Michigan).

Lotman, Jurij (Yuri) M. (1990). *The universe of mind: A semiotic theory of culture* (Ann Shukman, Trans.). Bloomington: Indiana University Press. The book deals with the relationship between semiotic theory and culture, in the broadest sense of the term. The first part of the book considers how signs in texts generate meaning, and the second part offers Lotman's theory of the "semiosphere" and spatiality. In this section he deals with symbolism found in St. Petersburg and with spatiality in Dante's *Divine Comedy* and Bulgakov's *The Master and Margarita.*

Propp, Vladimir. (1968). *Morphology of the folktale.* Austin: University of Texas Press. This classic "formalist" analysis of fairy tales, originally published in 1928, has implications for the analysis of all kinds of other mass-mediated culture.

Rapaille, Clotaire. (2006). *The culture code: An ingenious way to understand why people around the world buy and live as they do*. New York: Broadway Books. Rapaille argues that from the ages of 1 to 7, children become "imprinted" with certain codes that affect many aspects of life, from attitudes to cheese to shopping.

Saussure, Ferdinand de. (1966). *A course in general linguistics* (W. Baskin, Trans.). New York: McGraw-Hill. This book, originally published in 1915, is one of the central documents in semiotic analysis and the source of many of the concepts used in the field.

Scholes, Robert. (1974). *Structuralism in literature*. New Haven, CT: Yale University Press. This book provides an introduction to structuralism, with a focus on the analysis of literary texts but with obvious implications for other kinds of texts. The ideas of such thinkers as Jakobson, Lévi-Strauss, Jolles, Souriau, Propp, and Barthes are presented.

Sebeok, Thomas A. (Ed.). (1977). *A perfusion of signs*. Bloomington: Indiana University Press.

Sebeok, Thomas A. (Ed.). (1978). *Sight, sound and sense*. Bloomington: Indiana University Press.
These two volumes edited by Sebeok are important collections of applied semiotic theory. The topics addressed include clowns, medicine, faces, religion, nonsense, architecture, music, and culture.

Solomon, Jack. (1988). *The signs of our times: The secret meanings of everyday life*. New York: Harper & Row. This book presents a fascinating and perceptive application of semiotic analysis to everything from advertising, toys, and architecture to television, food, and fashion. It has an excellent concluding chapter on postmodernist art forms such as MTV and postmodernist works such as the film *Koyaanisqatsi*.

Wright, Will. (1975). *Sixguns and society: A structural study of the western*. Berkeley: University of California Press. This is an ingenious application of the ideas of Lévi-Strauss, Propp, and others to the western.

NOTES

1. For example, consider the difference order makes in the following two phrases, both of which contain the same words: "My husband was late . . ." and "My late husband was . . ."

2. Space constraints do not permit me to dwell any longer on Lévi-Strauss. Readers interested in learning more about Lévi-Strauss are referred to the annotated bibliography that accompanies this chapter for works by and about this author.

3. For an explication of these matters, see Berger (2012).

Marxist thought is one of the most powerful and suggestive ways available to the media analyst for analyzing society and its institutions. This chapter deals with such fundamental principles of Marxist analysis as alienation, materialism, false consciousness, class conflict, and hegemony—concepts that can be applied to media and can help us understand the ways media function. Particular attention is paid to the role of advertising in creating consumer lust, and some cautions are offered about the danger of being doctrinaire.

Marxist Analysis

Until a decade or so ago, there was rather little Marxist analysis in "mainstream" American literary and social thought. This is not to say there were no Marxists; rather, the Marxists were always "voices crying in the wilderness"—not very many people paid heed to these voices or took them seriously. This has been changing in recent years, and there are now increasing numbers of Marxist historians, political scientists, economists, and critics.

The situation is complicated by the fact that there are different schools of Marxism, and Marxist thought seems to be changing rapidly. In the pages that follow I discuss some of the more fundamental concepts of Marxism that can be applied to media and popular culture. Ironically, Marxism today often seems to have more interesting things to say about culture, consciousness, and related problems than it does about economics.

The discussion that follows leans heavily on the work of Erich Fromm, who has argued that Marx was a humanist whose argument was essentially a moral one. I might point out, in passing, that many Marxists do not approve of the societies created in Marx's name that pervert his doctrine, such as those in the former Soviet Union, Eastern Europe, Cuba, China, and elsewhere. For all practical purposes, communism is dead. Many countries that were Marxist, such as Russia and many Eastern European nations, have rejected Marxist doctrines and now are firmly in the capitalist market economy camp. China is nominally a communist country, and so is Vietnam, but in reality both have market-oriented capitalist economies. The only country that remains true to Marxist ideology, it seems, is Cuba, and many scholars predict that when Fidel Castro dies, Cuba, too, will abandon Marxism. It should be pointed out, however, that one can be a Marxist—and, for our purposes, a Marxist critic of the media—without being a communist and without believing in the necessity of revolution and the establishment of a classless society by violent means.

What follows is an outline of some of the most fundamental principles of Marxism—principles most useful to the media analyst. My goal here is to provide readers with a basic understanding of Marxism so that they can apply Marxist concepts to the public art forms carried by the media. Readers who find that this kind of analysis offers them valuable new perspectives and leads to new insights can pursue study of the subject further (for instance, by examining the books listed in the annotated bibliography that accompanies this chapter). I cite a number of helpful texts in the following discussion, but, because of the limitations of space, this chapter can form no more than an introduction to Marxist thought from which readers can apply Marxist analyses of media.

MATERIALISM

When we talk about Marxist thought being *materialistic*, we are using the term in a special way—not as it is traditionally used in the United States, where it suggests a craving for money and the things that money can buy. For Marxists, *materialism* refers to a conception of history and the way society organizes itself. Let me start here with some quotations of crucial importance from Marx's "Preface to a Contribution to the Critique of Political Economy," as published in his *Selected Writings in Sociology and Social Philosophy* (1964). First, his discussion of the relationship between society and consciousness:

> In the social production which men carry on they enter into definite relations that are indispensable and independent of their will; these relations of production correspond to a definite state of development of their material powers of production. The totality of these relations of production constitutes the economic structure of society—the real foundation, on which legal and political superstructures arise and to which definite forms of social consciousness correspond. The mode of production of material life determines the general character of the social, political and spiritual processes of life. It is not the consciousness of men that determines their being, but, on the contrary, their social being determines their consciousness. (p. 51)

The mode of production (economic relationships), then, is the base or the "determinant element" in our thoughts—although the relationship between our thoughts and society is a complicated one. This passage suggests that beneath the superficial randomness of things there is a kind of inner logic at work. Everything is shaped, ultimately, by the economic system of a society, which, in subtle ways, affects the ideas individuals have, ideas instrumental in determining the kinds of arrangements people make with one another, the institutions they establish, and so on.

Marx also wrote, in "The German Ideology" (1964),

> The production of ideas, of conceptions, of consciousness, is at first directly interwoven with the material activity and the material intercourse of men, the language of real life. Conceiving, thinking, the mental intercourse of men, appear at this stage as the direct efflux from their material behavior. The same applies to mental production as expressed in the language of politics, laws, morality, religion, and metaphysics of a people. Men are the producers of their conceptions, ideas, etc.—real, active men, as they are conditioned by the definite development of their productive forces and of the intercourse corresponding to these, up to its furthest forms. Consciousness can never be anything else than conscious existence. (pp. 74–75)

This passage is important because it brings people into the picture and suggests that although consciousness is socially produced, it is always filtered through the minds of real, live, active men and women and is not something that works automatically. There is always the possibility of individuals gaining an understanding of their situation and doing something about it. But more about this shortly. We have, now, our first important insight—namely, that "our" ideas are not entirely our own, that knowledge is social.

With all of this in mind, here are some questions we might ask now:

1. What social, political, and economic arrangements characterize the society in which the media are being analyzed?
2. Who owns, controls, and operates the media?
3. What roles do the various media play in the society where the media are being analyzed? And what are the functions of the various popular art forms carried by the media?
4. What ideas, values, notions, concepts, beliefs, and so on are spread by the media, and what ideas, values, and so on are neglected by the media? Why? Do the media "manipulate" people and shape their behavior, or do people have the capacity to use the media for their own purposes?
5. How have the Internet and sites such as YouTube and Twitter changed things? What impact has the Internet had on traditional media such as newspapers and magazines?
6. How are writers, artists, actors, and other creative people affected by the patterns of ownership and control of the media?

THE BASE AND THE SUPERSTRUCTURE

This section begins to develop ideas found in the passages quoted earlier. What Marx has described as the "base" represents the economic system found in a given society. This economic system, or mode of production, influences, in profound and complicated ways, the "superstructure," or institutions and values, of a given society. Here is a relevant quotation from Friedrich Engels's "Socialism: Utopian and Scientific" (1972) on this matter:

> The new facts made imperative a new examination of all past history. Then it was seen that *all* past history, with the exception of its primitive stages, was the history of class struggles; that these warring classes of society are always the products of the modes of production and of exchange—in a word, of the *economic* conditions of their time; that the economic structure of society always furnishes the real basis, starting from which we can alone work out the ultimate explanation of the whole superstructure of juridical and political institutions as well as of the religious, philosophical, and other ideas of a given historical period. Hegel had freed history from metaphysics—he had made it dialectical; but his conception of history was essentially idealistic. But now idealism was driven from its last refuge, the philosophy of history; now a materialistic treatment of history was propounded, and a method found of explaining man's "knowing" by his "being" instead of, as heretofore, his "being" by his "knowing." (p. 621, italics in original)

This passage offers an explanation of how ideas are transmitted to human beings: through the institutions, philosophical systems, religious organizations, and arts found in a given society at a given time—that is, through the superstructure. Capitalism is not only an economic system but also something that affects attitudes, values, personality types, and culture in general.

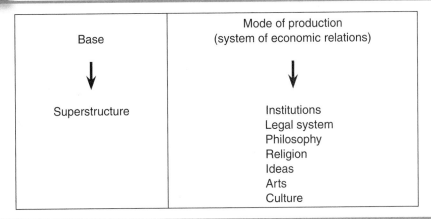

Figure 2.1   Influences on the Superstructure

How the base affects the superstructure is a problem that has caused Marxists a considerable amount of aggravation. Economic relations may be the ultimately determining ones, but they are not the only ones, and it is a great oversimplification to say that the superstructure is automatically shaped by the base and is nothing but a reflection of it—a position sometimes described as "vulgar Marxism." This point of view fails to recognize that an economic system is dynamic and always in a state of change—as is a given superstructure—and that people, leading real lives and capable of all kinds of actions, are involved also. In the following discussion of superstructure I focus on the public arts and the mass media, institutions that many Marxists claim are crucial to the understanding of how consciousness is determined, shaped, and manipulated.

Figure 2.1 displays the ideas I've just discussed in diagrammatic form. All of this might seem rather abstract and irrelevant until one recognizes that the consciousness of people has important social, economic, and political implications.

FALSE CONSCIOUSNESS

It is important for the ruling class to affect people's consciousness by giving them certain ideas; in this way the wealthy, who benefit most from the social arrangements in a capitalist country, maintain the status quo. Marx (1964) explains how the ruling class operates:

> The ideas of the ruling class are, in every age, the ruling ideas: i.e., the class which is the dominant *material* force in society is at the same time its dominant *intellectual* force. The class which has the means of material production at its disposal, has control at the same time over the means of mental production, so that in consequence the ideas of those who lack the means of mental production are, in general, subject to it. The dominant ideas are

nothing more than the ideal expression of the dominant material relationships, the dominant material relationships grasped as ideas, and thus of the relationships which make one class the ruling one; they are consequently the ideas of its dominance. The individuals compos-ing the ruling class possess among other things consciousness, and therefore think. Insofar, therefore, as they rule as a class and determine the whole extent of an epoch, it is self-evident that they do this in their whole range and thus, among other things, rule also as thinkers, as producers of ideas, and regulate the production and distribution of the ideas of their age. Consequently their ideas are the ruling ideas of their age. (p. 78, italics in original)

According to this thesis, the ideas of a given age are those promulgated and popularized by the ruling class in its own interest. Generally speaking then, the ideas people have are those the ruling class wants them to have.

The ruling class, we must recognize, believes its own messages. This is because it has within itself a group of conceptualizing ideologists who, as Marx (1964) puts it, "make it their chief source of livelihood to develop and perfect the illusions of the class about itself" (p. 79). By *ideology,* I mean any system of logically coherent and widely applicable sociopolitical beliefs. The ruling class, according to this theory, propagates an ideology that justifies its status and makes it difficult for ordinary people to recognize they are being exploited and victimized.

This notion—that the masses of people are being manipulated and exploited by the ruling class—is one of the central arguments of modern Marxist cultural analysis. As Donald Lazere (1977) notes,

> Applied to any aspect of culture, Marxist method seeks to explicate the manifest and latent or coded reflections of modes of material production, ideological values, class relations and structures of social power—racial or sexual as well as politico-economic—or the state of consciousness of people in a precise historical or socio-economic situation. . . . The Marxist method, recently in varying degrees of combination with structuralism and semiology, has provided an incisive analytic tool for studying the political signification in every facet of con-temporary culture, including popular entertainment in TV and films, music, mass circulation books, newspaper and magazine features, comics, fashion, tourism, sports and games, as well as such acculturating institutions as education, religion, the family and child-rearing, social and sexual relations between men and women—all the patterns of work, play, and other customs of everyday life. . . . The most frequent theme in Marxist cultural criticism is the way the prevalent mode of production and the ideology of the ruling class in any society dominate every phase of culture, and at present, the way capitalist production and ideology dominate American culture, along with that of the rest of the world that American business and culture have colonized. This domination is perpetuated both through overt propaganda in political rhetoric, news reporting, advertising and public relations, and through the often unconscious absorption of capitalistic values by creators and consumers in all the above aspects of the culture of everyday life. (pp. 755–756)

This passage suggests the all-encompassing nature of the Marxist approach and some of the most important objects of its attention. Quite obviously, the mass media and popular culture are centrally important in the spread of false consciousness, in leading people to believe that "whatever is, is right."

From this perspective the mass media and popular culture constitute a crucial link between the institutions of society (and the superstructure in general) and individual consciousness.

German media theorist Hans Magnus Enzenberger (1974) has attacked the notion of manipulation as being useful but perhaps a bit dated:

> The New Left of the sixties has reduced the development of the media to a single concept—that of manipulation. This concept was originally extremely useful for heuristic purposes and has made possible a great many individual analytical investigations, but it now threatens to degenerate into a mere slogan which conceals more than it is able to illuminate, and therefore itself requires analysis. (pp. 100–101)

Enzenberger argues that the notion of manipulation is ultimately grounded on the assumption (the unspoken premise) that "there is such a thing as unmanipulated truth" (p. 101), a notion he finds questionable, and one that is too limited. Ultimately, he argues, the left's antagonism toward mass media benefits capitalism.

Enzenberger's hope is, perhaps, somewhat utopian. His notion is that all media manipulate; it is in the very nature of media:

> There is no such thing as unmanipulated writing, filming, or broadcasting. The question is therefore not whether the media are manipulated, but who manipulates them. A revolutionary plan should not require the manipulators to disappear; on the contrary, it must make everyone a manipulator. (p. 104)

At this point we have moved away from analysis per se, and I will not pursue Enzenberger's thought any further. It may be that the theory of manipulation has deficiencies and drawbacks, but it still remains a central concept of Marxist media analysis for the simple reason that, as Marxists view society, the media are tools of manipulation. (The same argument about media manipulation can be used against socialist and communist countries, although Marxist critics as a rule do not like to concern themselves with such matters.)

IDEOLOGY

Karl Mannheim's *Ideology and Utopia: An Introduction to the Sociology of Knowledge* (1936), a classic work in political theory, offers an interesting insight into the nature of ideology. Mannheim writes,

> The concept "ideology" reflects the one discovery which has emerged from political conflict, namely, that ruling groups can in their thinking become so intensively interest-bound to a situation that they are simply no longer able to see certain facts which would undermine their sense of domination. There is implicit in the word "ideology" the insight that in certain situations the collective unconscious of certain groups obscures the real condition of society both to itself and to others and thereby stabilizes it. (p. 40)

Opposing the ideologists, for Mannheim, are people he describes as "utopians" who are drawn from groups that see only the bad things in society. Ideologists, we may say, see no evil and utopians see no good. Both are mistaken, for most societies have a combination of good and bad.

A more contemporary discussion of the concept of ideology is found in the Introduction to Meenakshi Gigi Durham and Douglas M. Kellner's *Media and Cultural Studies: Key Works* (2001). They write:

> The concept of *ideology* forces readers to perceive that all cultural texts have the distinct biases, interests, and embedded values, reproducing the point of view of their producers and often the values of the dominant social groups. Karl Marx and Friedrich Engels coined the term "ideology" in the 1840s to describe the dominant ideas and representations in a given social order. . . . During the capitalist era, values of individualism, profit, competition, and the market became dominant, articulating the ideology of the new bourgeois class which was consolidating its class power. Today, in our high tech and global capitalism, ideas that promote globalization, new technologies, and an unrestrained market economy are becoming the prevailing ideas—conceptions that further the interests of the new governing elites in the global economy. . . . Ideologies appear natural, they seem to be common sense, and thus are often invisible and elude criticism. Marx and Engels began a critique of ideology, attempting to show how ruling ideas reproduce dominant social interests trying to naturalize, idealize, and legitimate the existing society and its institutions and values. (p. 6)

If we direct our analysis of ideology to the media, we find that popular culture or mass-mediated culture found in capitalist nations has a mythologizing function. The media are owned and controlled by the

Theodor W. Adorno

ruling class and are used to generate false consciousness in the masses, or in Marxist terms, the proletariat. People generally are not aware they hold ideological beliefs because they seem so natural and pervasive. Ideology pervades the films, television programs, newspapers, magazines, and books found in bourgeois societies, and while people don't recognize that ideology and false consciousness shape their thinking, this does not mean the masses aren't affected by ideology. They haven't brought the ideologies they hold to consciousness and may not be able to articulate them, but from a Marxist perspective, most people in bourgeois societies have ideological beliefs that shape their thinking and behavior. The Frankfurt School, discussed next, offered a comprehensive Marxist critique of American media and culture that influenced many media over the years.

THE FRANKFURT SCHOOL

In Germany in the 1930s, a number of media theorists, known as "the Frankfurt School," applied Marxist theories to the study of media and culture. They came to the United States in the 1940s, escaping from Nazi Germany, and became very influential. Among them were thinkers such as Theodor W. Adorno, Herbert Marcuse, and Max Horkheimer. They believed that the mass media in the United States functioned as a means of generating false consciousness in the American people and thus prevented history from playing out as it should have, according to Marxist theory. The media distracted working-class Americans from recognizing the degree to which they were exploited by the ruling class and revolting against them. The ruling classes, according to the Frankfurt School, distracted the masses with mindless entertainments and bought them off by getting them involved with consumer culture.

Adorno (1957) offers a typical example of the Frankfurt School's perspectives on the mass media and mass culture:

> Rigid institutionalization transforms modern mass culture into a medium of undreamed of psychological control. The repetitiveness, the selfsameness, and the ubiquity of modern mass culture tend to make for automatized reactions and to weaken the forces of individual resistance. . . . The increasing strength of modern mass culture is further enhanced by changes in the sociological structure of the audience. The old cultured elite does not exist anymore, the modern intelligentsia only partially corresponds to it. At the same time, huge strata of the population formerly unacquainted with art have become cultural consumers. (p. 476)

The Frankfurt School has been criticized as being elitist. Some scholars have suggested that the Frankfurt School's hostility to popular culture and the "masses" was a result of their status loss and the shock of coming from hierarchical societies in Europe to an egalitarian one in the United States. There may also have been an element of nostalgia in members of the Frankfurt School for a period when members of cultural elites were awarded high status and treated with great deference, in contrast to the situation in the United States where economic elites are awarded high status. Whatever the case, the Frankfurt School did offer an important, though perhaps somewhat extreme, critique of the media and popular culture. Now, with the development of the Internet, the robotic "mass man" the members of the Frankfurt School wrote about seems to have disappeared and been replaced by an anarchic multitude of bloggers and video makers.

In his book, *Media Culture: Cultural Studies, Identity, and Politics Between the Modern and Postmodern*, Douglas Kellner (1995) offers an assessment of the Frankfurt School. He writes,

> Adorno's analysis of popular music, Lowenthal's studies of popular literature and magazines, Herzog's studies of radio soap operas, and the perspectives and critiques of mass culture developed in Horkheimer and Adorno's famous study of the culture industries (1972) provided many examples of the usefulness of the Frankfurt School's approach. Moreover, in their theories of the culture industries and critiques of mass culture, they were the first to systematically analyze and criticize mass-mediated culture and communications within critical social theory. . . . Yet there are serious flaws in the original program of critical theory which requires a radical reconstruction of the classical model of the culture industries. . . . Overcoming the limitations of the classical model would include: more concrete analysis of the political economy of the media and the processes of the production of culture; more empirical and historical research into the construction of media industries and their interaction with other social institutions; more studies of audience reception and media effects; and the incorporation of new cultural theories and methods into a reconstructed critical theory of culture and the media. (p. 29)

We must remember that the Frankfurt School flourished many years ago, and despite its flaws, Kellner (1995) concludes, "Although the Frankfurt School approach is partial and one-sided, it does provide tools to criticize the ideological and debased forms of media culture and the ways that it reinforces ideologies which legitimate forms of oppression" (p. 30).

CLASS CONFLICT

For Marx (1964), history is based on unending class conflict—unending, that is, until the establishment of a communist society, in which classes disappear and, with them, conflict.

> The history of all hitherto existing society is the history of class struggles. Freeman and slave, patrician and plebeian, lord and serf, guild-master and journeyman, in a word oppressor and oppressed, stood in constant opposition to one another, carried on an uninterrupted, now hidden, now open fight, a fight that each time ended either in a revolutionary reconstitution of society at large, or in the common ruin of the contending classes. (p. 200)

The two classes that Marx talks about are the bourgeoisie, who own the factories and corporations and form the ruling class, and the proletariat, the huge mass of workers exploited by this ruling class whose condition becomes increasingly more desperate.

The bourgeoisie, according to this theory, avert class conflict by indoctrinating the proletariat with ruling-class ideas, such as the notion of the "self-made man" and the idea that the social and economic arrangements in a given society are natural and not historical. If social arrangements are natural, they cannot be modified; thus one must accept a given order as inevitable. Marxists argue that the social and economic arrangements found in a given society at a given time are historical—created by people and therefore capable of being changed by people. The bourgeoisie try to convince everyone that capitalism is natural and therefore eternal, but this idea, say the Marxists, is patently false, and it is the duty of Marxist analysts to demonstrate this.

One of the approaches the ruling class uses to avert conflict is to convince people there are no classes in a given society or that class is somehow incidental and irrelevant. Thus in the United States we have the myth of a "classless" society because we have not had a hereditary aristocracy and because members of the upper class tend to be friendly in social encounters. The president of a major corporation might call the doorman or janitor by his first name, but this, to the Marxists, is a means of camouflaging real social relations—although the United States, with its large middle class, does present special problems to Marxist analysts, as the likelihood of a revolution seems rather distant.

Nevertheless, the mass media still perform their job of distracting people from the realities of U.S. society (poverty, racism, sexism, and so on) and of "clouding their minds" with ideas the ruling class wishes them to have. In some cases, the media offer heroes who reflect the bourgeois, ruling-class line and who reinforce and indoctrinate the masses who follow their activities in books, television programs, films, and so on. Generally speaking, the media serve either to mask class differences or to act as apologists for the ruling class in an effort to avert class conflict and prevent changes in the political order.

But the fact remains that for Marxists, classes exist, and members of opposing classes are locked into hostile and mutually destructive relationships. As Marx (1964) has written, "Society as a whole is more and more splitting up into two great hostile camps, into two great classes directly facing each other—bourgeoisie and proletariat" (p. 201). The resolution of this dialectic is, for Marxists, inevitable, even though the media controlled by the ruling class or bourgeoisie may temporarily prevent members of the proletariat from attaining true consciousness of their situation.

Henri Lefebvre (1968/1984), a French Marxist, has taken the concept of class conflict and manipulation and developed it into the notion that people in capitalist societies are living in a state of "terror." He explains this notion as follows. First, any society with radical class differences, with a small privileged class at the top and a mass of people living in poverty, has to be maintained through compulsion and persuasion. Second, such a class-stratified society is bound to become overly repressive and must develop sophisticated ways of masking repression and making unsuspecting individuals the instruments of their own repression and the repression of others. Finally, we arrive at the "terrorist" society, in which

HENRI LEFEBVRE

> compulsion and the illusion of freedom converge; unacknowledged compulsions besiege the lives of communities (and of their individual members) and organize them according to a general strategy. . . . In a terrorist society terror is diffuse, violence is always latent, pressure is exerted from all sides on its members, who can only avoid it and shift its weight by a super-human effort; each member is a terrorist because he wants to be in power (if only briefly). . . . [T]he "system" . . . has a hold on every member separately and submits every member to the whole, that is, to a strategy, a hidden end, objectives unknown to all but those in power, and that no one questions. (p. 147)

This notion that people in capitalist societies are living in a state of terror may seem extreme at first but could help to explain why many Americans feel pressured and anxious about their lives and prospects for the future.

Lefebvre first wrote the book from which I quoted in 1968, when Marxism seemed to have answers for people and when the critiques it made of bourgeois societies seemed terribly telling. Marxists spoke from a sense of moral superiority when they criticized class-ridden capitalist societies, full of exploited workers and impoverished people.

The events that took place in Eastern Europe and the Soviet Union in the 1990s showed that the Marxist-Leninist governments in these states only pretended to rule in the people's interest. They were class-ridden and corrupt, and grossly inefficient as well. The rapid decline of communism as a viable form of government has cast a dark shadow on Lefebvre's criticisms of capitalist societies. In reality, it could be argued that it was the communist societies that were terrorist, both overtly (in their use of military power and the secret police) and in terms of their impact on the psyches of their citizens.

And yet it strikes me that Lefebvre's argument has some merit and that his notion that people in bourgeois capitalist societies live in a state of psychological terror has some currency. In our everyday lives, we are under constant "attack" (by print advertisements, radio and television commercials, and programs carried by the mass media) even though we may not recognize that we are being besieged or may not be able to articulate our feelings. (The terrors raised by these attacks may include growing old in a youth-crazed culture, being fat in a thin-crazed culture, being poor in a wealth-obsessed culture, being a person of color in a white-dominated culture, being a woman in a male-dominated culture, always being told or shown that we are suffering from deprivation, whether relative or absolute, and so on, endlessly.)

Whether these pressures we feel (if you don't want to use the word *terror*) are primarily the result of living in complex, modern, urban societies or of our specific social, economic, and political arrangements is a question yet to be answered. For Lefebvre, the answer is clear.

ALIENATION

The term *alienation* suggests separation and distance; it contains within it the word *alien*, a stranger in a society who has no connections with others, no ties, no "liens" of any sort. This notion is of central importance to an understanding of Marxism, which derives alienation from the capitalist economic system. Capitalism may be able to produce goods and materialist abundance for large numbers of people (although, ultimately, at the expense of others), but it necessarily generates alienation, and all classes suffer from this, whether they recognize it or not.

There is a link between alienation and consciousness. People who live in a state of alienation (or condition of alienation) suffer from "false consciousness"—a consciousness that takes the form of the ideology that dominates their thinking. But in addition to this false consciousness, alienation may be said to be unconscious, in that people do not recognize that they are, in fact, alienated. One reason for this may be that alienation is so pervasive that it is invisible and hard to take hold of.

For Fromm and for many other interpreters of Marx, alienation is the core of Marx's theory. As Fromm (1962) has noted,

> The concept of alienation has become increasingly the focus of the discussion of Marx's ideas in England, France, Germany and the U.S.A. . . . The majority of those involved in this debate . . . take a position that alienation and the task of overcoming it is the center of Marx's socialist humanism and the aim of socialism; furthermore that there is a complete continuity between the young and the mature Marx, in spite of changes in terminology and emphasis. (pp. 43–44)

This is a debatable position, Fromm adds. Whatever the case, the concept of alienation is very useful to analysts of popular culture.

The following quotation from Marx (1964) serves to illustrate his views on alienation:

> In what does this alienation of labour consist? First, that the work is *external* to the worker, that it is not a part of his nature, that consequently he does not fulfill himself in his work but denies himself, has a feeling of misery, not of wellbeing, does not develop freely a physical and mental energy, but is physically exhausted and mentally debased. The worker therefore feels himself at home only during his leisure, whereas at work he feels homeless. His work is

not voluntary but imposed, *forced labour*. It is not the satisfaction of a need, but only a *means* for satisfying other needs. Its alien character is clearly shown by the fact that as soon as there is no physical or other compulsion it is avoided like the plague. Finally, the alienated character of work for the worker appears in the fact that it is not his work but work for someone else, that in work he does not belong to himself but to another person.

The *alienation* of the worker in his product means not only that his labour becomes an object, takes on its own existence, but that it exists outside him, independently, and alien to him, and that it stands opposed to him as an autonomous power. The life which he has given to the object sets itself against him as an alien and hostile force. (pp. 169–170, italics in original)

Thus people become separated or estranged from their work, from friends, from themselves, and from life. A person's work, which is central to identity and sense of self, becomes separated from him or her and ends up as a destructive force. Workers experience themselves as objects, things acted on, and not as subjects, active forces in the world. The things people produce become "commodities," objects separated, somehow, from the workers' labor. As people become increasingly more alienated, they become the prisoners of their alienated needs and end up, as Marx puts it, "the *self-conscious* and *self-acting* commodity" (qtd. in Fromm, 1962, p. 51, italics in original).

In this situation the mass media play a crucial role. They provide momentary gratifications for the alienated spirit, they distract the alienated individual from his or her misery (and from consciousness of the objective facts of his or her situation), and, with the institution of advertising, they stimulate desire, leading people to work harder and harder. There is a kind of vicious cycle here: If, as Marx argues, work in capitalist societies alienates people, then the more people work, the more they become alienated. In order to find some means of escaping their alienation (which they do not recognize as a condition, but the symptoms of which they feel), they engage in various forms of consumption, all of which cost money, so that they are forced to work increasingly hard to escape from the effects of their work. Advertising has replaced the Puritan ethic as the chief means of motivating Americans to work hard; thus advertising must be seen as occupying a central role in advanced capitalist societies.

There is a debate among Marxist critics about the status of Franz Kafka, author of *The Trial*, *The Castle*, and many other important works. Kafka's writings, critics suggest, show characters struggling with vast, anonymous bureaucracies and reflect the alienation so dominant in capitalist societies. The central question many critics argue about is whether it was Kafka's intent to suggest that alienation is a universal condition (and not just tied to capitalism).

Conservative Marxist critics attack Kafka for arguing that alienation is an inevitable condition of human beings and not recognizing that it could be overcome in socialist countries. Kafka did not understand, these critics argue, that alienation is historical, not natural, and he failed to suggest or to show in his stories how alienation might be overcome—through the establishment of socialist societies (i.e., classless ones ruled by communists). Liberal Marxist critics, in contrast, assert that Kafka's work shows that alienation can persist even in socialist countries (which are characterized by enormous bureaucracies) and that it is valuable because it points that out.

Kafka's stories make people aware of this alienation, and this ultimately suggests that changes should be made and that alienation can be eradicated.

This critical debate, let me suggest, has been settled by history. Today, very few people take seriously the notion that only socialist realism is acceptable in art and literature, and socialist realist criticism has all but disappeared.

THE CONSUMER SOCIETY

Advertising, as I have suggested, is an essential institution in advanced capitalist societies because it is necessary to motivate people to work hard so they can accumulate money, which they can then use to buy things. But in addition, people must be driven to consume, must be made crazy to consume, for it is consumption that maintains the economic system. Thus the alienation generated by a capitalist system is functional, for the anxieties and miseries generated by such a system tend to be assuaged by impulsive consumption. As Marx has written about the effects of capitalism,

> Every man speculates upon creating a *new* need in another in order to force him to a new sacrifice, to place him in a new dependence, and to entice him into a new kind of pleasure and thereby into economic ruin. Everyone tries to establish over others an *alien* power in order to find there the satisfaction of his own egoistic need. (Qtd. in Fromm, 1962, p. 50, italics in original)

Advertising generates anxieties, creates dissatisfactions, and, in general, feeds on the alienation present in capitalist societies to maintain the consumer culture.

There is nothing that advertising will not do, use, or co-opt to achieve its goals. If it has to debase sexuality, co-opt the women's rights movement, merchandise cancer (via cigarettes), seduce children, terrorize the masses, or employ any other tactics, it will. One thing that advertising does is divert people's attention from social and political concerns and steer that attention toward narcissistic and private concerns. Through advertising, individual self-gratification is developed into an obsession, and thus alienation is strengthened and the sense of community weakened.

Thus advertising is more than a merchandising tool; it takes control of everyday life and dominates social relationships. At the same time, advertising leads people to turn inward and to separate themselves from one another. It also imposes on society a collective form of taste. Advertising is a kind of popular art carried by the mass media, an art form that persuades and convinces and thus has both an immediate and a long-range mission. The immediate mission is to sell goods; the long-range mission is to maintain the class system. In order to sell goods, advertising has to change attitudes, lifestyles, customs, habits, and preferences while at the same time maintaining the economic system that benefits from these changes.

Wolfgang Fritz Haug, a German Marxist, has developed a concept relevant to this discussion. Haug suggests that those who control the industries in capitalist societies have learned to fuse sexuality onto commodities and thus have gained greater control of that aspect of people's lives that is of most interest to the ruling classes—the purchasing of goods and services. In his book *Critique of Commodity Aesthetics: Appearance, Sexuality, and Advertising in Capitalist Society*, Haug (1986) argues that the advertising industry, the servant of capitalist interests, has learned how to mold and exploit human sexuality, to alter human need and instinct structures. In his postscript to the eighth German edition of the book, he writes,

> It would be particularly absurd in the case of commodity aesthetics to ignore the fact that its current dominant form is the aesthetics of the monopoly-commodity, i.e., the form in which transnational enterprises in particular intervene directly in the collective imagination of cultures. (p. 11)

Thus this power to use the appearance of products as a means of stimulating desire for them (the aestheticization of commodities) is now a worldwide phenomenon, and people in many countries are affected by it as it "intervenes" in their cultures by capturing, so to speak, people's imaginations. People have the illusion that they make their own decisions about what to purchase and what to do, but, according to Haug, these decisions are made for them to a remarkable degree. Their acts turn out to be almost automatic responses to "stimuli" generated by advertisers and the commodities themselves.

On the cover of *Critique of Commodity Aesthetics* is a remarkable photograph of pigeons in St. Mark's Square in Venice. The photo, taken from above, shows pigeons arranged so that they spell out *Coca-Cola*. To get this effect, workers scattered birdseed to form the lettering, and the birds flocked to the seed. As Haug explains,

> The pigeons did not gather with the intention of forming the trademark but to satisfy their hunger. But equally the seed was not scattered to feed the pigeons but to employ them on its tracks as extras. The arrangement is totally alien and external to pigeons. While they are consuming their feed, capital is subsuming, and consuming, them. This picture, a triumph of capitalist advertising technique, symbolizes a fundamental aspect of capitalism. (p. 118)

This photograph is most instructive. We (human beings living in societies dominated by capitalism and commodity aesthetics) are like the pigeons in the photograph; we fly to the things we want to consume under the illusion we are making individual choices and decisions, whereas in reality we are being motivated and manipulated by forces beyond our control.

In a later book titled *Commodity Aesthetics, Ideology, and Culture* (1987), Haug modified his views somewhat, arguing for a paradigm shift from what was essentially an economistic reading of Marx, which derived ideology, everyday life, and mass culture fairly directly from economic conditions. Haug's new perspective focuses on the development of action "from below" and the capacity people have to resist domination and manipulation in the spheres of culture and economics, which he now sees as separate and distinct.

Nevertheless, the photograph of the pigeons strikes a chord. It shows how our actions can seem to be motivated purely by personal desire and interest yet in reality be shaped and controlled by others, for their own purposes. The main instruments of this manipulation of people (as of the pigeons) are advertising and the mass media, along with allied industries such as industrial design.

In his book *The Mechanical Bride: Folklore of Industrial Man* (1951/1967), Marshall McLuhan analyzes advertisements (and comics) as cultural indicators and offers a number of brilliant insights into what specific advertisements reveal about American culture. In a chapter titled "Love-Goddess Assembly Line," he compares Hollywood and advertising:

> So Hollywood is like the ad agencies in constantly striving to enter and control the unconscious minds of a vast public, not in order to understand it or to present these minds, as the serious novelist does, but in order to exploit them for profit. . . . The ad agencies and Hollywood, in their different ways, are always trying to get inside the public mind in order to impose their collective dreams on that inner stage. (p. 97)

The irony is that we are all convinced of our freedom to make our own choices, because we believe our minds are "inviolable," when in fact our choices have been imposed on us, in subtle ways, by the advertising industry. This illusion of autonomy makes us all the more susceptible to manipulation and exploitation.

Advertising is part of what Enzenberger (1974) has called "the consciousness industry" or "the mind industry." In a chapter titled "The Industrialization of the Mind," he describes the ultimate selling job done by advertising and the media:

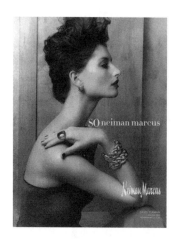

> The mind industry's main business and concern is not to sell its product: it is to "sell" the existing order, to perpetuate the prevailing pattern of man's domination by man, no matter who runs the society, and by what means. Its main task is to expand and train our consciousness—in order to exploit it. (p. 10)

Advertising can be seen as an industry that uses radical methods for conservative reasons. There is, then, a special irony to the famous phrase used in the advertising industry, "Let's run it up the flagpole and see if anyone salutes." This is meant to be a testimony to advertising's pragmatism and openness to new ideas. What people are "saluting" when they do salute, however, is the old order.

In the "So Neiman Marcus" advertisement, we see a beautiful woman, shown in profile, wearing what looks like gold jewelry, and a red dress. She represents, for many women, an ideal they wish to emulate and can aspire to, and, as John Berger explains, of whom women can be envious. Women, it is suggested, can transform themselves by patronizing Neiman Marcus and purchasing David Yurman products.

JOHN BERGER ON ADVERTISING

John Berger is an English Marxist who made a television series about advertising and consumer culture and also wrote an influential book, *Ways of Seeing*, based on the series. He offers an important insight into the way advertising, which he calls publicity, works. He writes,

> Publicity is not merely an assembly of competing messages: it is a language in itself, which is always being used to make the same general proposal. Within publicity choices are offered. . . but publicity as a system only makes a single proposal.

> It proposes to each of us that we transform ourselves, or our lives, by buying something more.

> This more, it proposes, will make us in some way richer—even though we will be poorer by having spent our money.

> Publicity persuades us of such a transformation by showing us people who have apparently been transformed and are, as a result, enviable. The state of being envied is what constitutes glamour. And publicity is the process of manufacturing glamour. . . . Publicity is never a celebration of pleasure-in-itself. Publicity is always about the future buyer. It offers him an image of himself made glamourous by the product or opportunity it is trying to sell. The image then makes him envious of himself as he might be. Yet what makes the self-which-he-might-be enviable? The envy of others. Publicity is about social relations, not objects. (1972, p. 131)

Berger's notion that advertising focuses on envy and the motivation to purchase the right product or service explains a great deal about how advertising works. We must recognize that, ultimately, it is the sign value of the things we buy that is crucial—not their supposed functions.

BOURGEOIS HEROES

A great deal of media analysis involves heroic figures—men, women, animals, robots—who have a number of different functions in films, television series, comic books, commercials, and other dramatic forms. For some people, heroes and heroines—and I am using these terms in the sense of characters who are important to dramas and other public art forms (so that villains must also be considered)—reflect their ages and societies. For others, heroes shape their ages and help transform their societies. In addition, heroes offer people models to imitate and thus help them attain identities. At times these models are deviant, so some heroes and heroines disturb whatever equilibrium society has obtained.

For Marxists, bourgeois heroes and heroines function to maintain the status quo by "peddling" capitalist ideology in disguised form and by helping keep consumer lust at a high pitch. One of the ideas bourgeois heroes sell is that of individualism, a value that takes many forms (the self-made man, the American dream, the "me generation," and so on) but is always connected to alienation, although few people see the connection. One of the early English Marxists, Christopher Caudwell, discusses heroes in his book *Studies and Further Studies in a Dying Culture* (1971). In his chapter on T. E. Lawrence he writes,

> If any culture produced heroes, it should surely be bourgeois culture. For the hero is an outstanding individual and bourgeoisdom is the creed of individualism. . . . Indeed, bourgeois history, for bourgeois schools, is simply the struggles of heroes with their antagonists and difficulties. (p. 21)

This view of heroism, according to Caudwell, is naive, because it does not recognize that heroes are connected, intimately, to their societies and social and economic phenomena. He continues:

> What is it that constitutes heroism? Personality? No; men with the flattest and simplest personalities have become heroes. Is it courage? A man can do no more than risk and perhaps lose his life, and millions did that in the Great War. Is it success—the utilization of events to fulfill a purpose, something brilliant and dazzling in the execution, a kind of luring and forcing Fortune to obey one, as with that type of all heroes, Julius Caesar? (p. 21)

None of these factors is adequate for heroism, as Caudwell sees it, for heroism is independent of people's motives and is based on the social significance of people's acts. The heroes we tend to celebrate are what Caudwell calls "charlatans," who, he suggests, may have power over men but not over matter. Charlatans lack a societal reference and exist as alienated and alienating curiosities. "Society," Marx (1964) has noted, "is not merely an aggregate of individuals; it is the sum of the relations in which these individuals stand to one another" (p. 96). Thus the hero, for the Marxist, is the man or woman who understands this and who fights for a new social order—one in which the bourgeois values of individualism, consumer lust, and upper-class domination are smashed.

HEGEMONY

Raymond Williams (1977) has described the development of the concept of hegemony as "one of the major turning points in Marxist cultural theory" (p. 108). In common usage, *hegemony* means domination or rule by one state or nation over another. Marxists use the term in a different manner: Rule is based on overt power and, at times, on coercion, but hegemony is subtler and more pervasive. As Williams explains, rule is political and, in critical times, is based on coercion or force. Hegemony, on the other hand, is a complicated intermeshing of political, social, and cultural forces. Hegemony transcends (but also includes) two other concepts: culture, which is how we shape our lives, and ideology, which, from a Marxist perspective, expresses and is a projection of specific class interests.

RAYMOND WILLIAMS

Hegemony transcends culture as a concept because culture can be seen as being tied to "specific distributions of power and influence," or the mode of production and relations that stem from it. And hegemony transcends ideology as a concept because ideology is limited to systematized and formalized meanings that are more or less conscious. Ideology may be masked and camouflaged in films and television programs and other works carried by mass media, but the discerning Marxist can elicit these ideologies and point them out.

This is valuable, but only to a point, because ideological analysis does not cover enough territory and does not lead to the kind of profound analysis that hegemonic analysis makes possible. Williams (1977) explains this as follows, saying about hegemony,

> It is distinct in its refusal to equate consciousness with the articulate formal system which can be and ordinarily is abstracted as "ideology." It of course does not exclude the articulate and formal meanings, values and beliefs which a dominant class develops and propagates. But it does not equate these with consciousness, or rather it does not reduce consciousness to them. Instead it sees the relations of dominance and subordination, in their forms as practical consciousness, as in effect a saturation of the whole process of living—not only of political and economic activity, nor only of manifest social activity, but of the whole substance of lived identities and relationships, to such a depth that the pressures and limits of what can ultimately be seen as a specific economic, political and cultural system seem to most of us the pressures and limits of simple experience and common sense. Hegemony is then not only the articulate upper level of "ideology," nor are its forms of control only those ordinarily seen as "manipulation" or "indoctrination." It is a whole body of practices and expectations, over the whole of living: our senses, our assignments of energy, our shaping perceptions of ourselves and our world. It is a lived system of meanings and values—constitutive and constituting—which as they are experienced as practices appear as reciprocally confirming. It thus constitutes a sense of reality for most people in the society, a sense of the absolute because of an experienced reality beyond which it is very difficult for most members of the society to move, in most areas of their lives. (pp. 109–110)

Hegemony thus is what might be described as "that which goes without saying," or the givens or commonsense realities of the world, which, it turns out, serve an ultimate purpose—that of maintaining the dominance of the ruling class.

The works carried by the mass media can be seen, then, not merely as carriers of ideology that manipulate and indoctrinate people with certain views. The media, as unwitting instruments of hegemonic domination, have a much broader and deeper influence—they shape people's very ideas of themselves and the world; they shape people's worldviews.

Thus when we use the concept of hegemony we must look very deeply into the work we are analyzing and elicit from it not only its ideological content but also its even more fundamental (and perhaps more insidious) ethnological, worldview-generating content. We might think of hegemonic analysis as analogous to the work psychoanalysts do when they probe beneath symptoms to underlying root causes in the personality structure of patients. Williams says that hegemonic analysis is "cultural" but in a special sense, in that it connects culture to the patterns of subordination and domination in a given society.

Let me offer another analogy that might be useful here. The concept of hegemony is similar to that of a paradigm, as used by philosophers of science. The term *paradigm* refers to an entire system of thought that characterizes a historical period and plays a major role in shaping the kind of science found in an era. Paradigm shifts occur in science every hundred years or so (or perhaps even less often), and with each paradigm shift, scientists see the world in new ways and work accordingly. Table 2.1 provides a comparison of paradigm and hegemony.

Table 2.1	Comparison of Paradigm and Hegemony
Paradigm	**Hegemony**
Theory	Ideology
Law	Popular arts
Science	Media analysis

With both a paradigm and hegemony, the ultimate determinant of thought and behavior is not recognized, because it is all-pervasive and fundamental. And just as the theory "explains" the law (or the event in nature that can be explained by law), so the paradigm encompasses all the theories held. Likewise, the concept of hegemony encompasses all that exists in a society—ideological notions, works of popular art carried by the media, and so forth. And this makes the analysis of media difficult, because it is hard to put your finger on all the things you take for granted and assume are simply part of reality. We are, all too often, captives of the categories of bourgeois thought—the very thought we hope to expose as the instrument of our own domination.

THE PROBLEM OF MEDIA CONSOLIDATION

One of the topics of most concern to Marxist critics of the media (and many non-Marxist critics as well) is the increasing global consolidation of the media. If the media have the ability to shape the consciousness of large numbers of people—and media organizations claim they have that power when they sell advertising space or time—then the fact that a relatively small number of people control the media (and thus have enormous power) is alarming.

As Ben Bagdikian, who was for many years dean of the School of Journalism at the University of California, Berkeley, noted in a 1987 article,

> In 1982, when I completed research for my book [*The Media Monopoly*], 50 corporations controlled half or more of the media business. By December 1986, when I finished revision for a second edition, the 50 had shrunk to 29. The last time I counted, it was down to 26.

Currently, something like half a dozen giant corporations dominate the media all over the world. Table 2.2 shows the top 10 media companies in the United States by sales for 2011. These giant organizations further consolidate their power through alliances with other media corporations.

Media giants such as those listed in Table 2.2 are concerned primarily not with the public interest but with profits. They also often have political agendas, such as favoring the election of politicians who will be friendly to them and pass laws favorable to their interests. Thus, for example, the major media

Table 2.2	Top 10 U.S. Media Companies by Sales, 2011	
Rank	**Company**	**Revenue in Billions**
1	GE	$151,628
2	Apple	$65,225
3	Walt Disney	$38,063
4	Comcast	$37,937
5	Amazon	$34,304
6	News Corp.	$32,778
7	Google	$29,321
8	Time Warner	$18,868
9	CBS	$14,059
10	Viacom	$13,497

Source: www.businessinsider.com/top-18-richest-media-companies-in-america-2011-5?op=1

corporations favored a recent change in Federal Communications Commission policy that made it possible for them to purchase television stations in certain markets where they already owned media outlets, making it possible for them to consolidate their power further.

Our media are now dominated by a small number of giant corporations. In recent years, with the development of Facebook, Twitter, and other social media, the situation has changed, and new technological developments are threatening the power of the television, music, newspaper, magazine, and publishing industries, as well as many other non-Internet mass media. Corporations such as Apple and Google and newer entities like Facebook and Twitter are now major players in the media world.

THE DANGER OF BEING DOCTRINAIRE

Marxism in general, and Marxist media analysis in particular, has a great deal of appeal, especially to people with a strong sense of social justice and a desire for a more egalitarian, humane world. Despite the awesome complexity that often characterizes Marxist thought, for Marxists, the world is basically divided into two camps: the bourgeoisie, who own the instruments of production and are ultimately responsible for alienation and a host of other ills from which all of society suffers, and the proletariat and their allies, who want to save themselves and society. This is a great oversimplification, of course, but it also has a grain of truth, and in any fight between "good guys" and "bad guys," it is only natural to root for the good guys.

In its best form, Marxism is a humanistic system of thought that seeks to make it possible for all people to lead productive, useful lives. However, Marxism also is an ideology that explains everything (or nearly everything) in the world on the basis of certain axioms or beliefs from which everything else follows. And that is its danger.

The danger for Marxist media analysts is that they know the answers *before* they ask the questions. That is, Marxists are also prisoners of the categories of their thought, and the questions they ask of a work of popular art carried by the media are often rather limited. Like the proverbial Frenchman (or Freudian) who sees sex in everything, the Marxist media analyst tends to see alienation, manipulation, and ideological exploitation in all of the public arts and tends to treat art of all kinds primarily in terms of its ideological content. Such analysis is terribly limiting, and it cannot do justice to most works of art.

Thus for the Marxist analyst there is a terrible danger of being doctrinaire, of seeing works of popular culture (or anything else) *only* in terms of Marxist concepts and notions. This is not to say that there is no ideological dimension to much or most (or all, many Marxists would argue) of the material produced for the mass media—there is, and media analysts must be mindful of it. But analysts must not neglect other aspects of these works—their psychological, moral, and aesthetic components, for example—and should not attempt to fit the material carried by the media into a Procrustean bed of Marxist notions.

There is also, of course, the possibility that Marx was wrong and that his notions about the economic system's relation to culture are not correct or are too simplistic to be worth much. There is something destructive about a great deal of utopian idealism, and Marx's fantasies of a communist society may ultimately do a great deal of damage to people who do not recognize that the best is often the enemy of the good. Marx (1964) has written,

> For as soon as the division of labor begins, each man has a particular, exclusive sphere of activity, which is forced upon him and from which he cannot escape. He is a hunter, a fisherman, a shepherd, or a critic, and must remain so if he does not want to lose his means of livelihood; whereas in communist society, where nobody has one exclusive sphere of activity, but each can become accomplished in any branch he wishes, production as a whole is regulated by society, thus making it possible for me to do one thing today and another tomorrow, to hunt in the morning, fish in the afternoon, rear cattle in the evening, criticize after dinner, in accordance with my inclination, without ever becoming hunter, fisherman, shepherd or critic. (p. 97)

In the name of achieving this kind of society, however, most of the allegedly socialist Marxist states set up repressive societies in which the media were used for manipulation to a much greater degree than in Western bourgeois societies. If Marxist media analysts are to be taken seriously as they point out the ways in which soap operas indoctrinate people into bourgeois values and mystify alienated housewives, this is an irony they must explain.

GRID-GROUP ANALYSIS

Aaron Wildavsky, who taught political science at the University of California in Berkeley for many years, offers us an introduction to grid-group analysis. As he wrote in an unpublished manuscript, "Conditions for a Pluralist Democracy, or Cultural Pluralism Means More Than One Political Culture in a Country" (1982),

> What matters to people is how they should live with other people. The great questions of social life are "Who am I?" (To what kind of a group do I belong?) and "What should I do?" (Are there many or few prescriptions I am expected to obey?). Groups are strong or weak according to whether they have boundaries separating them from others. Decisions are taken either for the group as a whole (strong boundaries) or for individuals or families (weak boundaries). Prescriptions are few or many indicating the individual internalizes a large or a small number of behavioral norms to which he or she is bound. By combining boundaries with prescriptions . . . the most general answers to the questions of social life can be combined to form four different political cultures. (p. 7)

In Table 2.3, I show how these two dimensions, grid and group, lead to four different political cultures or lifestyles, depending on the strength or weakness of the group boundaries and number of rules and prescriptions.

Different theorists have given these lifestyles different names, but the names all suggest what it is that characterizes the political culture or lifestyle. Michael Thompson, Richard Ellis, and Aaron Wildavsky's *Cultural Theory* (1990) discusses the ways in which political cultures are formed. In the book they discuss the ideas of Mary Douglas, a British social anthropologist, who was most responsible for developing grid-group theory. Thompson and his colleagues discuss the main points Douglas makes in her presentation of this theory:

> She argues that the variability of an individual's involvement in social life can be adequately captured by two dimensions of sociality: group and grid. *Group* refers to the extent to which an individual is incorporated into bounded units. The greater the incorporation, the more individual choice is subject to group determination. *Grid* denotes the degree to which an individual's life is circumscribed by externally imposed prescriptions. The more binding and extensive the scope of the prescriptions, the less of life that is open to individual negotiation. (p. 5)

Thompson and his colleagues describe how this grid-group typology generates four political cultures or ways of life, what Douglas calls "lifestyles":

> Strong group boundaries coupled with minimal prescriptions produce social relations that are egalitarian. . . . When an individual's social environment is characterized by strong group boundaries and binding prescriptions, the resulting social relations are hierarchical. . . . Individuals who are bound by neither group incorporation nor prescribed roles inhabit an individualistic social context. In such an environment all boundaries are provisional and

subject to negotiation. . . . People who find themselves subject to binding prescriptions and are excluded from group membership exemplify the fatalistic way of life. Fatalists are controlled from without. (pp. 6–7)

Mary Douglas on Shopping

We have to make a radical shift away from thinking about consumption as a manifestation of individual choices. Culture itself is the result of myriads of individual choices, not primarily between commodities but between kinds of relationships. The basic choice that a rational individual has to make is the choice about what kind of society to live in. According to that choice, the rest follows. Artefacts are selected to demonstrate the choice. Food is eaten, clothes are worn, cinema, books, music, holidays, all the rest are choices that conform with the initial choice for a form of society.

Source: Douglas, 1997, pp. 17–18

Each of these different ways of life is in conflict with the others, yet they all need one another. *Hierarchical elitists* believe in stratification and in the responsibility of those at the top to look after those below them. *Individualists* are interested primarily in themselves and want the freedom to compete fairly and be protected by the government. *Egalitarians* stress that people are equal in terms of their needs and that differences between people are social and not natural and should be played down. *Fatalists* believe in luck and opt out of the political system. All four groups are locked into complementary relationships, and all are necessary for the political order.

If we take the two dimensions—group boundaries (weak or strong) and grid aspects (few or many rules and prescriptions)—we can see in Table 2.3 how they generate the four ways of life or political cultures.

Table 2.3   Four Lifestyles According to Grid-Group Theory

Way of Life	Group Boundaries	Number and Kinds of Prescriptions
Hierarchical elitist	Strong	Numerous and varied
Egalitarian	Strong	Few
Competitive individualist	Weak	Few
Fatalist	Weak	Numerous and varied

As Thompson et al. (1990) note, social scientists are always looking for latent or hidden aspects of social phenomena. The authors use this insight to offer a comment on the Marxist view of societies:

> Things are never as they seem in class societies, Marx tells us, because exploitation must be disguised for the social order to be sustained. Since rulers do not like to think of themselves as exploiters, benefiting unjustly from the labor of others, and the exploited must be kept ignorant of their subjection lest they revolt, the truth must be kept from both rulers and ruled alike. (p. 149)

Marx, they argue, ties mystification to the capitalist economic system, whereas Thompson et al. suggest that mystification pervades every aspect and all ways of life, and it is the task of the social scientist to explore and explain this mystification. We can see that egalitarians are similar to Marxists in stressing that everyone should be treated the same way and have the same needs. But what Marx didn't recognize, Thompson et al. assert, is that egalitarianism can function as a useful critique of social relationships and arrangements only when it is out of power. If Marx had analyzed egalitarian political cultures as well as hierarchist and fatalist ones (read here as "bourgeois" and "proletarian"), these authors suggest, he would have developed different theories about sociopolitical institutions and the need for revolution.

Grid-group theory has direct applications to the media. Our media preferences are shaped, in good measure, by two things: a desire for the reinforcement of our basic values and beliefs by watching television programs, going to films, and reading books that support them and, second, a desire to avoid cognitive dissonance by not going to films or watching television shows that challenge our belief systems. Let me suggest, then, that the four political cultures and lifestyles shape our media choices, though we generally are not conscious of this, and we can use the four political cultures or lifestyles to figure out what members of each of these groups, if they were consistent and logical, would prefer. You can use grid-group theory and apply it to the media in the game "Playing Aaron Wildavsky," found in the appendix.

MARXIST CRITICISM IN THE POSTMODERN WORLD

Whether Marxism is the best—or even a credible—philosophy as a basis for analyzing and criticizing culture and the mass media continues to be debated. Ironically, it may be that the United States will turn out to be one of the few places where Marxism is taken seriously. More precisely, it is only in some departments in some American universities that Marxist theories—especially as they relate to the media and other sociocultural phenomena—have many adherents.

In the postmodern world there is some question about whether any logically coherent philosophy, such as Marxism, is widely accepted anymore. Jean-François Lyotard, a French scholar, offers one of the most widely quoted definitions of *postmodern* in his book *The Postmodern Condition: A Report on Knowledge* (1984):

> Simplifying to the extreme, I define *postmodern* as incredulity toward metanarratives. . . . To the obsolescence of the metanarrative apparatus of legitimation corresponds, most notably, the crisis of metaphysical philosophy and of the university institution which in the past relied on it. (p. xxiv)

Lyotard suggests that most people no longer accept the old overarching philosophical systems and metanarratives that helped individuals make sense of the world. These metanarratives, which were found in religions and political ideologies, no longer dominate our thinking. What we have now, Lyotard asserts, are competing narratives and ways of making sense of the world, and this has led to what might be called a crisis of legitimation. That is, it's hard to know what's right and what's wrong. To push matters to an extreme, postmodernist theorists assert that nobody knows what to believe, and many of these theorists argue further that it doesn't make any difference: It really doesn't matter what a person believes.

Postmodernism, whatever it may be (and there are many debates about that matter), is generally held to have replaced modernism around 1960, when there was a major cultural shift and the values and beliefs that characterized modernism—a belief in metanarratives, in rationality, in grand theories—suddenly were rejected. Let me suggest some of the differences between postmodernism and modernism. If modernism involves differentiation between the elite arts and popular culture, postmodernism breaks down the barriers between them and revels joyfully in mass culture. Modernism involves a "high seriousness" toward life while postmodernism involves an element of game playing and an ironic stance as well as a kind of playfulness. People in postmodernist societies "play" with their identities and change them when they feel bored with their old ones.

Modernism involves stylistic purity, as found in modernist architecture, with its slabs of steel, concrete, and glass, while postmodernism involves stylistic eclecticism and variety in architecture. In postmodernism, the pastiche is the dominant art form. Modernists believe we can know reality while postmodernists suggest that we are all confounded by illusions and hyperreality. Postmodernism is the realm of consumer culture, in contrast to what we might describe as a production culture of modernism. The great heroes of modernism are businessmen and statesmen while the heroes of postmodernism tend to be celebrities and entertainment figures, whose tastes and consumption habits are held up as models. It is because postmodernist thought has had such an impact on our lives that we are so interested in it.

Fredric Jameson, one of the most important theorists of postmodernism, describes in his book *Postmodernism: or, The Cultural Logic of Late Capitalism* (1991) media and pop culture as they relate to postmodernism. He offers the following description of postmodern pop culture:

> This whole "degraded" landscape of schlock and kitsch, of TV series and *Reader's Digest* culture, of advertising and motels, of the late show and grade-B Hollywood films, of so-called paraliterature, with its airport paperback categories of the gothic and the romance, the popular biography, the murder mystery, and even the science fiction or fantasy novel. (pp. 2–3)

Jameson, I should add, argues that postmodernism is just another name of a new form of capitalism and is tied intimately to consumer culture.

Ultimately, each of us has to decide whether Marxism still makes sense as a basis on which to analyze the mass media. If analysts find the concepts of Marxism useful and believe they explain things better than other perspectives, or offer useful insights, they should use them. If not, they approach media analysis from another viewpoint. Philosophies don't really die—they are abandoned when people turn their attention elsewhere. Whether Marxism will ultimately be dumped on the ash heap of history remains to be seen.

STUDY QUESTIONS AND TOPICS FOR DISCUSSION

1. What is meant by dialectical materialism?
2. Explain how the base relates to the superstructure.
3. What errors do "vulgar Marxists" make?
4. What is an ideology? How are ideologies related to false consciousness?
5. Why are the ideas of the ruling class the ideas of the masses?
6. How do all of the topics raised in questions 1 through 5 relate to the matter of class conflict? To alienation? To consumer lust?
7. What are the basic attributes of bourgeois heroes and heroines? How do these heroes differ from Marxist ones?
8. When Marxists do cultural analysis, what topics do they address?
9. What has been said about advertising in this chapter?
10. What are some of the problems associated with Marxist analysis?
11. To which of the four lifestyles do you belong? How has this lifestyle affected your consumption choices, your taste in media, and other choices you have made?

ANNOTATED BIBLIOGRAPHY

Adorno, Theodor W. (1948). *Philosophy of modern music.* New York: Seabury. Adorno deals with the work of Schoenberg and Stravinsky and topics such as consciousness, alienation, and fetishism in music.

Benjamin, Walter. (1999). *The Arcades Project.* Cambridge, MA: Belknap/Harvard University Press. An enormous (1,073 pages), inventive, and influential study of Paris and 19th-century Europe through quotations Benjamin assembled as a giant montage.

Berger, Arthur Asa. (Ed.). (1990). *Agitpop: Political culture and communication theory.* New Brunswick, NJ: Transaction. This volume presents a study of mass media and popular culture as they relate to political culture in the United States.

Berlin, Isaiah. (1963). *Karl Marx: His life and environment.* New York: Galaxy. This is a classic biography of Marx that also explains his ideas and their relation to his experiences.

Caudwell, Christopher. (1971). *Studies and further studies in a dying culture.* New York: Monthly Review Press. In this book a remarkable stylist deals with literary figures, personalities, and concepts. Caudwell's Marxism may be slightly "vulgar," or simplistic, but he has an incredible mind.

Dorfman, Ariel. (1983). *The empire's old clothes: What the Lone Ranger, Babar, and other innocent heroes do to our minds.* New York: Pantheon. Dorfman offers a Marxist critique of such topics as the Lone Ranger, the Babar books, and *Reader's Digest*, arguing that these texts and others are full of messages that spread capitalist ideology and help maintain the status quo.

Douglas, Mary. (1997). "In defence of shopping." In Pasi Falk & Colin Campbell (Eds.), *The shopping experience* (pp. 15–30). London: Sage. This essay is a seminal work that shows how lifestyles shape our choices when we shop and explains how lifestyles function in our everyday lives.

Eagleton, Terry. (1976). *Marxism and literary criticism*. Berkeley: University of California Press. A slim volume that shows how Marxist theory informs literary criticism.

Eagleton, Terry. (1978). *Criticism and ideology: A study in Marxist theory*. New York: W. W. Norton. Eagleton, a prominent British scholar, offers a Marxist analysis of literary theory that shows its ideological aspects and discusses how texts "produce" ideology.

Enzenberger, Hans Magnus. (1974). *The consciousness industry: On literature, politics and the media*. New York: Seabury. Enzenberger, an influential critic, presents some slightly unorthodox ideas.

Fischer, Ernst. (1963). *The necessity of art: A Marxist approach*. New York: Pelican. This book presents a sophisticated Marxist analysis of art, literature, and aesthetics, with interesting treatment of comics and other elements of popular culture.

Fromm, Erich. (1962). *Beyond the chains of illusion: My encounter with Marx and Freud*. New York: Touchstone. Fromm provides a comparison of the ideas of Marx and Freud that serves as a useful introduction to the thoughts of both men.

Haug, Wolfgang Fritz. (1986). *Critique of commodity aesthetics: Appearance, sexuality, and advertising in capitalist society*. Minneapolis: University of Minnesota Press. This volume offers a Marxist analysis of the role advertising plays in capitalist societies and the power design has to aestheticize objects and shape consumer behavior.

Haug, Wolfgang Fritz. (1987). *Commodity aesthetics, ideology, and culture*. New York: International General. In this collection of essays written from 1970 to 1983, Haug discusses his theory of commodity aesthetics and applies it to mass culture, workers, and ideology and offers a new paradigm that focuses on what he calls "cultural competence."

Jameson, Fredric. (1991). *Postmodernism; or, The cultural logic of late capitalism*. Durham, NC: Duke University Press. Jameson, a leading Marxist critic, uses Marxist theory to analyze postmodernism. He has a great deal to say about media and popular culture in this study.

Kellner, Douglas. (1995). *Media culture: Cultural studies, identity, and politics between the modern and the postmodern*. London: Routledge. This book deals with various aspects of media and culture, with discussions of disparate topics such as Spike Lee, advertising, the Gulf War, Madonna, and cyberpunk.

Lefebvre, Henri. (1984). *Everyday life in the modern world*. New Brunswick, NJ: Transaction. In this volume, originally published in 1968, Lefebvre offers a Marxist analysis of everyday life, including important discussions of advertising, fashion, and terror.

MacCannell, Dean. (1976). *The tourist: A new theory of the leisure class*. New York: Schocken. MacCannell combines semiotic analysis with Marxist theory to address tourism and sightseeing as important sociological and economic activities.

Marx, Karl. (1964). *Selected writings in sociology and social philosophy* (T. B. Bottomore & Maximilien Rubel, Eds.; T. B. Bottomore, Trans.). New York: McGraw-Hill, 1964. This is a collection of important passages from Marx's writings, organized and introduced by the editors.

Pappenheim, Fritz. (1959). *The alienation of modern man*. New York: Monthly Review Press. This volume presents a wide-ranging study of alienation and its relation to philosophy, literature, technology, and politics, written from a Marxist perspective.

Rius. (1990). *Marx for beginners*. New York: David McKay. This book of cartoons explains the fundamental ideas found in Marx's work and provides a dictionary of Marxist terms; recommended for those who like books with lots of pictures.

Thompson, Michael, Ellis, Richard, & Wildavsky, Aaron. (1990). *Cultural theory*. Boulder, CO: Westview. This book is not, by any means, a Marxist analysis, but the authors have very interesting things to say about Marxist theory. They also offer an important discussion of grid-group theory.

Tucker, Robert C. (Ed.). (1972). *The Marx-Engels reader.* New York: W. W. Norton. This volume, edited by one of the foremost scholars of Marxism, provides almost 700 pages of the works of Marx and Engels, showing the evolution of their thought.

Williams, Raymond. (1977). *Marxism and literature.* Oxford, UK: Oxford University Press. Williams, an influential British Marxist, addresses culture and literature. The book includes a useful bibliography of Marxist texts.

Sigmund Freud

Psychoanalysis is a therapeutic technique, but it is also a form of inquiry applied to many areas—politics, anthropology, and literary criticism, to name a few. The results psychoanalytic inquiry yields are interesting but also generally controversial. This chapter explores the most significant aspects of psychoanalytic theory and shows how the principles of psychoanalytic thought can be used to explain the hidden significance of cigarette lighters and *Hamlet*, among other things.

Psychoanalytic Criticism

THE UNCONSCIOUS

Psychoanalytic criticism is a form of applied psychoanalysis, a science concerned with the interaction between conscious and unconscious processes and with the laws of mental functioning. It should not be confused with psychotherapy, which is concerned with treating mental illness and behavioral problems, although many psychotherapists use analysis in their work. Rather, psychoanalytic criticism is one of many forms of study that use psychoanalytic concepts to understand subjects. Thus there are psychoanalytically inclined sociologists, anthropologists, and political scientists, as well as critics, and all of them use concepts and insights from psychoanalytic theory in their work.

Freud did not discover the unconscious; Plato, Nietzsche, Bergson, and many others discussed it before Freud. However, Freud developed the concept most thoroughly, and it is with Freud that all neo-Freudians, post-Freudians, anti-Freudians, and non-Freudians must come to grips. He was a seminal thinker of incredible power and scope, and his ideas and insights have fueled the work of generations of scholars in numerous fields. What I offer in this section is not a full-scale explication of Freudian thought but a selection of some of Freud's most important concepts—concepts that can be applied to the media to help clarify how the media work and affect us. Freud was most interested in helping people, but in the course of his amazing career he wrote on many other subjects, such as folklore, humor, and theater—pointing the way toward the development of psychoanalytic criticism.

One of the keystones in psychoanalytic theory is the concept of the unconscious. As Freud writes in his essay "Psychoanalysis" in *Character and Culture* (1963),

> It was a triumph for the interpretative art of psychoanalysis when it succeeded in demonstrating that certain common mental acts of normal people, for which no one had hitherto attempted to put forward a psychological explanation, were to be regarded in the same light as the symptoms of neurotics: that is to say they had a *meaning*, which was unknown to the subject but which could easily be discovered by analytic means. . . . A class of material was brought to light which is calculated better than any other to stimulate a belief in the existence of unconscious mental acts even in people to whom the hypothesis of something at once mental and unconscious seems strange and even absurd. (pp. 235–236, italics in original)

We are not, then, aware of everything going on in our minds. In fact, only a small portion of our mental lives is accessible to us.

conscious
subconscious
unconscious

It has frequently been suggested that an individual's mental life can be represented by an iceberg. The tip of the iceberg, that part seen above the water, is what the person is conscious of. The remainder of the iceberg, by far the greater part of it, lies hidden beneath the water. Although it is not seen, it is still there. "What is in your mind," Freud (1963) notes, "is not identical with what you are conscious of; whether something is going on in your mind and whether you hear of it, are two different things" (p. 189).

This means we are not in complete control of ourselves all the time, we are affected by events and circumstances in ways we cannot fathom, and we do things for reasons we do not understand or will not admit to ourselves. In short, we are not completely rational creatures who act only on the basis of logic and intelligence but instead are vulnerable to emotional and other kinds of nonrational or irrational appeals.

But why, you may ask, don't we become conscious of all that is going on in our minds? Why does all this material elude us? Why do our minds play such tricks on us? Freud offers an explanation that is both obvious (once it is pointed out) and ingenious: We *repress* this material because we do not want, for a variety of reasons, to become conscious of it. It would cause us pain or guilt or some other unpleasant feeling. Thus we create a barrier between our consciousness and our unconscious and do not allow repressed material to pass through that barrier.

Ernest Dichter is one of the founding fathers of the field known as motivation research. The goal of motivation research is to discover the unconscious or, it is assumed, the real reasons people do things, so that organizations, manufacturers, and so on can better shape people's behavior—that is, get them to buy particular products or do whatever else is asked of them. In his book *The Strategy of Desire* (1960), Dichter writes,

> Whatever your attitude toward modern psychology or psychoanalysis, it has been proved beyond any doubt that many of our daily decisions are governed by motivations over which we have no control and of which we are often quite unaware. (p. 12)

Dichter and other motivation researchers, then, mine the unconscious and put it to work, so to speak.

Dichter (1964) offers an example of the way in which unconscious desires and forces operate in a discussion of cigarette lighters:

> The reliability of a lighter is important because it is integrally connected with the basic [read "unconscious"] reason for using a lighter. (p. 341)

Let me interrupt here to ask what you think this "basic reason" might be. The answer most people would give is, "That's obvious—to light cigarettes." But that is the conscious, or "manifest," reason. The basic, or "real," reason and the "latent" and unconscious reason are sometimes not the same.

Let us return to Dichter, who tells us why people use lighters:

> The basic reason for using a lighter [is] . . . the desire for mastery and power. The capacity to summon fire inevitably gives every human being, child or grownup, a sense of power. Reasons go far back into man's history. Fire and the ability to command it are prized because they are associated not only with warmth, but also with life itself. As attested to by the Greek legend of Prometheus and many other myths, the ability to control fire is an age-old symbol of man's conquest of the physical world he inhabits.

> A cigarette lighter provides conspicuous evidence of this ability to summon fire. The ease and speed with which the lighter works enhances the feeling of power. The failure of a lighter to work does not just create superficial social embarrassment, it frustrates a deep-seated desire for a feeling of mastery and control. (p. 341)

Thus cigarette lighters are important to people because lighters fulfill powerful but unconscious needs and desires. The same can be said of many of the films we see, television programs we watch, novels we read, and other art forms we find so necessary to our lives. All of these things feed our unconscious lives, our psyches, in ways that few people understand.

But the need for mastery and power is only part of the story, for at a deeper level there is something else connected with the humble cigarette lighter. Dichter (1964) explains:

> Research evidence suggests that at a still deeper level the need for certainty that a cigarette lighter will work matters as much as it does because it is also bound up with the idea of sexual potency. The working of the lighter becomes a kind of symbol of the flame which must be lit in consummating sexual union. (p. 341)

This leads us to our next important subject—sexuality. Many people are aware that Freud was interested in sexuality, but they may know little more than that. And often the little knowledge they have of Freud's views is simplistic, which leads to absurd misconceptions.

This advertisement for Cabanaca Cachaca liquor is one of a series made by the company that makes a connection between the liquor and sexuality. The company has been criticized by some scholars for exploiting female sexuality in its advertisements, all of which have a powerful erotic component to them. The bottle and the woman combine to generate a sexually exciting image. The image of the woman in the advertisement is very striking and her pose is very suggestive. The photographs in the series are all very beautiful, but the way women are portrayed, many critics suggest, gives women unreal notions of what it is to be a woman.

SEXUALITY

It was his work on sexuality that generated a great deal of criticism of Freud. I believe, however, that much of this hostility is based on misunderstanding Freud's theories and also, in the United States at least, extreme sensitivity to the topic of sexuality. Americans resist intrusion into this most private and personal aspect of their lives and may even repress—refuse to admit to consciousness— ideas and insights that would explain sexuality in general and behavior in particular.

Freud calls the "force by which the sexual instinct is represented in the mind" the *libido* (qtd. in Hollitscher, 2002, p. 82). This term should be understood broadly and not restricted to sexual relations; that is, *libido* refers to various kinds of sensual pleasures and gratifications. According to Freud, all individuals pass through four stages in their development: the oral, the anal, the phallic, and the genital. In *The Encyclopedia of Psychoanalysis* these stages are described as follows:

> The mouth represents an erotogenic zone for the infant. Sucking and later eating represent the gratification of oral needs. The fact that the infant often sucks a pacifier indicates that he is not only concerned with the incorporation of calories. When the infant begins to have teeth, the need to bite expresses his sadistic desires. The second stage of development is usually referred to as the sadistic-anal, and is characterized by the infant's interest in excreting or retaining his stools. Finally, the third stage is referred to as the phallic, in which the boy is interested in his penis and the girl in her clitoris. The boy's interest in his penis appears to be responsible for his positive Oedipus complex, which is finally dissolved by the fear of castration. The girl reacts with penis envy, if she considers her clitoris to be an inferior organ to the penis.

> Freud pointed out that the stages are not clear-cut, and that the fourth stage, the genital phase, is achieved only with puberty. (Eidelberg, 1968, pp. 210–211)

During infancy and childhood, an individual's sexual life is rich but dissociated and unfocused. Focusing occurs at puberty.

One of the difficulties in explaining psychoanalytic theory is that one seems to have to know everything at the same time. In the previous quotation, for example, a number of concepts are mentioned that might need a bit of amplification, such as the matter of anality, the Oedipus complex, and the related concepts of castration anxiety and penis envy. These concepts are difficult for many people to accept and often strike those unfamiliar with Freud and psychoanalytic thought as fantastic and farfetched. Perhaps it is most useful to think of all of these ideas as concepts Freud developed to explain the phenomena and behaviors he encountered in his work. He describes psychoanalysis as "always incomplete and always ready to correct or modify its theories" (1963, p. 251).

Let us start with the matter of anal behavior, or what Freud calls "anal eroticism" in a fascinating paper titled "Character and Anal Eroticism" (Rieff, 1963). Freud connects a combination of personality traits developed to an extreme degree—orderliness, parsimoniousness, and obstinacy—with people who have had problems overcoming their anal stage and who may use these personality traits as a means of dealing with this fact. What is most fascinating is "connections which exist between the two complexes of interest in money and of defecation, which seem so dissimilar" that are, or appear to be, "most far-reaching" (Rieff, 1963, p. 30). Freud (1963) writes:

In reality, wherever archaic modes of thought predominate or have persisted—in ancient civilizations, in myth, fairy-tale and superstition, in unconscious thoughts and dreams, and in the neuroses—money comes into the closest relation with excrement. We know how the money which the devil gives his paramours turns to excrement after his departure, and the devil is most certainly nothing more than a personification of the unconscious instinctual forces. (p. 31)

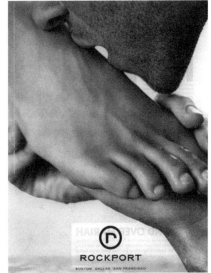

Ultimately there is an identification of gold with feces, "the most precious substance known to man and the most worthless" (p. 32).

The Rockport advertisement that shows a man kissing a foot brings to our consciousness the erotic aspects of the human foot. The masculinity of the man is enhanced by his facial hair. He has what looks like 2- to 3-day beard growth. We don't know the gender of the foot being kissed. The toenails are not polished, which means the foot could belong to a male or a female who doesn't use nail polish. The way the man grasps the foot and the nature of his kiss all contribute to the curious nature of the advertisement, which only has the word *Rockport* in it. The diagonal nature of the foot and the hand lead the eye to the name Rockport. The ad offers readers an arresting image, one that might spark our curiosity, and a design that directs our attention to the name of the company. The foot becomes a sexual object.

WILLIAM A. ROSSI ON SEXUAL ASPECTS OF THE FOOT AND SHOE

William A. Rossi's (1976) fascinating book *The Sex Life of the Foot and Shoe* regarding sexuality and the foot makes a number of remarkable claims. It begins as follows:

> The foot is an erotic organ and the shoe is its sexual covering. This is a reality as ancient as mankind, as contemporary as the Space Age. The human foot possesses a natural sexuality whose powers have borne remarkable influence on all peoples of all cultures through all history. (p. 1)

He offers a number of points about the foot to support his argument. I offer a selection of some of the more interesting ones. He writes (1976, pp. 4–5),

> It's one of the body's most sensitive tactile organs, possessing its own "sexual nerves"—and capable of the most intimate sensations in touching and being touched.

It has played a major role in the evolution and development of many of the erogenous features of the human anatomy—buttocks, bosom, legs and thighs, abdomen, hips, etc. What we refer to as "the figure" or the voluptuous architecture of the body, owes much of its sensuous character to the foot, which was responsible for the upright posture that altered the entire anatomy.

The unusual structure of the human foot which made the upright posture possible, also made possible frontal human copulation, a coital position unique in all nature.

Of all the known sex-related fetishes, those associated with the foot, toes, and shoes are by far the most common.

The erotic foot created a podosexual mania among five billion Chinese that lasted nearly one thousand years.

One reason the Chinese bound women's feet, he asserts, is so Chinese men could have sexual play with the foot. In the book, Rossi deals with many psychosexual aspects of feet and shoes. The point he makes is that human sexuality takes many diverse, and in some cases perverse, forms, and we should recognize that shoes, along with many other objects we purchase, have a hidden sexual aspect to them.

THE OEDIPUS COMPLEX

The Oedipus complex represents the core of neurosis for Freud; this concept explains a great deal. In a famous letter Freud wrote on October 15, 1897, to Wilhelm Fliess, he described how he came to recognize the existence and importance of the Oedipus complex:

Being entirely honest with oneself is a good exercise. Only one idea of general value has occurred to me. I have found love of the mother and jealousy of the father in my own case too, and now believe it to be a general phenomena of early childhood, even if it does not always occur so early as in children who have been made hysterics. . . . If that is the case, the gripping power of *Oedipus Rex*, in spite of all the rational objections to the inexorable fate that the story presupposes, becomes intelligible, and one can understand why later fate dramas were such failures. Our feelings rise against any arbitrary individual fate. . . but the Greek myth seizes on a compulsion which everyone recognizes because he has felt traces of it in himself. Every member of the audience was once a budding Oedipus in fantasy, and this dream-fulfillment played out in reality causes everyone to recoil in horror, with the full measure of repression which separates his infantile from his present state.

The idea has passed through my head that the same thing may lie at the root of *Hamlet*. I am not thinking of Shakespeare's conscious intentions, but supposing rather that he was impelled to write it by a real event because his own unconscious understood that of his hero. How can one explain the hysteric Hamlet's phrase "So conscience doth make cowards of us all," and his hesitation to avenge his father by killing his uncle, when he himself so casually sends his courtiers to their death and dispatches Laertes so quickly? How better than by the torment roused in him by the obscure memory that he himself had meditated the same deed against his father because of passion for his mother—"use every man after his desert, and who should scape whipping?" His conscience is his unconscious feeling of guilt. (Qtd. in Grotjahn, 1966, pp. 84–85)

According to psychoanalytic theory, every individual passes through a stage in which he or she desires the parent of the opposite sex—all of this, of course, on an unconscious level. Most people learn to master their Oedipus complexes; neurotic individuals are plagued by theirs. In little boys this mastery is aided by an unconscious fear of castration—castration anxiety—and in little girls it is aided by jealousy of men and what is termed penis envy.

Little boys, according to Freudian theory, sexualize their love for their mothers and wish to displace their fathers and monopolize their mothers' affection. Their fear of retaliation by their fathers then leads them to renounce their love of their mothers, to identify with the masculinity of their fathers, to rechannel their love outside of the family, and to direct their interest toward other females.

With little girls, the situation is different. They do not have to fear castration (some theorists suggest they believe they have already lost their penises) and so do not relinquish their Oedipal desires as quickly as boys do. But girls do fear the loss of the love of both their parents and so avoid this loss by reidentifying with their mothers and turning, eventually, to males other than their fathers as a means of obtaining babies (and, indirectly, their lost penises).

Freud also wrote about several other related complexes of interest here. For example, the Heracles complex is characterized by a hatred of the father for his children. The father sees the children as rivals for the affection of his wife and so wishes to get rid of the children. The Jocasta complex (named for the mother of Oedipus) is characterized by abnormal attachment of the mother to her son; it is found in varying degrees of intensity, from simple overattachment to incestuous relations.

One of the ways in which young children deal with their Oedipal anxieties is through exposure to fairy tales. In *The Uses of Enchantment*, Bruno Bettelheim (1977) devotes a chapter to Oedipal conflicts and resolutions in which he argues that fairy tales can help children resolve these problems. Children identify with the heroes and heroines of such stories and learn important things about life as well. Fairy tales, Bettelheim suggests, speak to children indirectly and symbolically—the stories are often about some unlikely hero who "proves himself by slaying dragons, solving riddles, and living by his wits and goodness until eventually he frees the beautiful princess, marries her, and lives happily ever after" (p. 111). In stories that speak to little girls, there is usually some evil stepmother or enchantress who is intensely jealous of the heroine and tries to prevent some hero, such as Prince Charming, from finding his princess. Sometimes in these tales the mother is split into two characters—an evil stepmother and a good mother (or fairy godmother).

Fairy tales are important because they help children cope with the psychological difficulties they experience. As Bettelheim (1977) explains,

Through the centuries (if not millennia) during which, in their retelling, fairy tales became ever more refined, they came to convey at the same time overt and covert meanings—came to speak simultaneously to all levels of the human personality, communicating in a manner which reaches the uneducated mind of the child as well as that of the sophisticated adult. Applying the psychoanalytic model of the human personality, fairy tales carry important messages to the conscious, preconscious and unconscious mind, on whatever level each is functioning at the time. By dealing with universal human problems, particularly those which preoccupy the child's mind, these stories speak to his budding ego and encourage its develop-ment, while at the same time relieving preconscious and unconscious pressures. As the sto-ries unfold, they give conscious credence and body to id pressures and show ways to satisfy these that are in line with ego and superego requirements. (pp. 5–6)

Fairy tales, as well as other texts very much like them (which may be, in truth, modernized fairy tales), have important functions as far as our psyches are concerned.

I cannot resist pointing out in passing that the relationship between Luke Skywalker and Darth Vader in *Star Wars* is (we eventually discover) Oedipal. *Star Wars* is, to a great degree, a modernized fairy tale about a princess in distress, a young man who rescues the princess, and a powerful father figure, Darth Vader. There are many other elements in the film as well—Germanic storm trooper villains and World War II airplane battles, for example—but the core of the film is, I would suggest, a fairy tale. George Lucas, who directed the film, is known to have studied myths in preparing the film. Of interest is the relationship between the name *Lucas* and the hero of the film, Luke (Lucas) Skywalker.

All of the phenomena discussed in this section operate beyond our consciousness and are kept buried through our power to resist and repress things that would disturb us. We empathize with Hamlet and with countless other heroes and heroines because, unconsciously, we recognize that their battles are our battles and their difficulties are our difficulties.

ON THE IMPORTANCE OF MYTH

The Oedipus complex, as Freud pointed out, is named after a mythological hero. The fact that Freud named this complex after a mythical figure suggests the important role that myths play in our con-sciousness and lives.

The story of Oedipus begins with the marriage of King Laius of Thebes to his distant cousin, Jocasta. An oracle makes a prophecy that Laius will be killed by his son, so when Jocasta gives birth to Oedipus, Laius binds the infant's feet and orders that he be left on a mountaintop to die. Laius is unaware that Oedipus has been rescued from the mountain by a shepherd and taken to King Polybus of Corinth, who raises him as his son. Oedipus believes Polybus is his father, so when, as a young man, he hears Apollo has said Oedipus is fated to kill his father, he leaves Corinth to avoid harming Polybus. As he travels to Thebes and meets Laius at a crossroads, the two men get into a fight, and Laius is killed. Oedipus then goes on to Thebes, which is being plagued by the Sphinx, a monster that looks like a winged lion and has the face of a woman. The Sphinx devours any wayfarer who cannot answer this riddle: What creature goes on four feet in the morning, two at noon, and three in the evening?

Oedipus seeks out the Sphinx and correctly answers the riddle she poses: The creature is man, who crawls in infancy, walks on two legs in the prime of life, and uses a cane to walk in old age. When Oedipus answers the riddle, the Sphinx kills herself and Thebes is saved. Oedipus is then welcomed into the city with great fanfare, and the Thebans make him their king. He marries the wife of the former king, Jocasta—not realizing she is his mother—and they have two children. When the children are grown up, Thebes is visited by another plague. Oedipus sends Jocasta's brother, Creon, to consult the oracle at Delphi to find out what might be done to lift the plague. Creon comes back with the answer: Whoever murdered King Laius must be punished. Oedipus then sends Tiresias, a blind prophet (who had once been a woman), to the oracle to find out the name of the king's murderer. When Tiresias returns, he at first refuses to tell Oedipus what he has learned. When Oedipus accuses Tiresias of not telling him the answer because Tiresias himself was involved in the killing of King Laius, Tiresias finally tells Oedipus, "You are the murderer." When it becomes clear that Oedipus has killed his own father and married his mother, Jocasta kills herself and Oedipus blinds himself in his grief.

This myth, Freud suggests, is a template that explains the developmental processes all children undergo. The child is attracted to the parent of the opposite sex and becomes hostile toward the parent of the same sex. Most children are able to resolve their Oedipal difficulties and lead normal lives, but those who can't end up with many psychological difficulties. For Freud, Oedipal conflicts are the core of neuroses.

Freud's argument is that myths affect our psychological development. These sacred stories shape many of the things we do, although we are unaware of this influence. As Mircea Eliade explains in *The Sacred and the Profane: The Nature of Religion* (1957/1961), "The modern man who feels and claims that he is nonreligious still retains a large stock of camouflaged myths and degenerated rituals" (pp. 204–205). Thus many films and television programs and many of our rituals, such as holding New Year's Eve parties, have unrecognized sacred or mythological content. Myths are an important component of our psyches, our media and popular culture, and our everyday lives. As Raphael Patai, an anthropologist and biblical scholar, explains in his book *Myth and Modern Man* (1972),

Myth . . . is a traditional religious charter, which operates by validating laws, customs, rites, institutions and beliefs, or explaining socio-cultural situations and natural phenomena, and taking the form of stories, believed to be true, about divine beings and heroes. (p. 2)

What is important to recognize, Patai adds, is that myth not only validates many of our activities but also plays a role in creating many of them, even if we aren't aware of it.

MEDIA AND THE OEDIPUS COMPLEX

The reason I spent so much time on the story of Oedipus is because we can use it to understand relationships in many contemporary films, television programs, and other mass-mediated texts. Whenever you have a trio of a younger man, an older man, and a woman, or a younger woman, an older woman, and a man, there is reason to suspect that the Oedipus complex may be motivating, to varying degrees, the characters. At the very least, we can find Oedipal themes in such stories.

Let me offer Ian Fleming's James Bond novels and the numerous Bond films as an example. In many Bond texts he is captured by an older man who attempts to kill him in horrible ways or do other terrible things to him. In the novel *Dr. No*, Bond is captured by one of No's henchmen and imprisoned. His love interest, Honeychile Rider, is to be killed by crabs on the island in an insane experiment Dr. No wants to carry out. Some media critics have suggested that M in the novels is a woman and that the letter stands for *mother*. In recent Bond films, Judi Dench plays M, and the character's role has increased in importance.

In their book *Bond and Beyond: The Political Career of a Popular Hero* (1987), Tony Bennett and Janet Woollacott discuss Bond's Oedipal problems. They write:

> In *You Only Live Twice*, Bond is going through a peculiarly acute phase in his ever-ongoing, never-to-be-resolved Oedipal crisis. Indeed, between them, *You Only Live Twice* and its sequel *The Man with the Golden Gun* offer a fairly explicit rehearsal of the Oedipus myth. Bond is sent away to a foreign land, is given another name, loses his memory so that like Oedipus, he lacks a knowledge of his true identity and parentage, eventually leaves those who have adopted him (Kissy) and journeys back to his homeland where (having been captured and brainwashed by the KGB *en route*) he attempts, in the opening pages of *The Man with the Golden Gun*, to kill M. (pp. 125–126, italics in original)

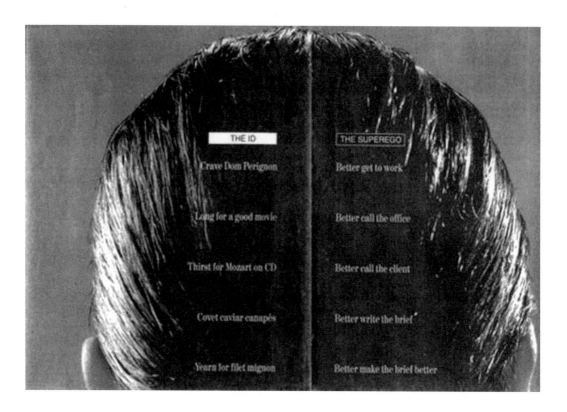

Bond, as the authors point out, is continually threatened by symbolic castration by the powerful figures that capture him in various adventures. Bennett and Woollacott suggest we find these Oedipal themes in the Bond adventures because Fleming had not resolved his Oedipal problems; he was excessively fond of his mother and hostile toward his father. In Bond novels and films, he meets and is attracted to a beautiful woman. Later, a powerful and older male figure captures Bond and plans to kill him. Bond always finds a way to escape and kill the villain and then is able to have a sexual relationship with the woman.

We can find the Oedipus complex or Oedipal themes in many texts. This can be explained relatively easily. If Freud is correct about the Oedipus complex, everyone experiences it, and residues of this experience then linger in the unconscious of scriptwriters and filmmakers and all the people who experience their work. From a psychoanalytic perspective, we can say that one reason we are drawn to stories, regardless of the medium, is that these stories either help us resolve our Oedipal problems or confirm that we have resolved them.

ID, EGO, AND SUPEREGO

The image in this advertisement, of the confrontation between id impulses and superego restraints, does an excellent job of showing us how the mind deals with conflicting pressures. The id wants Dom Perignon, and the superego says, "Better get to work." By putting the list of desires and the list of restraints on the back of the man's head, we are meant to understand that this conflict is taking place in his mind. No matter what the id desires, the superego says he'd better do something else. This advertisement is directed toward target audiences sophisticated enough to recognize the endless conflict that takes place in our minds. The ego is not mentioned; perhaps it is assumed that the ego will tell the man to use United Airlines next time he has to fly.

The id, ego, and superego are part of what is usually referred to as Freud's structural hypothesis about mental functioning. Charles Brenner (1974) offers the following brief description of these three entities:

> We may say that id comprises the psychic representatives of the drives, the ego consists of those functions which have to do with the individual's relation to his environment, and the superego comprises the moral precepts of our minds as well as our ideal aspirations.
>
> The drives, of course, we assume to be present from birth, but the same is certainly not true of interest in or control of the environment on the one hand, nor of any moral sense or aspirations on the other. It is obvious that neither of the latter, that is neither the ego nor the superego, develops till sometime after birth.
>
> Freud expressed this fact by assuming that the id comprised the entire psychic apparatus at birth, and that the ego and superego were originally parts of the id which differentiated sufficiently in the course of growth to warrant their being considered as separate functional entities. (p. 38)

Each of these entities—the id, ego, and superego—is extremely complicated, and Freud and others have written a great deal about how each develops and functions and the importance of each to the individual's psychic life.

Freud's structural hypothesis superseded his earlier theory of mental functioning, known as the topographic, which divided the psyche into three systems: conscious, preconscious, and unconscious. (I have dealt with these notions already, although I left out the preconscious in order to simplify matters.) In essence, according to the structural hypothesis, the psyche is in constant struggle, as the id and superego war against one another. The poor ego tries to mediate between the two—between the desire for pleasure and the fear of punishment, between drives and conscience.

Freud's description of the id in his *New Introductory Lectures on Psychoanalysis* is most graphic:

> We can come nearer to the id with images, and call it chaos, a cauldron of seething excitement. We suppose that it is somewhere in direct contact with somatic processes, and takes over from them instinctual needs and gives them mental expression, but we cannot say in what substratum this contact is made. These instincts fill it with energy, but it has no organization and no unified will, only an impulsion to obtain satisfaction for the instinctual needs, in accordance with the pleasure-principle. (Qtd. in Hinsie & Campbell, 1970, p. 372)

This bubbling cauldron of sexual desire, passion, and lust must not be allowed to determine an individual's actions because we live in societies, and civilization demands we control our behavior. In fact, the demands civilization makes on us are so great, according to Freud, that we suffer from great psychological pain.

The superego corresponds, as Brenner (1974) notes, "in a general way to what we ordinarily call conscience. It comprises the moral functions of the personality." He lists the functions of the superego:

> 1. the approval or disapproval of actions and wishes on the grounds of rectitude. 2. critical self-observation. 3. self-punishment. 4. the demand for reparation or repentance of wrongdoing. 5. self-praise or self-love as a reward for virtuous or desirable thoughts and actions. Contrary to the ordinary meaning of "conscience," however, we understand that the functions of the superego are often largely or completely unconscious. (pp. 111–112)

The superego assumes, then, a position in opposition to the id. In between these two polarities, the ego tries to mediate, operating always with the aim of self-preservation. The ego carries out its function by storing up experiences in the memory, avoiding excessively strong stimuli through flight, adapting to moderately strong stimuli, and bringing about changes in the world through activity.

We can use the concepts of the id, ego, and superego to help us understand texts. In certain texts, characters may be seen as primarily id figures or ego figures or superego figures. For example, in *Star Trek*, I would suggest that Spock is, essentially, an ego figure, Kirk (in German, interestingly, the name means *church*) is a superego figure, and McCoy is an id figure. Spock, the emotionless Vulcan, represents pure rationality. Kirk, the commander of the *Enterprise*, more or less determines what is to be done and so represents the superego. And McCoy, who is very emotional and often operates on the basis of his feelings, represents the id.

In some texts it is easy to identify characters as id, ego, or superego figures. Superman, Dick Tracy, Luke Skywalker, and countless other heroes and heroines and caped crusaders are obviously superego figures. But others, such as James Bond and Indiana Jones, are more complicated; they may be more id and ego figures, perhaps, than superego. Villains, of course, are almost always id figures; they lack superego development and are interested only in gratifying their desires. They may be intelligent and shrewd, but they lack a sense of right and wrong.

We can also examine genres in terms of the Freudian structural hypothesis. Certain kinds of films and television programs, such as news shows, interview programs, and documentaries, can be classified as essentially ego texts. Texts that feature the police or that have religious messages are obviously superego texts. And soap operas and other television programs and films that involve sexuality (pornography, MTV) tend to be id texts. It is not always possible to label a text as clearly representing the id, ego, or superego, but in some cases, especially when the work is formulaic, it does make sense.

THE STRUCTURAL HYPOTHESIS APPLIED TO CULTURE

In Table 3.1, I use Freud's structural hypothesis to suggest how the id, ego, and superego can be applied to a number of media and cultural phenomena.

It is also possible to analyze films, songs, social media, heroes, and many other phenomena using Freud's id/ego/superego theory. We can see, then, that various texts in the mass media and areas of society and culture can be analyzed and found to have id, ego, and superego elements in them. Las Vegas advertises that what happens in Las Vegas stays in Las Vegas. This campaign can be seen as an overt invitation for people to let their ids loose in any number of ways without having to worry about their superegos chastising them or anyone finding out what they've been doing.

Table 3.1 Applications of Freud's Structural Hypothesis

Topic	Id	Ego	Superego
Star Trek	McCoy	Spock	Captain Kirk
Cities	Las Vegas	Boston	Vatican City
Toys	Barbie Doll	Science toys	Superhero toys
Clothes	Bikini	Scientist's white coat	Clerical garb
Books	Vampire novels	Science books	Bible, Koran

SYMBOLS

Psychoanalysis is, remember, an interpretive art. It seeks to find meaning in the behavior of people and in the art they create. One way we can apply psychoanalytic theory is by understanding how the psyche works and learning how to interpret the hidden significance of what people and characters in fiction do. We ask ourselves questions such as, "What does it mean when Hamlet says this or that?" or "What does it mean when Hamlet is unable to act?" We want to know *why*.

This is where symbols come in. Symbols stand for something else and may be hidden or at least not obvious. A symbol can stand for an institution, a mode of thought, an idea, a wish—any number of things. Heroes and heroines are often symbolic and thus can be interpreted in terms of the things they stand for. And much of what is most interesting about symbols is their relation to the unconscious. Symbols are keys that enable us to unlock the doors shielding our unconscious feelings and beliefs from scrutiny. Symbols are messages from our unconscious.

Hinsie and Campbell (1970) define symbolism as follows:

> The act or process of representing an order or idea by a substitute object, sign, or signal. In psychiatry, symbolism is of particular importance since it can serve as a defense mechanism of the ego, as where unconscious (and forbidden) aggressive or sexual impulses come to expression through symbolic representation and thus are able to avoid censorship. (p. 734)

According to this theory, then, we mask our unconscious sexual and aggressive desires through symbolization, which enables us to escape guilt from the superego.

Interpreting symbols can involve a number of difficulties. (I might point out that there are many theories in psychology about symbols, and they have, like many other aspects of psychoanalytic thought, generated a great deal of controversy.) First, symbols are often ambiguous, and how they are explained depends on one's orientation. For instance, some people see Hamlet's inability to act as symbolic of the power of an unresolved Oedipus complex, whereas others believe it symbolizes his skepticism and overintellectualism. Some think Hamlet is paralyzed by grief; others think he is insane. (If you are interested in the "problem" of Hamlet, I recommend you read *Hamlet and Oedipus*, by Ernest Jones [1949]. Jones provides a fascinating, although doctrinaire, Freudian interpretation of this symbolic hero.)

Symbols may be classified as conventional, accidental, or universal. Conventional symbols stand for things. In contrast to these are accidental symbols, which are personal, private, and connected to an individual's life history. For example, for a man who fell in love for the first time in Paris, Paris may become an accidental symbol for love. (The accidental symbols found in dreams are what make the interpretation of dreams so complicated, although dreams contain more than accidental symbols.) Finally, universal symbols are those rooted in the experience of all people. Many of these are connected to our bodies and to natural processes. Attempting to understand symbols is often complicated by the fact that the logic behind symbolization is frequently not the same logic people use in their everyday reasoning processes.

A broad comparison can be drawn between dreams and the works carried by the mass media. For a long time, neither were considered very important; neither dreams nor media texts were thought to have any effect on us, and so neither attracted much serious attention. Now we know better. Dreams are visual, so they are best compared to such media as film, television, and comics. And just as dreams can be interpreted through analysis of their symbolic content, so can the mediated dreams we find in the cinema or on the television screen. In both cases we ask the same questions: What is going on? What disguises are there? What gratifications do we get? What do the various symbolic heroes and heroines tell us about ourselves and our societies?

DEFENSE MECHANISMS

Defense mechanisms are techniques the ego employs to control instincts and ward off anxieties. All of us make use of these mechanisms from time to time, although we are seldom conscious of doing so. In like manner, much of what the media bring us involves human beings in varying kinds of relationships, so many of the characters we see or read about can be interpreted (often) in terms of their defense mechanisms. That is, their behavior may make more sense to us if we can relate it to the defenses people use to maintain their equilibrium. We can also understand our fascination with mass media in terms of defense mechanisms.

Following is a list of some of the most important defense mechanisms, with a brief description of each.

- *Ambivalence.* A simultaneous feeling of love and hate or attraction and repulsion toward the same person or object. Sometimes these feelings alternate in rapid succession in people who wish to be able to gratify contradictory wishes.
- *Avoidance.* Refusal to become involved with subjects that are distressing because they are connected to unconscious sexual or aggressive impulses.
- *Denial or disavowal.* Refusal to accept the reality of something that generates anxiety by blocking it from consciousness or by becoming involved in a wish-fulfilling fantasy.
- *Fixation.* Obsessive preoccupation or attachment to something, generally the result of some traumatic experience.
- *Identification.* The desire to become like someone or something in some aspect of thought or behavior.
- *Projection.* An attempt to deny some negative or hostile feeling in oneself by attributing it to someone else. Thus a person who hates someone will project that hatred onto another, perceiving that person as being the one who hates.
- *Rationalization.* The offering of logical reasons or excuses for behavior generated by unconscious and irrational determinants. (This term was introduced into psychoanalysis by Ernest Jones.)
- *Reaction formation.* This occurs when a pair of opposing attitudes generates problems, so one element is suppressed and kept unconscious by overemphasis on the other (its opposite),

although it doesn't disappear. For example, a person might have ambivalent feelings of love and hatred toward another; the hate may be made unconscious and kept unconscious by an overemphasis on love, so that it appears to be replaced by love.

- *Regression*. The individual's return to an earlier stage in life development when confronted with a stressful or anxiety-provoking situation.
- *Repression*. The barring from consciousness of instinctual wishes, memories, desires, and the like. This is considered the most basic defense mechanism.
- *Suppression*. The purposeful putting out of the mind and consciousness something the individual finds painful. This is the second most basic defense mechanism. (Because suppression is voluntary, suppressed material can be recalled to consciousness fairly easily, unlike repressed material, which is very difficult to bring to consciousness.)

Let me suggest how a media analyst might apply knowledge of defense mechanisms by presenting an example involving regression. In an analysis I conducted some years ago, I contrasted Pac-Man with other video games that preceded it, such as Space Invaders. For more than a year, Pac-Man was the most popular video game in the United States, which is one of the reasons I analyzed it.

In Space Invaders, players fly through the open skies, zapping invading aliens. Two things about Space Invaders are important to this analysis: First, there is freedom to fly about; second, the game is phallic. In Pac-Man, on the other hand, the play is restricted to an enclosed area, and the "attacks" involve eating. In other words, aggression in Pac-Man is oral. What we have in Pac-Man, then, is a regression from the phallic (guns) to the oral (biting) as a means of fighting and a change from the freedom to race around the skies to confinement in a maze. From a developmental perspective, Pac-Man is regressive.

The significance of this regression raises interesting questions. When it is not pathological, regression often involves an attempt to escape from anxiety of some kind and is a perfectly normal kind of behavior that functions in the service of the ego. It may be that the popularity of Pac-Man suggested that, somehow, large numbers of American young people (although they were not the only ones playing it) were experiencing anxieties and that they were using the game to assuage those anxieties. Curiously, there is often a connection between regression and fixation, so the fact that so many people played the game over and over again should not be too surprising.

Regression and all of the other defense mechanisms listed earlier are concepts that can be applied to the behavior of characters in films, television programs, and other texts and to various other aspects of the media. These concepts can help us understand human motivation and can enrich and deepen our ability to analyze the media.

Defense mechanisms are functions of the ego, which uses them against the id. When the id threatens the ego, generating anxiety, the ego uses whatever it can to neutralize the id. There is a considerable amount of disagreement among psychoanalysts as to what can legitimately be called a defense mechanism (the ego also has other techniques for mastering the id), but the ones listed earlier are generally accepted as the most important.

MARTIN GROTJAHN ON HORROR FILMS

Martin Grotjahn, a Freudian psychiatrist, offers a fascinating discussion of horror television texts that shows how defense mechanisms play an important role, at the unconscious level, in our attraction to these programs—to which we can add horror in other media: novels, video games, and films. He writes in *The Voice of the Symbol* (1971),

> The fascination of horror shows for so many people can be explained only when we consider the dynamic of the child's attraction to and fear of them. Horror is experienced when an old and long-repressed childhood fear seems to come true. The child fears ghosts or dead people returning. He fears that thoughts may come true; or that magic-mystic beliefs may prove to be effective. Fantasies may no longer be restricted to the unconscious but may become true events before our eyes on the television screen. We all are full of dangerous, bad wishes and thoughts which suddenly may emerge from repression and seem to become real and true; we can actually see them happening on the screen. The projection of repressed trends into symbols on the television screen would offer rare opportunity for working through of unconscious conflicts. Television could develop new means of art expression and an entirely new field of communication could be opened. (p. 9)

Grotjahn feels that television focuses its energy on entertaining us, in contrast to live theater, which, he suggests, makes us confront our conscious and unconscious conflicts more directly.

In his analysis of horror television shows we gain an understanding of why horror appeals to so many people and of the way horror is involved with defense mechanisms such as repression and projection. Let me suggest that in returning to our childhood fears, there is an element of regression involved in our fascination with horror. This means that at the unconscious level, we attempt to conquer our childhood fears by watching horror programs and films. We may also derive some pleasure from a regression to a period when life was simpler, when we may have experienced unconditional love and admiration from our parents and others, and we didn't have to struggle with problems of attaining an identity, earning a livelihood, and the responsibilities of maturity.

DREAMS

It is possible, without stretching things too much, to make a comparison between dreams and many of the fictions brought to us by the media—especially the moving-image media, such as film and television. Dreams are like films and television productions in that they are made up of images, generally have a narrative structure (although it may be obscure and bizarre), and are frequently hard to fathom. According to Erich Fromm (1957),

> Dreams are understood to be the hallucinatory fulfillment of irrational wishes and particularly sexual wishes which have originated in our early childhood and have not been fully transformed into reaction formations or sublimations. These wishes are expressed as being fulfilled when our conscious control is weakened, as is the case in sleep. (p. 67)

The situation is complicated by the fact that we don't allow ourselves to dream about certain things, which implies that some kind of censoring agent is at work that prevents certain forbidden thoughts to appear undisguised. This is where symbols (which I've already discussed) come in—they allow us to sneak "forbidden" material past our internal censors. Most of these symbols are sexual, as Fromm (1957) points out:

> The male genital is symbolized by sticks, trees, umbrellas, knives, pencils, hammers, airplanes, and many other objects which represent it either by their shape or by their function. The female genital is represented in the same manner by caves, bottles, boxes, doors, jewel cases, gardens, flowers, etc. Sexual pleasure is represented by activities like dancing, riding, climbing, flying. The falling out of hair or teeth is a symbolic representation of castration. Aside from sexual elements, symbols are expressive of the fundamental experiences of the little child. Father and mother are symbolized by king and queen or emperor and empress, children as little animals, death as a journey. (pp. 68–69)

These sexual symbols are one part of Freudian theory that often strikes people as ridiculous, and it has given Freud and psychoanalytic theory a bad name in many circles. However, Freud is often disparaged for this aspect of his theory by people who have not read his work at all or who have read very little of it. To the average person, and to many others who have read only a little in the field, the idea of seeing pencils and cigars as penises is simply absurd. One of the nice things about psychoanalytic theory is that this kind of behavior can be explained as repression—the refusal to acknowledge one's sexuality and other aspects of the psyche.

Many of Freud's critics take comfort in quoting a statement that has been attributed to him: "Sometimes a cigar is just a cigar." They generally employ this remark when someone else has used a Freudian interpretation of symbols to describe some object or artifact as a phallic symbol. I once suggested that the Washington monument, a great shaft erected in honor of the *father* of our country, is quite obviously a phallic symbol—although I don't believe the people responsible for creating the monument thought of it as such. "Ha!" replied a critic, who then offered the cigar quote.

My point here is that if sometimes a cigar is just a cigar, at other times a cigar is *not* just a cigar. You can't have it both ways. The notion that certain objects represent, to the unconscious mind, penises (and other objects, of course, represent vaginas or wombs) may strike you as absurd, but if you are going to argue that suggesting something is a phallic symbol is incorrect in some cases, you must accept the notion that in other cases, suggesting something is a phallic symbol may be correct.

In any case, dreams require interpretation, and that interpretation must be keyed to the dreamer's life. The dreamer can help an analyst discover a dream's true meaning by participating in free association—revealing all the thoughts that come into his or her mind—and by restructuring the dream. Fromm (1957) writes,

> This true dream, which is the expression of our hidden desires, Freud calls the "latent dream." The distorted version of the dream as we remember it is the "manifest dream" and the process of distortion and disguise is the "dream-work." The main mechanisms through which the dream-work translates the latent into the manifest dream are condensation, displacement and secondary elaboration. By condensation Freud refers to the fact that the manifest dream is much shorter than the latent dream. It leaves out a number of elements of the latent dream, combines fragments of various elements, and condenses them into one new element in the manifest dream. . . . By displacement Freud refers to the fact that an element of the latent dream, and often a very important one, is expressed by a remote element in the manifest dream and usually one which appears to be quite unimportant. (pp. 69–70)

The process of secondary elaboration involves filling in gaps in the dream, repairing inconsistencies, and so on, so the manifest dream *seems* consistent and coherent. Two things make analyzing dreams especially difficult: the fact that elements in dreams often stand for their opposites and the fact that the manifest dream is not a coherent narrative but a series of disconnected images. Thus a dream represents a formidable problem to the analyst, who must understand how dreams disguise and distort things and be able to relate what is found in dreams to the dreamer's personal life.

Jacques Lacan, a French thinker, has suggested that the semiotic concepts of metaphor and metonymy are useful for understanding dreams. Condensation, according to Lacan, is similar to what I have described in Chapter 1 as metaphor, and displacement is similar to metonymy. In condensation and in metaphor, we tie concepts together; in displacement and in metonymy, we substitute one thing for something else. Lacan differs with Freud over the nature of the unconscious. According to Freud, the unconscious is chaotic and preverbal, whereas for Lacan (1966) the unconscious is organized more or less like a language, which suggests that semiotics and linguistics might be useful in understanding how the unconscious works.

Recently, some researchers have suggested that Freud's theories about dreams being responses to experiences and being based on wish fulfillment might be inadequate. Whatever the case, his notions about how dreams function and the roles condensation and displacement play in dreams have interesting implications for the study of how the media affect individuals and, through individuals, society.

As I have noted, many of the products of the mass media can be viewed as similar to dreams—in analyzing these products, we must look for distortions and disguises, we must concern ourselves with the unconscious and with censorship, and we must relate what we discover in mediated works to the personal histories of the dreamers (which involve both their biographies and their social situations). We must also recognize the influences of the psyches of the creators and interpreters of these works. Clearly, the situation is quite complicated.

We can assume that apart from the surface communication between the artist or creator and the audience or receiver, there is also communication from the subconscious or unconscious of one to that of the other, so that some of the most important aspects of what we get from media may be submerged and not readily observable. This is why knowledge of the psyche and how it functions is so important.

CONDENSATION AND DISPLACEMENT

As noted earlier, the symbolic content of dreams is represented in two important ways—through condensation and displacement. Charles Brenner defines condensation in his book *An Elementary Textbook of Psychoanalysis* (1974): "The term 'condensation' is used to indicate the representation of several ideas or images by a single word or image, or even a part of one" (p. 51). Freud offers a description of the process in *The Interpretation of Dreams* (1900/1965):

> The first thing that becomes clear to anyone who compares the dream content with the dream thought is that a work of *condensation* on a large scale has been carried out. Dreams are brief, meagre and laconic in comparison with the range and wealth of dream thoughts. If a dream is written out it may perhaps fill half a page. The analysis setting out the dream thoughts underlying it may occupy six, eight or a dozen times as much space. (pp. 312–313, italics in original)

And even this is incomplete, says Freud. It's never possible to be sure, he suggests, that a dream has been completely analyzed and interpreted.

Brenner (1974) defines displacement as "the representation of a part by the whole, or vice versa, or, in general, the substitution of one idea or image by another which is associatively connected with it" (p. 51). We use displacement in our dreams because we don't wish to confront certain phenomena directly, as this might wake us, and so we find symbolic substitutes that are less threatening. And what is it that we seek to displace? Brenner (1974) writes:

> The list of what may be represented by a symbol is not very long. It comprises the body and its parts, particularly the sexual organs, buttocks, anus, urinary and alimentary tracts, and the breasts; members of the immediate family, such as mother, father, sister and brother; certain bodily functions and experiences, such as sexual intercourse, urination, defecation, eating, weeping, rage, and sexual excitement; birth; death; and a few others. The reader will notice that these are things which are of great interest to the small child, in other words that they are things important to an individual at a time when his ego is still immature. (p. 52)

CONCAVE

It's important to recognize that these processes are also found in mass-mediated dreamlike texts, such as sitcoms, soap operas, commercials, advertisements, sporting events, spy stories, crime shows, and many others, which helps explain why the media fascinate us so much. Hollywood has been called a "dream factory," and two of the processes that play important roles in films are condensation and displacement.

AGGRESSION AND GUILT

In *Civilization and Its Discontents* (1962), one of his last books, Freud discusses aggressiveness in people:

> Men are not gentle creatures who want to be loved, and who at the most can defend themselves if they are attacked; they are, on the contrary, creatures among whose instinctual

endowments is to be reckoned a powerful share of aggressiveness. As a result, their neighbor is for them not only a potential helper or sexual object, but also someone who tempts them to satisfy their aggressiveness on him, to exploit his capacity for work without compensation, to use him sexually without his consent, to seize his possessions, to humiliate him, to cause him pain, to torture and to kill him. *Homo homini lupus* [Man is a wolf to man]. (p. 58)

In this passage Freud suggests that aggressiveness is instinctual but secondary to more basic instincts, as his use of the phrase "a powerful share" indicates.

This aggressiveness could threaten to disrupt or even destroy society and civilization as we know it, so a powerful opposing force is brought into play. This force is guilt, which, Freud (1962) explains, is aggression turned back on itself:

Another question concerns us. . . . What means does civilization employ in order to inhibit the aggressiveness which opposes it, to make it harmless, to get rid of it, perhaps? . . . [Man's] aggressiveness is introjected, internalized; it is, in point of fact, sent back to where it came from—that is, it is directed toward his own ego. There it is taken over by a portion of the ego, which sets itself over against the rest of the ego as super-ego, and which now, in the form of "conscience," is ready to put into action against the ego the same harsh aggressiveness that the ego would like to satisfy upon other, extraneous individuals. . . . Civilization, therefore, obtains mastery of the individual's dangerous desire for aggression by weakening and disarming it and by setting up an agency within him to watch over it, like a garrison in a conquered city. (pp. 70–71)

In fact, Freud argues, we are made to feel so guilty that at times we become overwhelmed with guilt and forfeit our sense of happiness. The "cost" of civilization is generally too great for us; we are forced to renounce too much (especially our sexuality), and we suffer from too much guilt.

This is where humor comes in, for in humor we have developed a way to allow ourselves to enjoy certain kinds of aggression by masking them and thus evading guilt. Freud (1960) analyzes humor in great detail in *Jokes and Their Relation to the Unconscious*, one of his most impressive works. Freud was drawn to the study of humor—a subject that has never been satisfactorily explained—because of his interest in the psyche, the unconscious, and human aggressiveness. Freud suggested that humor involves masked aggression; the humor disguises the aggression and thus allows id elements to enjoy the aggression without having to worry about the superego generating guilt over the aggression. Martin Grotjahn deals with humor in his book *Beyond Laughter: Humor and the Subconscious* (1966), which expands on Freud's ideas about humor and applies them to a number of related topics such as humor and creativity, clowns, and humor and therapy.

CONTENT

CON OF THE COB
(BOSTON JOKE)

L(N₵o(L)N

VATICON

CONDOM

STEREOTYPES AND AGGRESSIVE HUMOR

We can see stereotyping very clearly in jokes about nationalities, races, occupations, sexual orientations, and religions. Stereotypes are positive, neutral, or negative beliefs people have about group members. In jokes about stereotypes, the content tends to be negative. I offer some jokes and humorous texts that involve stereotypes.

The United Nations asked a number of different nationalities to write books about elephants. They receive the following books. The French write a book titled *The Love Life of Elephants*. The English write *The Elephant and English Social Classes*. The Germans write a five-volume series titled *A Short Introduction to the History of the Elephant*. The Italians write *The Elephant and the Renaissance*. The Americans write *How to Raise Bigger and Better Elephants*. And the Israelis write *Elephants and the Jewish Question*.

Two men and a woman are shipwrecked on a desert island. If they are Spanish, the men will fight a duel and the survivor gets the girl. If French, one man becomes the husband, and the other the lover. If English, nothing will happen because no one is there to introduce them so they won't speak. If Italian, they will play cards to decide who will have the girl. If Greek, they will start fighting over politics and forget the girl. If Turks, one will have the front way and the other the back passage.

A ship goes down in the Pacific. Nobody survives except two men and a woman. They save themselves on a small island. What happens if the two men are Italian? One murders the other in order to possess the woman for himself. If they are Frenchmen, they live peacefully a *trois*. If they are English or Germans, then the men move to another island and leave the woman alone. If they are Russians, they set a bottle afloat for Moscow for further instructions.

All of these jokes are slurs on different nationalities. A good deal of stereotyped humor is much nastier and more hostile than these jokes, such as those about Poles and Jewish American princesses. Jokes and riddles play an important part in spreading stereotypes, along with films and television programs that use stereotypes as a quick way of showing character behavior and motivation.

FREUD AND BEYOND

Over the many decades since Freud started investigating the human psyche, there have been many new developments in psychoanalytic theory. In their book *Freud and Beyond: A History of Modern Psychoanalytic Thought*, Stephen A. Mitchell and Margaret J. Black (1996) write,

> Very little of the way Freud understood and practiced psychoanalysis has remained simply intact. The major pillars of his theorizing—instinctual drives, the centrality of the Oedipus complex, the motivational primacy of sex and aggression—have all been challenged and fundamentally transformed in contemporary psychoanalytic thought.
> And Freud's basic technical principles—analytic neutrality, the systematic frustration of the patient's wishes, a regression of an infantile neurosis—have likewise been reconceptualized, revised, and transformed by current clinicians. (p. xvii)

In psychoanalytic theory, as in all theories, there have been a number of reconceptualizations and transformations, but Freud's ideas and his pioneering discoveries still remain at the heart of the enterprise for media critics. We turn now to the work of one of the other giants in psychoanalytic theory, Carl Jung.

JUNGIAN PSYCHOANALYTIC THEORY

Carl Jung is, after Freud, probably the most important psychoanalytic theorist. He was originally associated with Freud but moved away from Freud's ideas and founded his own school of analytic psychology. Jung elaborated a number of concepts that have led to different ways of helping people and, for our purposes, of analyzing texts. The following are some of these concepts.

Archetypes

An archetype is a universal theme found, according to Jung, in dreams, myths, religions, and works of art. Archetypes exist independent of the personal unconscious of individuals. They are connected, Jung theorized, to past history and an alleged collective unconscious found in all people. Jungians argue we become aware of them only as the result of images that come to us in dreams, works of art, or everyday emotional experiences that connect us to them in ways that, suddenly, we recognize. As Jung (1964) explains,

> What we properly call instincts are physiological urges, and are perceived by the senses. But at the same time, they also manifest themselves in fantasies and often reveal their presence only by symbolic images. These manifestations are what I call the archetypes. They are without known origin; and they reproduce themselves in any time or in any part of the world—even where transmission by direct descent or "cross fertilization" through migration must be ruled out. (p. 69)

Jung suggests that "the hero figure is an archetype, which has existed since time immemorial" (p. 73), and so the same applies to the myth of paradise or of a past "golden age," when people lived in peace and abundance.

The Collective Unconscious

The source of Jung's archetypes is what he describes as the collective unconscious. As Jung (1964) explains, making an analogy with instincts,

> We do not assume that each new-born animal creates its own instincts as an individual acquisition, and we must not suppose that human individuals invent their specific human ways with every new birth. Like the instincts, the collective thought patterns of the human mind are innate and inherited. They function, when the occasion arises, in more or less the same way in all of us. (p. 75)

This explains, Jungians argue, why myths are universal and certain themes and motifs are found in works of art throughout history and everywhere in the world. Jung's notions about archetypes, the collective unconscious, and the universality of myths, I should add, are very controversial, and many psychologists and others take issue with them. It is impossible to demonstrate, for instance, that a collective unconscious actually exists.

The Myth of the Hero

Heroes, which are archetypes and manifestations of the collective unconscious, play an important role in Jungian thought. As one prominent Jungian, Joseph L. Henderson (1964), notes,

> The myth of the hero is the most common and the best-known myth in the world. We find it in the classical mythology of Greece and Rome, in the Middle Ages, in the Far East, and among contemporary primitive tribes. It also appears in our dreams.

These hero myths vary enormously in detail, but the more closely one examines them the more one sees that structurally they are very similar. They have, that is to say, a universal pattern, even though they were developed by groups or individuals without any direct cultural contact with each other. Over and over again one hears a tale describing a hero's miraculous but humble birth, his early proof of superhuman strength, his rapid rise to prominence or power, his triumphant struggle with the forces of evil, his fallibility to the sin of pride (*hybris*), and his fall through betrayal or a "heroic" sacrifice that ends in his death. (p. 110)

This description applies to so-called tragic heroes. Most heroes, especially those found in the mass media, generally don't succumb to the sin of pride; they usually survive to fight, in endless succession, new villains, who keep appearing with incredible regularity. The myth of the hero, according to Henderson, has the function of helping individuals develop consciousness of their ego, which enables them to deal with problems they confront as they grow older. Heroic figures help young people with problems of separation and individuation from their parents and other tutelary figures, which explains why heroes are found throughout history and why they are so important.

The Shadow Element in the Psyche

What Jungians call the shadow refers to the dark side of the human psyche, which we generally keep hidden from consciousness, although it is something we must eventually recognize and deal with. Henderson (1964) explains Jung's understanding of the shadow:

Dr. Jung has pointed out that the shadow cast by the conscious mind of the individual contains the hidden, repressed, and unfavorable (or nefarious) aspects of the personality. But this darkness is not just the simple converse of the conscious ego. Just as the ego contains unfavorable and destructive attitudes, so the shadow has good qualities—normal instincts and creative impulses. Ego and shadow, indeed, although separate, are inextricably linked together in much the same way that thought and feeling are related to each other. (p. 110)

There is, then, according to Jungians, a battle for deliverance between the shadow and the ego that occurs in the psyche. Heroes provide the means (or are the vehicles) by which, symbolically, the ego "liberates the mature man from a regressive longing to return to the blissful state of infancy in a world dominated by his mother" (Henderson, 1964, p. 111).

Freudians do not use this concept, but it is easy to see that it is vaguely analogous to what they describe as the unconscious. The struggle for dominance between the shadow and the ego may be compared with the battle that Freudians assert goes on between the id and the superego, which the ego tries to mediate. Jung's shadow seems to be more negative than Freud's id, but both are considered to be the source of creative activity.

The Anima and the Animus

In Jungian thought, the anima represents the female element found in all males, and the animus represents the male element found in all females. This duality, according to Jungians, is symbolized in hermaphrodites (people with sexual organs of both sexes) and in witches, priestesses, medicine men, and shamans. M.-L. von Franz (1964), a Jungian theorist, discusses the anima and animus in terms of their impact on personality, the arts, and related phenomena:

> The most frequent manifestation of the anima takes the form of erotic fantasy. Men may be driven to nurse their fantasies by looking at films and strip-tease shows, or by day-dreaming over pornographic material. This is a crude, primitive aspect of the anima, which becomes compulsive only when a man does not sufficiently cultivate his feeling relationships—when his feeling attitude toward life has remained infantile. (pp. 179–180)

Von Franz suggests that the anima has a positive side, however, that enables men to do such things as find the right marriage partner and explore their inner values, leading them to more profound insights into their own psyches. The animus functions in much the same way for women. It is formed, von Franz suggests, essentially by the woman's father and can have positive and negative influences. It can lead to coldness, obstinacy, and hypercritical behavior, but, conversely, it can help a woman to develop inner strength, to take an enterprising approach to life, and to relate to men in positive ways.

A useful summary of Jung's theories and contributions can be found in Ellis Cashmore and Chris Rojek's *Dictionary of Cultural Theorists* (1999):

> For Jung, as for Freud, a basic part of his analytical process was based upon dream analysis, and he published extensively on this topic. Jung also considered and defined the process of individuation as the path to individual self-knowledge. According to Jung, everyone has an innate desire to achieve this self-realization, and the prevention of this through external influences (from other people in close contact with the individual or from societal pressures) is the root cause of an individual's dysfunctional behavior. According to Jung, a person's personality can be described in terms of the persona and shadow: the persona representing the mask which mediates between a person and the world and the shadow representing that part of the personality which the individual will not allow himself or herself to express. An individual also has both a masculine and feminine side, labeled animus and anima. For a man the masculine side (animus) is resident in the conscious mind with the anima being present in the unconscious, while for a woman, the reverse is the case. In his later career, Jung became extremely interested in and knowledgeable concerning the religions, myths and rituals of primitive societies and, as a result, after his break with Freud, he became more concerned with the interpretation of society rather than individual psychology. . . . Much of his later work has a mystical aspect to it and this aspect of his work has led to a resurgence in popularity in Jungian psychology in recent years among alternative communities. Indeed, the psychology of Jung provides much of the foundations of "New Age" psychology and spirituality. (p. 262)

Jung published many books over the course of his long career. One of the most accessible is the book from which many of the quotations in this chapter are found, *Man and His Symbols* (1964).

PSYCHOANALYTIC ANALYSIS OF MEDIA: A CAUTIONARY NOTE

A subject as vast and complicated as the psyche poses enormous problems for a writer who wants to suggest how psychoanalytic concepts can be applied to analyzing the mass media. As with any other subject, there is always the problem of oversimplification and reductionist thinking. In this chapter I have attempted to suggest how the most fundamental concepts in psychoanalytic literature can be applied to the media—how they may help us to understand human motivation and perhaps also our reactions to what we read, see, and hear.

Because there are so many competing schools of psychoanalytic thought, and because the general public, which is not familiar with many of the concepts used by psychoanalytic thinkers, is often hostile to these concepts, psychoanalytic criticism is a difficult pursuit. But how else can we understand the way *King Kong* or *Star Trek* or *Hamlet* (or any other work in print or film media) has the power to seize our attention and move us in profound and interesting ways?

What Simon Lesser says about literature in *Fiction and the Unconscious* (1957) can be applied to just about all media:

> The supreme virtue of psychoanalysis, from the point of view of its potential utility for literary study, is that it has investigated the very aspects of man's nature with which the greatest writers of fiction have been preoccupied: the emotional, unconscious or only partly comprehended bases of our behavior. Unlike other psychologies, but like Sophocles and Shakespeare, Tolstoy and Dostoevsky, Melville and Hawthorne, it has concerned itself with the surging, non-rational forces which play so large a part in determining our destiny as well as the part of our being which tries, often in vain, to control and direct them. It offers us a systematic and well-validated body of knowledge about those forces. (p. 15)

Lesser goes on, then, to say something about what we would call the audience and the way it responds to fiction and media in general:

> It is my assumption that as we read we unconsciously *understand* at least some of a story's secret significance; to some extent our enjoyment is a product of this understanding. But some readers go on to try to account for the effect a story has had upon them, and to report what they discover. It is in connection with these later critical activities, which must be sharply differentiated I believe from the reading experience itself, that psychoanalytic concepts are likely to prove invaluable. They make it possible to deal with a portion of our response which was not hitherto accessible to criticism—permit us to explain reactions which were intuitive, fugitive and often non-verbal, and supply the key to the elements in the story responsible for those reactions. (p. 15, italics in original)

To conclude, I would like to emphasize that my purpose in this chapter has been not to provide a comprehensive review of psychoanalytic techniques but to propose the usefulness of psychoanalytic criticism for helping us to understand and interpret both what we find carried by the mass media and our responses to it—a suggestion worth some thought.

STUDY QUESTIONS AND TOPICS FOR DISCUSSION

1. What is meant by the unconscious?
2. The mental life of a human being is often compared to an iceberg. Draw this iceberg and show how it can be understood to represent mental life.
3. How did Dichter explain the use of cigarette lighters? How does this explanation relate to the psyche?
4. List and discuss the four stages of development that people pass through, according to Freud.
5. What, according to Freud, are the characteristics of anal eroticism?
6. Contrast Freud's topographic hypothesis with his structural hypothesis.
7. What is the Oedipus complex, and how has it been used to explain Shakespeare's *Hamlet*?
8. What did Freud say about symbols and how symbols function in dreams?
9. Describe and explain condensation, displacement, and secondary elaboration.
10. List and briefly describe six of the most important defense mechanisms and tell what roles they play.
11. How does the psyche handle guilt? How is humor related to this process?
12. What do Jungians believe about archetypes, the collective unconscious, the shadow, and the anima and animus? Pretend you are a Jungian critic and offer a Jungian analysis of *Star Wars* or some other text.
13. What cautions should one observe in approaching analysis of media (or anything else) from a psychoanalytic perspective?

ANNOTATED BIBLIOGRAPHY

Appignanesi, Richard. *Freud for beginners*. (1979). New York: Pantheon. This comic book explains the basic principles of Freudian thought.

Berger, Arthur Asa. (2000). *The Hamlet case: The murders at the MLA*. New York: Xlibris. In this comic academic novel, a demented English professor murders all the members of the editorial board of *Shakespeare Studies*, the journal he edits, but not before each of them (a semiotician, a psychoanalytic theorist, a Marxist critic, a sociological critic, a feminist critic, a historical critic, and a literary theorist) has offered a different interpretation of *Hamlet*.

Bettelheim, Bruno. (1977). *The uses of enchantment: The meaning and importance of fairy tales*. New York: Vintage. This is an excellent example of the application of psychoanalytic theory (Freudian, in particular) to an important literary genre. Extended and perceptive readings of some of the most important Western fairy tales appear in the second half of the book.

Brenner, Charles. (1974). *An elementary textbook of psychoanalysis*. Garden City, NY: Doubleday. This is a classic textbook on psychoanalytic theory, authoritative and relatively easy to read and understand.

Freud, Sigmund. (1963). *Character and culture* (Philip Rieff, Ed.). New York: Collier. This collection of Freud's work focuses on folklore, myth, literature, and the arts—that is, applications of his theories to cultural phenomena.

Freud, Sigmund. (1965). *The interpretation of dreams*. New York: Avon. This book, originally published in 1900, is considered Freud's greatest publication—a fascinating and controversial analysis of the nature of dreams and the role they play in our lives. Freud's discussions of symbols, condensation, displacement, and distortion are of particular interest to those interested in visual communication.

Fromm, Erich. (1957). *The forgotten language: An introduction to the understanding of dreams, fairy tales and myths*. New York: Grove. Fromm provides an interesting study of myths and dreams, with an extended comparison of the ideas of Jung and Freud.

Garber, Marjorie. (1993). *Vested interests: Cross-dressing and cultural anxiety.* New York: HarperPerennial. Encyclopedic, erudite, and fascinating, this book deals with various aspects of cross-dressing as it is found in print fiction, film, television, and everyday life.

Grotjahn, Martin. (1966). *Beyond laughter: Humor and the subconscious.* New York: McGraw-Hill. This fascinating study of humor and popular culture in general covers a lot of territory and has interesting things to say about many different topics such as horror films and our interest in mysteries.

Grotjahn, Martin. (1971). *The voice of the symbol.* New York: Delta. This classic study of the role of symbolism in media, the arts, dreams, and psychoanalytic theory includes chapters on television, Oedipus as a symbol, medieval Christian art, and symbolism in psychoanalytic theory.

Erikson, Erik. (1963). *Childhood and society.* New York: W. W. Norton. Erikson's classic study of the meaning of childhood and the problems children face as they mature.

Erikson, Erik. (1968). *Identity, youth and crisis.* New York: W. W. Norton. Here, Erikson focuses his attention on the crises we face as we grow up and search for a satisfying identity.

Jones, Ernest. (1949). *Hamlet and Oedipus.* New York: W. W. Norton. This book is a classic Freudian interpretation of *Hamlet* written by the author of an important biography of Freud. It is an excellent example of how psychoanalytic theory can be applied to an important text.

Jung, Carl G., with von Franz, M. L., Henderson, Jolande Jacobi, & Jaffé, Aniela. (1964). *Man and his symbols.* Garden City, NY: Doubleday. This book, conceived and edited by Jung, contains chapters by Jung and some of his followers on myths, dreams, heroic types, and other Jungian concerns. Many illustrations are provided.

Key, Wilson Bryan. (1974). *Subliminal seduction: Ad media's manipulation of a not so innocent America.* New York: Signet. This remarkable (some would say notorious) volume offers all kinds of notions about the role of subliminal communication in advertising. Key's thesis is that advertisers manipulate people by sending messages that have impacts below the level of consciousness. The book includes an introduction by Marshall McLuhan.

Klein, Melanie, & Riviere, Joan. (1964). *Love, hate and reparation.* New York: W. W. Norton. A classic study of the cycle of love, hate, and reparation that people go through in their lives by two influential psychoanalytic theorists.

Kolbenschlag, Madonna. (1980). *Kiss Sleeping Beauty goodbye: Breaking the spell of feminine myths and models.* Garden City, NY: Doubleday. This book argues that some women identify too strongly with the heroines in fairy tales and thus fail to develop themselves as persons. According to the author, many women wait, like Sleeping Beauty, for the perfect man to come and rescue them from lives that are boring and uneventful.

Kris, Ernst. (1964). *Psychoanalytic explorations in art.* New York: Schocken. This is an important book on the creative process, literary criticism, the comics, and art.

Lesser, Simon O. (1957). *Fiction and the unconscious.* Boston: Beacon. This psychoanalytic study of fiction is useful for those interested in popular culture and the public arts.

Mitchell, Stephen A., & Black, Margaret J. (1996). *Freud and beyond: A history of modern psychoanalytic thought.* New York: Basic Books. This book deals with psychoanalytic theory and new developments in the field in the years after Freud's death.

Phillips, William. (Ed.). (1963). *Art and psychoanalysis: Studies in the application of psychoanalytic theory to the creative process.* New York: Meridian. This is a collection of essays on art, literature, the creative process, psychological criticism, and related matters.

Rank, Otto. (1979). *The double: A psychoanalytic study.* New York: Meridian. This book presents a fascinating study of the double (doppelgänger) motif as it is found in myths and literary and artistic texts.

Spector, Jack J. (1974). *The aesthetics of Freud: A study in psychoanalysis and art.* New York: McGraw-Hill. This is a study of Freud's theories of art and his influence on art and literature, with attention paid to biographical matters.

Winick, Charles. (1995). *Desexualization in American life.* New Brunswick, NJ: Transaction. In this provocative and controversial book, Winick argues that in the past 30 years a remarkable process of desexualization has taken place in U.S. society that is reflected in fashion, sports, the media, and popular culture. He asserts, in essence, that symbolically men are becoming weaker and women are becoming stronger.

Much of the debate about media in contemporary society has a sociological dimension, so this chapter addresses, first, the sociological concepts that have the most immediate applicability to media analysis. This is followed by a discussion of uses and gratifications theory that includes a list of some of the reasons people use the mass media—that is, the uses and gratifications connected to the media. The chapter ends with a discussion of content analysis and offers a simple content analysis exercise that may yield interesting results.

Sociological Analysis

Someone once defined a sociologist as a person who tells everyone things they already know in language they can't understand. I use the term *sociological* in this chapter in the broadest sense possible. The focus here is on the social relationships of men and women, in contrast, for example, to psychological matters such as the consciousness of individuals. We examine the public arts with a concern for human interactions and personal relationships, asking, "Who does what to whom and why?" and "What patterns are discernible in the materials we study?"

It is useful to differentiate sociology from other social sciences, such as anthropology, political science, and psychology, by looking at the core concepts of these differing fields. The basic concern in sociology is how groups and institutions function (institutions are generally understood to be ways of patterning and organizing social life). The core concepts in psychology, as I have mentioned previously, are the individual psyche and the unconscious. For anthropologists, the core concept is culture; for political scientists, the core concepts are power and government. Disciplines are also often combined, so we have social psychologists, political sociologists, social anthropologists, and so on.

Table 4.1 shows (in highly simplified form) the core concepts found in four of the social sciences and the terms used by social scientists in these areas for the processes through which individuals are turned into members of society. These processes don't always take place in all individuals; thus we speak of people who are improperly socialized or who, because they have not received sufficient enculturation into a given society (travelers or aliens, for example), experience "culture shock."

Table 4.1   Core Concepts and Processes in Four Social Sciences

	Sociology	Psychology	Political Science	Anthropology
Core concept	Groups, institutions	Psyche, consciousness	Power, government	Culture
Process	Socialization	Identification	Indoctrination	Enculturation

The term *sociology* was coined by French philosopher Auguste Comte (1798–1857), who conceived of it as a means of integrating theoretical and practical knowledge about human beings. The purpose of sociology is, according to Comte, "to know in order to predict in order to control." Comte wanted to discover the laws by which people live, so that a rational and humane social order could be established. Since Comte's time, sociology has evolved, and we find sociologists studying everything from collective behavior, deviance, and religion to the ways bureaucracies function and how social change occurs.

Émile Durkheim

ÉMILE DURKHEIM ON OUR SOCIAL NATURE

Émile Durkheim, one of the most important sociological theorists and one of the founding fathers of French sociology, offers an important insight into the relationship between individuals and societies. An individual's intellectual activity is not as rich or as complex as a society's intellectual activity, because a society's thought is enriched by historical tradition. Durkheim points out that the individual has a complex relationship to society. He writes about this relationship in his classic study *The Elementary Forms of the Religious Life* (1915/1965):

> There are two beings in him: an individual being which has its foundation in the organism and the circle of whose activities is therefore strictly limited, and a social being which represents the highest reality in the intellectual and moral order that we can know by observation—I mean society. This duality of our nature has as its consequence in the practical order, the irreducibility of a moral ideal to a utilitarian motive, and in the order of thought, the irreducibility of reason to individual experience. In so far as he belongs to society, the individual transcends himself, both when he thinks and when he acts. (p. 29)

For Durkheim, then, each of us is "double." We are members of society and therefore in society, but, on the other hand, society is in us. Each of us has our own physical body and personality—that is, we are individuals—but we also are social animals who are members of society. And although we may not be aware of it, much of what we think is influenced by our societal membership.

According to Durkheim, the ideas we have are, to a large degree, shaped by what we are taught in school and by the way we are socialized by our peers, parents, priests, and favorite pop stars. So there is a strong social dimension to our thinking, even if we believe that somehow we are "self-made" men and women and that society is just an abstraction that has little impact on our lives. We should keep Durkheim's insight into the relationship between the individual and society in mind when we consider the role the mass media play in our lives and in our societies.

A more contemporary sociologist, Pierre Bourdieu, professor of sociology at the Collège de France, makes a similar argument. In his book *Sociology in Question* he writes (1993),

Sociology reveals the idea of personal opinion (like the idea of personal taste) is an illusion. From this it is concluded that sociology is reductive, that it disenchants, that it demobilizes people by taking away all their illusions. . . . If it is true that the idea of personal opinion itself is socially determined, that it is a product of history reproduced by education, that our opinions are determined, then it is better to know this; and if we have some chance of having personal opinions, it is perhaps on condition that we know our opinions are not spontaneously so. (p. 27)

This notion, that our opinions and taste are socially determined, strikes many people as far-fetched or absurd. But it is central to sociological theory. We should keep Bourdieu's discussion of opinion and taste in mind when we analyze texts since our analyses are tied to our personal history, our socioeconomic class, and other such phenomena. The same argument is made by many feminists who argue that gender is socially determined and not natural and by other social scientists that race is socially constructed.

In the remainder of this chapter, I first discuss some of the basic concepts and tools of analysis that sociologists use when they study societies. These concepts and tools enable us to see things we might have neglected previously. For example, take the concept of roles. Only in recent years have media critics paid much attention to the roles given to women in films and television programs, as well as to such related matters as the numbers of women relative to the number of men seen in these media, the ages of the women portrayed, and what happens to them. An understanding of some important sociological concepts can help an analyst examine the mass media in new ways.

Following this discussion of basic concepts, I address the gratifications the public arts offer to people and the needs people meet through their use of the mass media. In recent years there has been a good deal of interest in this uses-and-gratifications approach (sometimes also called the needs-and-gratifications approach). The focus here is on how people use the media and the gratifications the media offer them. I suggest a number of needs and gratifications that are met by the public arts; this list may shed some light on why certain television programs, films, and other media products are so popular, as well as the roles they might play in society.

The chapter ends with a discussion of a standard sociological technique, content analysis. In conducting content analysis, researchers use statistical methods to make inferences about what they find in the media. Take the matter of violence in children's television programs as an example. Once we decide on a working definition of *violence*, we can examine a sampling of children's television programs and count the incidents of violence we find. This enables us to move from saying, "There's a lot of violence on children's television," to something like, "There are *X* incidents of violence per hour on children's television."

Frequently, researchers using content analysis adopt a historical frame of reference. They might examine, for instance, earlier samples of children's programs in order to make comparisons concerning the violence they contain. Using content analysis techniques, researchers can determine whether there is more violence in children's television programs now than there was at some earlier time. If there is more violence now, what does that mean?

SOME BASIC CONCEPTS

Following are brief discussions of some fundamental sociological concepts, all of which can be applied to analysis of the public arts. The explanations are as concise as I can make them; I hope that in my effort to be clear I have not oversimplified matters too greatly. Try to apply these terms to characters in films and television shows and to the styles of texts you find interesting. Is Spider-Man alienated or anomic or both? What role do socioeconomic class and stereotyping play in situation comedies or the many British television series broadcast on National Public Television? What are the functions, latent and manifest, of televised football programs? Are certain races and ethnic groups overrepresented or underrepresented in the mass media? What roles are women generally given in texts? Are certain pop singers like Madonna or Lady Gaga deviant? Is a film such as *Cloud Atlas* postmodern? Keep questions like these in mind as you read my discussion of some of the more important concepts of sociological thought and think about how you can apply them to various texts.

Alienation

Alienation means, literally, "no ties" and refers to a feeling of estrangement and separation from others. A person who is alienated feels like a stranger (or alien), with no connections to his or her society. Feelings of alienation are connected, in many instances, to the bureaucracies that develop in organizations. Bureaucracies are often necessary to deal with large numbers of people in a fair and efficient manner, but they are also impersonal and tend to generate feelings of alienation. Students in large universities, for example, are frequently known to the administration only by their social security numbers, and our language concerning students also has an alienating tone. We sometimes talk about young men and women as being "college material," for instance.

We can use the concept of alienation to understand the behavior of characters in texts such as *Death of a Salesman*, the cult television show *The Prisoner*, and social groups and subcultures (teenagers, punk rockers, and so on). When we apply this concept we must connect it, very specifically, to acts of characters or the behaviors of groups and subcultures.

Anomie

The word *anomie* is derived from the Greek word *nomos*, meaning "norms." It means, literally, no (*a*) norms (*nomos*). Anomie and alienation are not the same. A group of thieves, for example, might have a strong sense of fellowship and thus not be alienated, but because they have no respect for the laws of society, they would be described as anomic. In *Masters of Sociological Thought*, Lewis A. Coser explains what Émile Durkheim described as anomie. Coser writes (1971):

MAX WEBER

> When social regulations break down, the controlling influence of society on individual propensities is no longer effective and individuals are left to their own devices. Such a state of affairs Durkheim calls anomie, a term that refers to a condition of relative normlessness in a whole society or in some of its component groups. Anomie does not relate to a state of mind, but a property of the social structure. It characterizes a condition in which individual desires are no longer regulated by common norms, and where, as a consequence, individuals are left without moral guidance in the pursuit of their goals. (pp. 132–133)

One way societies attempt to deal with anomie is by setting up rules of conduct in life, and to facilitate this, they develop bureaucracies, our next important sociological concept. Members of criminal gangs are anomic, but they are not alienated, in that they belong to closely knit groups that have strong bonds between members. One of the reasons gangs are so difficult to deal with is that members join them to escape from alienation.

Bureaucracy

As society becomes larger and more complex, it becomes increasingly difficult to regulate, and keeping things running with any degree of efficiency can be a problem. Bureaucracies are collections of more or less anonymous people who follow fixed rules and routines in running organizations. Bureaucracies are typically characterized by hierarchies of authority, impersonal handling of problems, and a great deal of red tape.

Max Weber, the great German sociologist, suggested that as societies evolve and become more complex, they move from being led by charismatic individuals to being led by politicians and bureaucrats in what he described as a "rational-legal system." One of the inevitable by-products of bureaucracies is depersonalization, which results in a sense of powerlessness and alienation. Our anxieties about bureaucracies inform the narratives of many books, television programs, and films, including Kafka's classic novels *The Trial* and *The Castle*, the television series *The Prisoner*, and the film *The Matrix* and its sequels.

Socioeconomic Class

A class is a group of people with something in common. When used in a sociological context, the term usually refers to socioeconomic class—a person's class level or place in the hierarchy of classes in society. W. Lloyd Warner (1953), a distinguished sociologist and anthropologist, has suggested six classes in American society: upper-upper, lower-upper, upper-middle, lower-middle, upper-lower, and lower-lower. Warner estimates the distribution of membership in these classes in the United States as follows:

Upper-upper, 1.4%

Lower-upper, 1.6%

Upper-middle, 10%

Lower-middle, 28%

Upper-lower, 33%

Lower-lower, 25%

Warner suggests that the lower-middle and upper-lower classes constitute the "common man." Although these figures are dated, they give an idea of the class makeup of U.S. society that is still fairly accurate.

Socioeconomic class is determined by a number of components, including education, income, and occupation, and different social classes have different lifestyles, ways of raising children, and values.

As of the early 1980s, it was estimated that the wealthiest 1% of American families owned more than 40% of all the corporate stock in the country, and the top 10% controlled almost 70% of the total wealth. This 10% owned around half the value of all real estate and more than 90% of corporate stocks and business assets and bonds. There were approximately 80 million families in the United States at that time, but 400,000 households controlled 27% of the wealth. Since these figures were compiled, the concentration of wealth has increased.

In terms of income, the lowest 25% of American families have been losing ground. The middle class has also been losing ground, as wages—in terms of real income—have been static in the last 10 years or so.

Thus, although many Americans tend to think of the United States as an essentially "classless" or "all-middle-class" society, it is actually very much a highly stratified, class-based society. Although a substantial middle class exists, members of the economic elite in the United States definitely have enormous political power.

Social Class in Britain

The British Broadcasting System recently published the results of a survey in April 2013 of 160,000 people in Britain and found there are now seven social classes there. Before this survey, Britain was thought to have three classes: upper, middle, and lower. An article in the *Guardian* lists these seven social classes. The sociologists who conducted the survey, Mike Savage and Fiona Devine, explain the three kinds of what they call "capital" in Britain that help differentiate the classes:

Economic capital: income, value of home, and savings

Social capital: number and status of people they know

Cultural capital: cultural interests (often elite culture) and activities

The seven social classes are the following. I have added the percentage of the population they represent, taken from other sources.

Elite. This is the most privileged class in Great Britain who has high levels of all three capitals. Their high amount of economic capital sets them apart from everyone else (6%).

Established middle class. Members of this class have high levels of all three capitals, although not as high as the elite. They are a gregarious and culturally engaged class (25%).

Technical middle class. This is a new small class with high economic capital but seemingly less culturally engaged. They have relatively few social contacts and so are less socially engaged (6%).

New affluent workers. This class has medium levels of economic capital and higher levels of cultural and social capital. They are a young and active group (15%).

Emergent service workers. This new class has low economic capital but high levels of "emerging" cultural capital and high social capital. This group is young and often found in urban areas (19%).

Traditional working class. This class scores low on all three forms of capital, although they are not the poorest group. The average age of this class is older than the others (14%).

Precariat. This is the most deprived class of all, with low levels of economic, cultural, and social capital. The everyday lives of members of this class are precarious (15%).

Source: www.guardian.co.uk/society/2013/apr/03/great-british-class-survey-seven

Culture

In recent years, scholars' interest in the concept of culture has grown considerably. A field of inquiry known as cultural studies, for example, has become a very important part of many universities' curricula, especially in media studies, communication, and literature departments. Stuart Hall, a British communication scholar, explains why we've become so interested in culture in the introduction to his book *Representation: Cultural Representations and Signifying Practices* (1997):

> What has come to be called "the cultural turn" in the social and human sciences, especially in cultural studies and the sociology of culture, has tended to emphasize the importance of *meaning* to the definition of culture. Culture, it is argued, is not so much a set of *things*—novels and paintings or TV programmes and comics—as a process, a set of *practices*. Primarily, culture is concerned with the production and the exchange of meanings—the "giving and taking of meaning"—between the members of a society or group. To say that two people belong to the same culture is to say that they interpret the world in roughly the same ways and can express themselves, their thoughts and feelings about the world, in ways which will be understood by each other. . . . It is participants in a culture who give meaning to people, objects and events. Things "in themselves" rarely if ever have one, single, fixed and unchanging meaning. (pp. 2–3)

This means that learning how to interpret and analyze our culture's mass-mediated texts, the content of the mass media, is a way of learning about our culture and, indirectly, because we are members of this culture, about ourselves. Notice also that Hall's perspective is essentially semiotic, focusing on the importance of signifying processes and meaning. Hall is talking about the anthropological definition of culture, which roughly deals with how people live and transmit their pictures of the world and ways of doing things from generation to generation.

Another definition of culture involves the arts. Postmodernists don't make any distinction between what are commonly known as elite culture and popular culture, but most scholars do. *Elite culture* refers to art forms such as opera, ballet, symphonic music, poetry, and what might be called "serious" novels and other literature; *popular culture* refers to mass-mediated texts such as sitcoms, radio and television commercials, print advertising, genre novels (science fiction, romance, western, detective), various kinds of pop music (country-western, rock, hip-hop), and sports contests. It is important to understand both kinds of culture, I would suggest, if we want to understand the fundamental beliefs and values found in a society.

In recent decades, a field of inquiry known as cultural studies has developed in which scholars use many disciplines to analyze media, culture, and anything else of interest to them. *Media Analysis Techniques* can be seen as a contribution to this field in that it uses a number of disciplines in the humanities and social sciences to analyze texts and mass-mediated culture.

Deviance

Deviance refers to behavioral patterns different from typical or conventional (some would say *normal*) ones. Attitudes toward different forms of deviance change over time. For instance, homosexuality was once considered criminal, later defined as deviant, and now is accepted as a natural phenomenon by

most people. Deviance generates anxiety in people because it forces them to consider the validity of their own practices as well as their own attitudes about what is normal.

Elites

Elites are at the top of the social pyramid, the upper-class and lower-upper-class people who hold positions of power, are affluent, and generally work in professional or executive occupations. (The opposite of elites are common men and women.) It has been documented that the heroes on television tend to be relatively young, well-educated, White professionals; the entertainment media present very few working-class heroes. We might wonder what effects this overrepresentation of elites has on the viewing audience.

Ethnicity

Ethnicity is conventionally understood to mean certain cultural traits, religious beliefs, and traditions that distinguish groups in society. In the United States, people whose grandparents or parents were from foreign countries—groups such as Italians, Poles, Germans, Finns, Jews (who are a special case), Chinese, Vietnamese, Mexicans, and countless other groups—are considered to have an ethnic identity. They are often identified as Italian Americans, Polish Americans, and so on. In the past, many people in the United States tried to camouflage their ethnic identities, but today ethnic pride is more common. Ethnic groups are often stereotyped in the media, but this practice is now under attack. Ethnicity is often confused with race.

Functionalism

Sociologists say that something is *functional* when it contributes to the maintenance and stability of whatever entity it is part of; likewise, something is *dysfunctional* if it is destabilizing or destructive. If something has no particular effect on the entity of which it is a part, it is said to be *nonfunctional.* The fact that something may be both functional and dysfunctional complicates matters. For example, television in general may be functional in that it provides a great deal of information to people, helps fuel consumption, and stresses certain values, but it may be dysfunctional in that it portrays some types of people in negative roles, suggests that the world is more violent than it really is, and creates feelings of anxiety and discontent in people who cannot afford all of the good (and bad) things advertised. Functional analysis has a conservative bias in that it emphasizes the maintenance and stability of society instead of focusing on changes that might be made.

We can also examine phenomena in terms of whether their functions are intended or unintended, conscious or unconscious. Thus the *manifest function* of television news programs might be to inform, whereas the *latent function* of these programs might be to indoctrinate viewers with certain political values and beliefs. Reporters and newscasters, I should point out, may not be aware they are indoctrinating people; they may believe all they are doing is reporting the news.

Media analysts are interested in the roles that individual performers play in texts and in the roles assigned to women, members of ethnic and racial minorities, old and young people, and representatives of other groups (sexual, political, religious, socioeconomic) as well. Viewers of films and television programs often identify with the heroes and heroines in these texts and incorporate what they see in creating their own identities. Many observers believe the mass media generate a considerable amount of "social teaching."

Many critics argue that the roles women play in the media are often demeaning. Women are all too frequently treated only as sexual objects, used for display, or portrayed as dummies who get excited about some brand of toilet paper. They are much less often shown as professionals or other productive citizens who should be taken seriously. Frequently, they appear only as passive figures that react to the initiatives of others, usually males. Such roles give audience members images of what women are like and how they should be treated that can have negative consequences, not only for women but for men as well. If space here permitted, I could also discuss the negative ways in which Blacks, Asians, Latinos, Jews, disabled persons, and members of countless other groups are portrayed in the media.

When media analysts look at roles in the media from a sociological perspective, then, they must examine the roles assigned to people (who must be seen as representatives of social groups) and the impacts media dissemination of these roles might have on individuals and on society in general.

Another concept of interest in the area of functionalism is that of *functional alternatives*. Sociologists use this idea to explain situations in which, for example, an original institution loses its viability (to some extent) and is replaced by a substitute institution. According to functionalist theory, institutions are created and evolve because certain things have to be done to keep a society operating properly. If a given institution no longer works, something must be found to take its place. Let us assume, for example, that people have a need for some kind of religious experience, some form of connection with powers beyond the human. This need, in the United States, has traditionally been taken care of by organized religions. But as mainline organized religions have lost popularity, something else has been needed to take their place, and professional football has to a degree filled that function. Professional football might be seen, from this perspective, as a functional alternative to organized religion. (I discuss this idea in more detail in Chapter 6.)

The aspects of functional analysis may be summarized as follows:

- *Functional*: maintains an organization, society, or the like
- *Dysfunctional*: destabilizes an organization, society, or the like
- *Nonfunctional*: plays no role
- *Manifest function*: intended and recognized by people
- *Latent function*: not intended and not recognized by people
- *Functional alternative*: substitute for original institution, practice

Lifestyle

Lifestyle is a comprehensive term that covers a person's tastes in fashion, cars, entertainment and recreation, literature, and related matters. *Style* suggests fashion, and *lifestyle* is used to describe how people fashion their lives. Our lifestyles are often connected to our socioeconomic class and are reflected in our "images." Mary Douglas, in her article on shopping (1997) and in other writings, uses the concept to distinguish between four competing lifestyles—individualists, hierarchists, egalitarians, and fatalists—that shape our behavior in various areas of life.

People's lifestyles are the sum of their various taste decisions: the kinds of cars they drive, the breeds of dogs or cats they own, the magazines they read (or at least display on their coffee tables), where they live, what their homes are like (how big, the colors of the walls, the kinds of furniture), their occupations, the kinds of food they eat and the restaurants they frequent, the kinds of vacations they take—the list is endless. All of these phenomena tend to be class specific and are reflections of an individual's so-called level of sophistication. The institution that tutors us about these matters is advertising, one of the basic functions of which is to make sure, to the extent it can, that expenditure always rises to meet, if not exceed, income.

Marginalization

Marginalization is the process by which individuals and groups with (in some cases deviant) values and beliefs that differ from the norm in societies are delegitimated and given secondary status. This may involve being ignored, being persecuted, or both. As the United States becomes an increasingly diverse and segmented multicultural society containing numerous linguistic, racial, sexual, and other subcultures, there is some question as to whether dominant elites and majority members will continue to be able to marginalize members of "out groups" and subcultures with different demographics.

Mass Communication and Mass Media

Sociologists and communication scholars distinguish between mass communication and mass media. We live in an age in which mass communication is held to be of major importance in our lives. Mass communication involves the use of mass media—print media such as newspapers and magazines and electronic media such as radio, television, and film (and now the Internet)—to communicate with large numbers of people at the same time. These media reach people in groups or individually.

Sociologists have developed numerous models to explain how mass communication works. These models are highly abstract representations of the process of communication, the role of media in communication, and related concerns. One of the most famous of these is Harold Lasswell's theory, which asks, "Who? Says what? In which channel? To whom? With what effect?" (qtd. in McQuail & Windahl,

1993, p. 13). Communication researchers debate whether the mass media are weak or powerful and what effects they have on individuals and societies.

Mass Society

A number of years ago, some sociologists argued that the United States had become what they described as a mass society—that is, a society in which large numbers of people live in given areas but have little involvement with one another, making them susceptible to manipulation. As Herbert Blumer, a prominent sociologist, wrote in 1936,

> [The mass] has no social organization, no body of customs and traditions, no established set of rules or rituals, no organized group of sentiments, no structure or status roles, and no established leadership. It merely consists of an aggregation of individuals who are separate, detached, anonymous. (Qtd. in Friedson, 1953, p. 314)

Many social scientists today do not accept this notion of a mass society; they assert that it is based on theory and not on the ways people behave in contemporary societies. Let me offer an example that suggests the mass society thesis is incorrect: Janice Radway's work on readers of romance novels.

Radway's book, *Reading the Romance: Women, Patriarchy, and Popular Literature* (1991), is a study of romance novel readers that began as a way of discovering the uses and gratifications romance novels offer readers. After spending some time with romance readers, Radway changed her focus:

> What the book gradually became, then, was less an account of the way romances as texts were interpreted than of the way romance reading as a form of behavior operated as a complex intervention in the ongoing social life of actual social subjects, women who saw themselves first as wives and mothers. (p. 7)

Her research, she writes, was influenced by the cultural studies movement at the Birmingham University Centre for Contemporary Cultural Studies, which used ethnographic field studies as a means of finding out how people used and were affected by mass media.

She offers some observations about the ability readers have to resist the power of those who control the media:

> If we can learn, then, to look at the ways in which various groups appropriate and use the mass-produced art of our culture, I suspect we may well begin to understand that although the ideological power of contemporary cultural forms is enormous, indeed sometimes even frightening, that power is not yet all-pervasive, totally vigilant, or complete. Interstices still

FREDRIC JAMESON

exist within the social fabric where opposition is carried on by people who are not satisfied by their place within it or by the restricted material and emotional rewards that accompany it. (p. 222)

By studying a group of romance novel readers, Radway learned it is possible, and perhaps often the case, that people are able to resist the power of mass media to shape their own consciousness. In this regard, consider what happened in Eastern European countries when the Soviet Union broke apart. Even though the people who lived in these countries had been subjected to something like 40 years of constant procommunist media propaganda, when they realized they could do so without fear of a Red Army invasion, they threw out the communist leaders who had been ruling them and established democratic forms of government.

Postmodernism

The term *postmodernism* has been defined in so many ways that some scholars suggest it can mean anything you want it to mean. According to some critics, postmodernism has had profound effects on U.S. culture and society and has played a major role in shaping Americans' consciousness. Fredric Jameson (1991), a literature professor at Duke University, has suggested that postmodernism is a "cultural dominant" that represents the latest stage of capitalism. Others take issue with this notion.

One of the best descriptions of postmodernism comes from sociologist Todd Gitlin (1989):

It self-consciously splices genres, attitudes, styles. It relishes the blurring or juxtaposition of forms (fiction-nonfiction), stances (straight-ironic), moods (violent-comic), cultural levels (high-low).

One postmodernist trope is the list, as if culture were a garage sale, so it is appropriate to evoke postmodernism by offering a list of examples, for better or worse: Michael Graves' Portland Building, Philip Johnson's AT&T, and hundreds of more or less skillful derivatives; Robert Rauschenberg's silk screens; Andy Warhol's multiple-image paintings, photo-realism . . . ; Disneyland, Las Vegas, suburban strips, shopping malls, mirror-glass office building facades; William Burroughs, Tom Wolfe, Donald Barthelme, Monty Python, Don DeLillo, Joe Isuzu "He's Lying" commercials, Philip Glass, Star Wars, Spalding Gray, David Hockney, . . . Max Headroom, David Byrne, Twyla Tharpe (choreographing Beach Boys and Frank Sinatra songs), Italo Calvino. (pp. 52–53)

What this list points out is the extent to which our consciousness has been shaped by postmodernism. If the postmodernist theorists are correct, many Americans who have never even heard the term *postmodernism* (although it is showing up now increasingly in popular magazines and newspapers) are living, although they may not realize it, postmodern lives. To adopt a medical analogy, Gitlin's list reflects the symptoms; postmodernism is the disease.

Postmodernism has implications for our study of the media. Postmodernists don't accept the modernist notion of hierarchy in the arts and reject the idea of an important difference between elite culture and mass-mediated popular culture. There are just arts, postmodernists suggest, and one is as good as another, whether we are talking about operas, symphonies, classic novels, romance novels, or comic books. This means, also, that originality is no longer considered important.

Pastiche is a dominant trope in postmodernism, and eclecticism rules. This perspective is reflected in an observation from Jean-François Lyotard's book *The Postmodern Condition: A Report on Knowledge* (1984):

> Eclecticism is the degree zero of contemporary general culture: one listens to reggae, watches a western, eats McDonald's food for lunch and local cuisine for dinner, wears Paris perfume in Tokyo and "retro" clothes in Hong Kong; knowledge is a matter for TV games. (p. 76)

If there are no overarching religious and philosophical beliefs to shape behavior, anything goes. Whether this freedom to do anything you want to do and believe anything you want to believe is satisfying and something on which human beings can build decent societies is another matter.

Lyotard points out that in the absence of aesthetic standards, the only thing important is the profit that works of art yield, which suggests that although postmodernists seem to be indifferent to everything, they are not indifferent to the value of the almighty dollar, euro, or whatever currency is used where they live and work.

Race

Race is contentious. It was once defined as dealing with people with a common genetic heritage, and three broad classifications were used: Negroid, Mongoloid, and Caucasoid. In recent years, we have abandoned this kind of thinking. Race, it must be added, is not the same thing as ethnicity, which is connected to nationality and not genetic makeup. I mention the subject of race because historically there has been a considerable amount of racism in the public arts, and it is still a problem.

In recent years, many scholars have argued that race is socially constructed. That is, race is not a biological category—given that, genetically, human beings are all the same—but a sociological and ideological one. These scholars also note that genetic variations make it difficult to identify anyone as a member of a particular race, and racial identity is further complicated by such phenomena as migration and intermarriage.

From a semiotic perspective, it can be said that we use the idea of race to deal with *otherness*, as a lens through which to view people who look different from us and in many cases come from cultures different from ours. All too often, unfortunately, we think of people different from us in terms of overgeneralizations known as stereotypes. In American mass-mediated texts, African Americans as well as members of many other ethnic and racial groups are underrepresented. When members of these groups do have roles in films and television shows, their roles are often stereotypical; thus it may be argued that the media ultimately contribute to racist attitudes in their audiences.

In her book *Black Looks: Race and Representation* (1992), social critic bell hooks (formerly Gloria Watkins) addresses the way African Americans are portrayed in the media:

> If we compare the relative progress African Americans have made in education and employment to the struggle to gain control over how we are represented, particularly in the mass media, we see that there has been little change in the area of representation. Opening a magazine or book, turning on the television set, watching a film, or looking at photographs in public spaces, we are most likely to see the images of black people that reinforce and reinscribe white supremacy. Those images may be constructed by white people who have not divested of racism or by people of color/black people who may see the world through the lens of white supremacy—internalized racism. (p. 1)

Thus hooks asserts that the media victimize Black people in two ways: through images created by White people who hold racist views and through images created by Black people who have internalized the racist views of Whites. In both cases, however, this racism is unconscious and thus not recognized. Most White people, hooks argues, get their unrealistic ideas of what Blacks are like from images in mass-mediated texts, such as films and television programs, in which they play certain roles. In addition, these images give Black people a distorted view of themselves. The election of Barack Obama to the presidency has played a major role in the way people regard Black people now and suggests that race is no longer a factor that prevents people of any race from becoming president.

Thus, although we may not be aware of it, media images have implicit social and ideological dimensions. That is why it is so important for us to examine the media's depictions of racial groups (and ethnic, gender, and other groups) and to understand the ideological content of those depictions.

Social Role

We are all familiar with the term *role* as it is used in theater, television, and film; the concept of social role is in some ways similar. Social roles are formed by the behavior we learn relating to expectations people have of us in specific situations. An individual's social roles are determined, in part, by that person's place in society. In the course of a day, the average individual plays many roles: parent, worker, companion, and so on. As we grow up, we learn—from our parents, media, and other sources—how various roles are to be played. It is part of the socialization process. Adolescence in America (and many other countries as well) is a period generally characterized by "role experimentation" as young people try different roles as they seek to define themselves.

Sex and Gender

Sex and gender are important sociological concepts when linked to roles and some of the other concepts discussed here. Many media critics argue that the mass media are sexist and have consistently assigned women to destructive roles. This is certainly an important issue for media analysts to keep in mind.

Sociologist E. Barbara Phillips conducted an instructive content analysis. She analyzed the roles of women portrayed in random selections from two magazines—*Ms.* and *Family Circle*—and discovered considerable differences between them. For example, the women who were subjects of articles in *Family Circle* were all homemakers; *Family Circle* included no articles about women involved in politics or social concerns. The articles in *Ms.*, on the other hand, didn't deal with any women as homemakers (although many of the subjects were married and had families); rather, they focused only on the ways women were involved in social, cultural, and political life and public service. The two magazines projected different roles for women, and, no doubt, each helped to support and reinforce the value systems of its readers.

Judith Butler's *Gender Trouble: Feminism and the Subversion of Identity* (1990) is considered a major contribution to our understanding of gender. In her preface to the book, she suggests that our notions of gender aren't as fixed as they used to be. She writes:

> Precisely because "female" no longer appears to be a stable notion, its meaning is as troubled and unfixed as "woman,"
> Judith Butler
> and because both terms gain their troubled significations only as relational terms, this inquiry takes as its focus gender and the relational analysis it suggests. Further, it is no longer clear that feminist theory ought to try to settle the questions of primary identity in order to get on with the task of politics. (p. xxix)

Butler's book is not easy to read, but it offers a highly nuanced study of gender and, as she points out in her discussion of writing the book, "It was cited as one of the founding texts of queer theory" (p. vii).

Socialization

Socialization is the process by which people are taught the rules, roles, and values of their society. It may be seen as a kind of indoctrination done formally through institutions such as the family, school system, and church and informally through the media. What is important about informal socialization is that people generally do not recognize they are being taught (some would say programmed) what roles to play and how to play them, what values to espouse, what attitudes to have, what goals to strive for, and so on.

There are two ways to get people to do what they are supposed to do—that is, to act in socially desirable ways. One is to use force, but that is very difficult and very expensive. If you can get children to internalize the values you want them to have, so that they act the way you want them to act, then it is much easier to create a stable society. As we grow up, we internalize rules and prohibitions depending on a number of variables, such as the socioeconomic class into which we are born, the education of our parents, our race, our religious upbringing, our gender, and our psychological makeup.

Our identities are shaped by what sociologists call our "significant others"—our parents, siblings, teachers, and friends—who give us feedback on who we are and what we are like. The feedback we get from these significant others is connected to the cultures or subcultures in which we are raised. As we grow up, we internalize the dominant values of our society and social groups that are most important for us, and we search for models to imitate.

Clotaire Rapaille

This is where the media come in. We unconsciously, as we watch television programs, read comic books, go to the movies, and otherwise consume our daily media diet (now estimated at around 8 hours of media exposure per day), find models to imitate. We internalize their values and imitate, to varying extents, their behavior. A number of media critics have suggested that most of the models we find in the media are not positive; they assert that the impact of media exposure on our well-being and on society's need for order is primarily negative.

If we are indeed being socialized by the media, the question we must ask is, "How does the violence that pervades mass-mediated texts, the woman-hating lyrics found in so much rap music, and the sexploitation found in commercials and print advertising affect us?" We may not be aware of this socialization and may think of media content as nothing but entertainment, but such a dismissive view, it may be argued, makes us all the more susceptible to the media's influence. The media, we can suggest, reflect basic values and beliefs that resonate with viewers of films and television shows and other kinds of media.

Clotaire Rapaille (2006), a French cultural anthropologist and marketing expert, wrote in *The Culture Code* that nations imprint different codes into children, which shape their behavior in their adult lives. As he explains, "Most of us imprint the meanings of the things most central to our lives by the age of seven. This is because emotion is the central force for children under the age of seven" (p. 21). He argues that three kinds of unconscious shape our behavior: a Freudian individual unconscious, a Jungian collective unconscious, and a cultural unconscious, which represents the codes imprinted on us that shape our behavior. He explains the relationship between codes as imprints:

> An imprint and its Code are like a lock and its combination. If you have all the right numbers in the right sequence, you can open the lock. Doing so over a vast array of imprints has profound implications. It brings to us the answer to one of our most fundamental questions: why do we act the way we do? Understanding the Culture Code provides us with a remarkable new tool—a new set of glasses, if you will, with which to view ourselves and our behaviors. It changes the way we see everything around us. What's more, it confirms what we have always suspected is true—that, despite our common humanity, people around the world really are different. The Culture Code offers a way to understand how. (p. 11)

His book discusses differences between Americans and people in other cultures. One of the most interesting differences is reflected in the way American and French people relate to cheese. The American code for cheese is "dead," and so they wrap it in plastic and store it in morgues known as refrigerators, he explains. The French code for cheese is "alive," and so the French store their cheese in containers (cloches) and don't refrigerate it. Every culture has its codes, and finding the codes that inform each culture helps us understand why people in that culture act the way they do.

Status

Status is often confused with role, but the two are different although connected. *Status* refers to the position a person has in some group or organization and the prestige attached to that position. Status is thus associated with a person's role. Within universities, for example, full professors have more status than assistant professors and play different roles. Within society in general, those who have certain occupations have great status (doctors, lawyers, professors, bankers), and those who work at "lesser" jobs have little status (ditch diggers). Status is a powerful force in society used to control people in subtle ways.

Stereotypes

O'Sullivan, Hartley, Saunders, Montgomery, and Fiske (1994) define a stereotype in *Key Concepts in Communication and Cultural Studies* as

> the social classification of particular groups of people as often highly simplified and generalized signs, which implicitly or explicitly represent a set of values, judgments and assumptions concerning their behavior, characteristics or history. (pp. 299–300)

Stereotypes can be positive, negative, or mixed, but regardless, they give millions of people oversimplified and sometimes pernicious images of Blacks, Jews, Frenchmen, doctors, police officers, women—the list is endless. No matter what form they take—racial, occupational, sex role—stereotypes are oversimplifications and overgeneralizations that minimize individual differences and tend to be destructive. The media use them extensively, which feeds on notions people have about the groups being stereotyped. As we have seen in the discussion of humor and stereotypes, they are often quite nasty and frequently used in an attempt to mask aggression.

Values

Values are the attitudes people have relative to what they believe to be desirable and undesirable, good and bad; they cover a wide spectrum of social phenomena, including sex, politics, and education. In indirect ways, people's values affect their behaviors. Media critics must be aware of the values demonstrated by characters portrayed in mass-mediated productions and should examine what these values suggest about society.

The preceding minicourse in sociological concepts is meant to alert you to some of the concerns sociologists (and other social scientists) have and their focus when examining the public arts. As I have pointed out, frequently it is useful to combine concepts, so we might consider such matters as sex role stereotyping, socioeconomic class and status, racism and sexism (and all the other *isms*), and the values of deviants. Readers interested in exploring these concepts in more detail and within the structure of sociological theory in general should consult any standard introductory sociology textbook; also, the annotated bibliography at the end of this chapter lists some important books that take a "media sociology" approach.

Herbert Gans

I should note here that media analysts need to bear in mind that they are concerned with works of art when they examine sitcoms, soap operas, commercials, and other genres found in the public arts. These texts cannot be considered merely documents to be viewed in terms of their sociological content; analysts must take other considerations into account as well, such as artistic conventions and the difficulties involved in dealing with some artistic or creative personalities.

HERBERT GANS ON TASTE CULTURES

Herbert Gans, a sociologist with an interest in media and popular culture, describes five "taste cultures" in the United States. As he writes in his book *Popular Culture and High Culture: An Analysis and Evaluation of Taste* (1974),

> I suggest that America is actually made up of a number of taste cultures, each with its own art, literature, music, and so forth, which differ mainly in that they express different aesthetic standards. . . . The underlying assumption of this analysis is that all taste cultures are of equal worth. . . . Because taste cultures reflect the class and particularly education attributes of their publics, low culture is as valid for poorly educated Americans as high culture is for well-educated ones, even if the higher cultures are, in the abstract, better or more comprehensive than the lower cultures. (pp. x–xi)

These five taste cultures are the following:

high culture

upper-middle culture

lower-middle culture

low culture

quasi-folk low culture

This classification system is similar, in many respects, to the six socioeconomic classes W. Lloyd Warner found when he analyzed American society.

In his book Gans lists some of the texts each of his taste cultures prefers. Keep in mind that the book was published in 1974, so the texts mentioned are those that were popular in the sixties and early seventies. Gans defended the media and popular culture preferences of the members of each of his taste cultures and suggested that we shouldn't look down on any of their choices, since each text was appropriate for the people who belonged to each taste culture. The following are examples of each of the cultures.

High Culture

(Made up of serious writers, artists, and creative types and highly educated people in the upper and upper-middle classes)

Formalistic modern music

Primitive art

Abstract expressionism

Finnegan's Wake by James Joyce

Serious essays

Upper-Middle Culture

(Made up of members of the upper-middle class, including professionals and executives from prestige universities and colleges)

Time

Newsweek

Psychology Today

Biographies of achievers

Feminist books

The New Yorker

Harper's

Vogue

Playboy

Lower-Middle Culture

(For Gans, the dominant taste culture in the United States. It is made up of lower-middle-class and lower-class people in low-status professions or who hold the lowest-level white-collar jobs.)

Life

Look

Reader's Digest

Saturday Evening Post

Novels by Harold Robbins, Jacqueline Susann

Bonanza

All in the Family

Maude

Mary Tyler Moore Show

Low Culture

(Made up of lower-middle-class people, skilled and semiskilled factory and service workers, those with a high school degree, and high school dropouts)

Westerns

Lucille Ball

Lawrence Welk

Ed Sullivan Show

Beverly Hillbillies

Tabloids

Quasi-Folk Low Culture

(Here we find unskilled blue-collar and service workers whose education often ended in grade school; they are often rural and people of color.)

Comic books

Old westerns

Simple action films and soap operas made in Mexico

Church and street festivals

Young people who are often graffiti artists

Gans (1974) devotes a few pages in his book to youth cultures, Black cultures, and ethnic cultures but doesn't go into detail about any of them because he believes they are only "temporary offshoots from the taste cultures described previously" (p. 94). There are some questions we might think about here. One question involves the kinds of texts members of each of Gans's taste cultures would like in contemporary America. The second is whether Gans's typology or five taste cultures is the best way to characterize the American media public—or any media public, for that matter. Is his theory simplistic? Are there more than five "taste cultures" in the United States? If so, what are they? We must also consider the postmodernist position that there's only one taste culture because postmodernists don't recognize any difference between elite and popular culture.

USES AND GRATIFICATIONS

Uses-and-gratifications theory has been the subject of a good deal of controversy, but the same can be said about every other theory related to media. Despite the fact that much of the research so far conducted on mass media has been empirical and concerned with the media's effects on attitudes (and many other matters), there has been a considerable amount of interest in the ways people use media and the gratifications media offer to people. Katz, Blumler, and Gurevitch (1979) mention some early works on the subject:

Herzog (1942) on quiz programs and the gratifications derived from listening to soap operas; Suchman (1942) on the motives for getting interested in serious music on radio; Wolfe and Fiske (1949) on the development of children's interest in comics; Berelson (1949) on the functions of newspaper reading; and so on. Each of these investigations came up with a list of functions served either by some specific contents or by the medium in question: to match one's wits against others, to get information or advice for daily living, to provide a framework for one's day, to prepare oneself culturally for the demands of upward mobility, or to be reassured about the dignity and usefulness of one's role. (p. 215)

Regardless of whether you think soap operas are stupid or situation comedies are silly, the functions these programs—and others—perform for people may in some cases be quite important. Shortly, I list and briefly describe a number of the possible gratifications the media offer and some needs they may help to fill. A good deal of scientific work remains to be done on people's needs, on the gratifications individuals seek, and on the roles the mass media play in meeting people's needs, but it seems obvious that people do use media in varying ways (although they may not be aware they are doing so).

The material that follows is informed by a number of sources, but I am particularly indebted to my colleague Stuart Hyde, who has addressed in his work a number of the needs and desires people have and the ways they use the public arts to deal with them. It is difficult to decide, in some cases, whether a given reason people use the media involves needs, uses, gratifications, or desires, so in the following list I avoid these terms altogether, leaving those issues for you to determine. The list is also incomplete; you may be able to add to it in ways that help you understand more fully how the media function.

To be amused. We seem to want to be entertained, to find things to laugh about, to be put in a happy spirit. The media are a source of pleasure.

To see authority figures exalted or deflated. American society has its roots in egalitarian values, and many Americans tend to regard authority as invalid. Thus we like to see authority figures deflated and ridiculed, especially politicians, soldiers, professors, and psychiatrists. We tend to exalt some authority figures, however: clergymen, surgeons, and detectives, to name a few. The media play an important role in teaching us how to relate to authority and deal with authority figures.

To experience the beautiful. We give high status to beautiful music, beautiful works of art, and people who are physically attractive—in particular, beautiful women. What is beautiful is another matter, however, and definitions of beauty change over time.

To share experiences with others (community). One of the more important functions of the mass media is to give people a common cultural (or pop cultural) frame of reference. In some cases, such as when we go to football games in huge stadiums, we are actually with others in a momentary kind of community. And this experience is often shared with millions of others who may listen to the game on the radio or watch it on television. In other cases we merely watch a program along with millions of others. It has been discovered that one of the most important topics of conversation among Americans is the content of the media; thus sharing the same programs or films may help people relate to one another.

To satisfy curiosity and to be informed. This has to do with our wish to know what's going on, to be up to date, to follow stories as they develop, and so on. The satisfaction of curiosity probably has to do with human beings' natural inquisitiveness, whereas the desire to know what's going on and to be informed has to do with surveillance and the anxiety we feel when we are "in the dark." One thing is certain—we learn a great deal from the media, both directly and indirectly.

To identify with the deity and the divine plan. Many people hold some form of what might be called "the God concept," and the media often help people gain a sense of the nature of life, the power of spiritual forces, and so forth.

To find distraction and diversion. Many people find that the public arts help them escape (if only momentarily) from worry and anxiety and pass the time when they are bored. This kind of thing is sometimes described as "killing time" by those who feel the public arts tend to be mindless and destructive, but from a uses-and-gratifications perspective, the public arts are never used only to kill time. We may *seem* to be doing nothing (and even think we are doing nothing) when we watch television or listen to rock music, but in truth a great deal is going on.

To experience empathy. We share in the joys and sorrows of others through the media, and from this we derive psychological pleasure—often catharsis, or relief. Although we relate to the characters we see in the media vicariously, we still are able to share in their emotional experiences, and this enriches us greatly. It also helps us prepare ourselves emotionally for the difficulties we all face in real life at one time or another.

To experience, in a guilt-free and controlled situation, extreme emotions, such as love and hate, the horrible and the terrible, and similar phenomena. This is slightly different from experiencing empathy, which involves identifying with characters. This concerns our desire to experience powerful emotions without being carried away by them or having to feel guilt about them. The media enable us to have powerful experiences without paying for them, so to speak, and to take risks without having to worry about being devastated. (There is some question, however, as to whether all individuals do escape being affected by their media experiences. Despite the "controls," some people may end up with morbid residues, thoughts that may trigger violence, or other effects of which they are unaware.)

To find models to imitate. These models help us gain a sense of identity, teach us how to cope in certain situations, and, informally, socialize us. One problem here is that some people may identify with villains rather than heroes and heroines and may pick up ideas, attitudes, and behavior patterns that are harmful and destructive. For example, there is a great deal of fear that children who watch television programs full of violence will learn to be violent and to use violence as a means of solving problems.

To gain identity. *Identity* can be defined as a coherent sense of self, a personal style, a defined personality. The United States is no longer a traditional society, and as our traditions wither, as we become more mobile, modern, and materialistic, we find it increasingly difficult to form identities. This is where the media come in—in particular, the heroic and unheroic figures we follow in the comics, watch on television, read about in popular novels, and so on. They help us manufacture identities, so to speak. But whether or not these identities are suitable, long lasting, and good for us is another matter.

To gain information about the world. In some cases this is obvious: In the media we hear economists talk about economic problems, professors and other experts are called on to explain things to us, documentaries deal with topics of interest, and televised college courses are offered. But we also learn a great deal incidentally from the media all the time, such as how to behave in certain situations. The media offer us heroic figures to emulate, and they reinforce certain values. The media are always teaching us something, even when they are not intentionally doing so and even when we don't realize it. A good question we might keep in mind, then, is, "What are we learning from the media?"

To reinforce belief in justice. It doesn't always work out this way, but generally speaking we like to see heroes defeat villains and see evil punished and virtue rewarded. In other words, we want to believe the universe is moral and crime doesn't pay.

To reinforce belief in romantic love. Although our belief in the power of love may be waning, we still tend to see romantic love as a wonderful thing and a prime motivating force in relationships. Implicit in the belief in romantic love is the notion that emotions are powerful forces capable of overwhelming logic, reason, class differences, age differences, racial differences, and anything else. We learn sometimes, however, that romantic love doesn't always lead to happiness.

To reinforce belief in magic, the marvelous, and the miraculous. This belief, which probably stems in great measure from childhood (fairy tales, magicians, and so on), explains our interest in horror stories, science fiction, and the like. It also represents a way of dealing with the demonic. The popularity of vampire stories in books, television, and other media suggests that our fascination with magic and the demonic remains strong.

To see others make mistakes. To err is human, it has been said. We all make mistakes, and when we see others make the same or similar mistakes we feel less guilty or upset about our own, because we can conclude that our errors are perfectly natural. In certain instances we also gain a sense of superiority, because we haven't been "stupid" enough to make *those* mistakes. In addition, we can learn by watching others make mistakes and pay for them—mistakes we can try to avoid.

To see order imposed on the world. We want to believe that the universe makes sense, that there are reasons for things being the way they are, and that we can plan ahead. The media constantly help us gain a sense of the orderliness of the world by teaching us about such things as the laws of nature, human psychology and motivation, and social phenomena.

To participate vicariously in history. We all want to be on the scene when important events take place—to be there when the big ball games are played, to hear what politicians have to say when history is being made—and the media help us do this. We can even spend our evenings overhearing (so to speak) celebrities chatting about their love lives. I would argue that this desire to participate in history is a powerful force in our lives that stems from our feelings of alienation and insignificance. Television allows the nobodies, huddled in front of their sets, to watch the somebodies on the talk shows.

To be purged of unpleasant emotions. The media often provide for catharsis, or purging of emotions, through art. We can discharge anger, anxiety, hostility, and a host of other negative feelings by watching plays, football games, or movies; by listening to music; and so on. Some public art forms, such as soap operas and professional wrestling, provide clearly defined "hate" figures to help viewers with this purgation.

To obtain outlets for sexual drives in a guilt-free context. In recent years a number of people have attacked television programming for its allegedly excessive amount of violence. This has led television executives (and those responsible for the content of other media as well) to try to find other ways of attracting and maintaining audience interest. One of the ways they have done so is with humor; another is with sex. Sexuality is treated much more explicitly in films than on television, where sexual activities tend to be implied but where "wiggle and jiggle" or "tits and ass" now are major elements in programming. Our sexual experiences are always vicarious when it comes to media. Whether these vicarious experiences provide relief or generate anxiety and negativity (because, for example, our significant others are not sex gods or goddesses) is a matter for conjecture.

To explore taboo subjects with impunity and without risk. Because the news and entertainment media allow us to examine taboo subjects "from a distance," we are able to obtain double benefits. We can explore certain subjects and derive whatever excitement or titillation they may generate, and we can gain a sense of moral satisfaction by condemning particular practices or coming to some kind of conclusions about them. When the media examine, either dramatically or in documentary style, topics such as incest, spousal abuse, rape, drug abuse, and child beating, we get the "thrill" of finding out about these crimes and the reward of being able to condemn those involved.

To experience the ugly. This is the opposite side of our desire to experience the beautiful. People have always been fascinated with ugliness, grotesques, and monsters in rather complex ways. We are both attracted to and repelled by ugliness. I should also point out that our attitudes toward what is beautiful and what is ugly are complicated by the fact that our definitions of beauty and ugliness are constantly changing.

To affirm moral, spiritual, and cultural values. Values, as noted earlier, are our beliefs (which we learn from our families, friends, and religious and other institutions) about what is good and bad, desirable and undesirable, just and unjust. Our actions and conduct are based on our values, which we tend to view as "ultimate." That is, they are the bedrock on which we build our lives and societies. Two of the most important values in American society are egalitarianism and achievement. We may not always put these values into practice, but they are goals toward which we work. The media tend to reinforce certain values and neglect others. Media analysts must be mindful of the values they find in texts and consider whether these are positive or negative, why they are being championed, and what they reveal about the social order.

To see villains in action. Villains are often more interesting than heroes and heroines, who must be good, moral, and thoughtful—at least most of the time. (In recent years, this matter has become less simple; we often find "good-bad" heroes and "bad-good" villains.) Villains can do all kinds of things, have much more room to maneuver than do heroes, and can be of all sorts and natures. We like to see all the terrible things villains are capable of doing, but we also like to see them punished. This gives us two satisfactions for the price of one.

To summarize, I have discussed the following reasons people use the mass media:

1. To be amused
2. To see authority figures exalted or deflated
3. To experience the beautiful
4. To share experiences with others (community)
5. To satisfy curiosity and to be informed
6. To identify with the deity and the divine plan
7. To find distraction and diversion
8. To experience empathy
9. To experience, in a guilt-free situation, extreme emotions
10. To find models to imitate
11. To gain identity
12. To gain information about the world
13. To reinforce belief in justice
14. To reinforce belief in romantic love
15. To reinforce belief in magic, the marvelous, and the miraculous
16. To see others make mistakes
17. To see order imposed on the world
18. To participate vicariously in history
19. To be purged of unpleasant emotions
20. To obtain outlets for sexual drives in a guilt-free context
21. To explore taboo subjects with impunity and without risk
22. To experience the ugly
23. To affirm moral, spiritual, and cultural values
24. To see villains in action

When you examine a text from a uses-and-gratifications point of view, you must try to determine which uses and gratifications are most important and which are secondary. Also, you should be able to cite an event in the text (the film, situation comedy, soap opera, comic book, or whatever) for each use or gratification that you assert the text fulfills.

One problem with the uses-and-gratifications approach is that critics often see a particular event (in a film, for instance) differently or identify different gratifications. This is because the uses to which people put the media are somewhat ambiguous. The uses-and-gratifications approach, however, helps us understand the power the mass media have. One question analysts must continually keep in mind when they think about the public arts: They do a great deal *for* us, but what are they doing *to* us?

GENRES AND FORMULAS

In Table 4.2, I suggest the uses and gratifications supplied by various genres—a genre being a kind of text, such as murder mysteries, soap operas, advertisements, documentaries, and so on.

This table suggests that the reason certain genres are popular is because they offer many gratifications to people who like them and use them for a variety of purposes. The popularity of these genres is, to a degree, a function of the gratifications they supply.

Table 4.3 covers the formulaic aspects of some important genres: the kinds of characters we find in them, their plots and themes, and so on. Thinking about stories in terms of their formulas, and what happens in certain genres, helps us understand something about their appeal. The conventions shown in Table 4.3 establish what a genre means for people and enable them to understand the texts without a lot of thinking. Of course some works in a given genre are more formulaic than others; there is some latitude within genres for experimentation, but most mass-mediated texts tend to be formulaic, with stereotyped characters and conventional plots. I assume people learn a genre's conventions as they are exposed to them.

Genres also come and go. In the seventies in the United States, more than 30 westerns were broadcast on television each week, and western films were popular as well. In contemporary America, few

Table 4.2	Uses and Gratifications of Genres	
Uses and Gratifications	**Genres**
To satisfy curiosity and be informed	Documentaries, news shows, talk shows, quiz shows
To be amused	Situation comedies, comedy shows
To identify with the deity and divine	Religious shows
To reinforce belief in justice	Police shows, law shows
To reinforce belief in romantic love	Romance novels, soap operas
To participate vicariously in history	Media events, sports shows
To see villains in action	Police shows, action-adventure shows
To obtain outlets for sexual drives in a guilt-free context	Pornography, fashion shows, titillating commercials, soap operas
To experience the ugly	Horror shows
To find models to imitate	Talk shows, action shows, award shows, sports shows, commercials
To experience the beautiful	Travel shows, art shows, culture shows (symphony concerts, operas, ballet)

Table 4.3	Formulaic Aspects of Genres			
Aspects \ Genre	Romance	Western	Science Fiction	Spy
Time	Early 1900s	1800s	Future	Present
Location	Rural England	Edge of civilization	Outer space	World
Hero	Lords, upper-class types	Cowboy	Space man	Secret agent
Heroine	Damsel in distress	Schoolmarm	Space woman	Female spy
Secondary	Friends of heroine	Townspeople, Indians	Technicians	Assistant agents
Villains	Supposed friends	Outlaws	Aliens	Moles
Plot	Heroine finds love	Restore law and order	Repel aliens	Find moles
Theme	Love conquers all	Justice and progress	Save humanity	Save free world
Costume	Gorgeous dresses	Cowboy hat	Space gear	Trench coat
Locomotion	Cars, horses, carriages	Horse	Rocket ship	Sports car
Weaponry	Fists	Six-gun	Ray gun Laser gun	Pistol with silencer

westerns are made for television or film. This is probably because the conventions of the genre no longer resonate with Americans and because other genres have evolved that do a better job of providing the gratifications people are looking for from media.

CONTENT ANALYSIS

Content analysis is a research technique that involves measuring something (such as counting instances of violence or determining percentages of Blacks, women, professional types, or whatever) in a random sampling of some form of communication (such as comics, sitcoms, soap operas, news shows). The basic assumption implicit in content analysis is that an investigation of messages and communication will allow some insight into some aspect (e.g., beliefs, values) of the people who receive these messages.

Leo Lowenthal on Content Analysis

A description of an early content analysis conducted using magazine stories may be instructive. Sociologist Leo Lowenthal (1944) studied biographies of popular heroes found in two magazines: *Collier's* and the *Saturday Evening Post*. He classified the biographies in terms of whether they dealt with political life, business and the professions, or entertainment. Lowenthal discovered several interesting things. First, there was an increase in the number of biographies over the years. Second, the number of articles on politicians, businesspeople, and professionals declined, and the number of articles on entertainers increased. Third, the articles on entertainers shifted their focus from serious artists and writers to popular entertainers of one sort or another. As he explains in "Biographies in Popular Magazines" (1944),

> As an experiment in content analysis, a year's publication of *The Saturday Evening Post (SEP)* and of *Collier's* for the period from April 1940 to March 1941 was covered. It is regrettable that a complete investigation could not be made for the most recent material, but samples taken at random showed that no basic change in the selection or content structure has occurred since this country's entry into the war. . . . We put the subjects of the biographies into three groups: the spheres of political life, of business and the professions, and of entertainment (the latter in the broadest sense of the word). Looking at our table we find for the time before World War I very high interest in political figures and an almost equal distribution of business and professional men, on the one hand, and of entertainers on the other. The picture changes completely after the war. The figures from political life have been cut by 40 per cent; the business and professional men have lost 30 per cent of their personnel while the entertainers have gained 50 per cent. This numerical relation seems to be rather constant from 1922 up to the present day. . . . We called the heroes of the past "idols of production"; we feel entitled to call the present day magazine heroes "idols of consumption." Indeed, almost every one of them is directly, or indirectly, related to the sphere of leisure time: either he does not belong to vocations which serve society's basic needs (e.g., the heroes of the world of entertainment and sport), or he amounts, more or less, to a caricature of a socially productive agent. (pp. 508, 510, 516)

Lowenthal found that earlier biographical articles focused on "idols of production" (providing education and orientation) whereas later articles focused on "idols of consumption," such as movie stars and other entertainment figures. The later articles dealt with what we would describe now as the lifestyle preferences and consumption patterns of these figures. Lowenthal discusses how these "idols of consumption" relate to such matters as attitudes toward childhood, success, adjustment, and the socializing function of these biographies. His 40-page article is frequently cited by sociologists.

Some of the advantages of content analysis as a research technique are as follows:

- It is inexpensive to conduct.
- It is usually relatively easy to get material.
- It is unobtrusive (and thus doesn't influence its subjects).
- It yields data that can be quantified.
- It can be used to examine current events, past events, or both.

The problems associated with content analysis include the following:

- It is hard to be certain that the sample studied is representative.
- It is often hard to obtain a good working definition of the topic being studied (for example, what is violence?).
- It isn't always easy to find a measurable unit, such as a frame in a comic strip. What does one do about films or magazine articles?
- It isn't possible to prove that the inferences made on the basis of a content analysis are correct.

Despite its drawbacks, content analysis can often be used to conduct interesting and useful experiments. Analysts who are just beginning to use this method will find it best to choose a medium that is relatively easy to deal with. That is why the following exercise involves the analysis of comic strips. Comics offer the content analyst a number of advantages: Most people are familiar with them, the characters are easily classifiable, and the strips are easy to obtain and simple to work with. Unlike texts found in the electronic media, which flit by rapidly, comics stay stuck to the page, and an analyst can spend as much time examining them as he or she likes.

You should choose your categories for analysis based on what you want to discover. Let me suggest some possible topics:

- Physical characteristics of heroes and heroines, villains and villainesses
  - Color of hair
  - Color of eyes
  - Height
  - Weight
  - Age
  - Body structure
  - Sex
  - Race

- Social characteristics of characters
  - Occupation
  - Education
  - Religion
  - Socioeconomic class
  - Status
  - Role
  - Ethnic background (nationality)

- Emotional nature of characters
  - Warm or cold
  - Anxious or calm
  - Stable or unstable
  - Authoritarian or dependent
  - Hostile or friendly
  - Powerful or weak

- Loving or hateful
- Individualist or conformist
- Vivacious or apathetic

These are just some of the things you might concern yourself with in a content analysis of the comics that focuses on the characters in these stories. You should also keep in mind thematic issues, such as the amount of violence (and its use), the values of the characters, allusions to social and political events, and reflections of cultural matters.

There is one other aspect of content analysis I should mention here: Content analyses are most useful when they include historic or comparative dimensions. Although it is interesting to know, for example, how much violence there is in the daily newspaper's comics pages, it is even more interesting to know how much violence there was in that newspaper's comics pages 10 years ago, 20 years ago, 30 years ago, and so on. By taking a historical point of view, an analyst can discern trends and determine whether there have been significant changes in attitudes about (or stereotypes of) women, members of particular ethnic groups, or any of the other topics listed earlier. By taking a comparative point of view, media analysts can discover how one culture's or society's values and beliefs differ from those of others.

To conduct an interesting exercise in content analysis, choose a comics page from some newspaper (making sure that back editions of the same paper are available on microfilm or online) and examine it in terms of the topics listed earlier as well as in terms of the average number of characters per frame, the percentages of male and female characters on the page, the number of words spoken by male and female characters, and the number of acts of violence. Make a comparison between what you find on the present-day page of comics and what you find on the comics page of the same paper 20, 30, or 40 years ago.

With this discussion of content analysis I bring to a conclusion my introduction to sociological perspectives on the media. It is, at best, a start, but it should provide you with a sense of the kinds of things sociologists look for when they examine media and the public arts. There is a degree of overlap with Marxist analysis here that might be expected, given that Marxist concepts inform a good deal of sociological thought. The uses-and-gratifications approach also has psychological dimensions.

STUDY QUESTIONS AND TOPICS FOR DISCUSSION

1. Explain the following basic sociological concepts: bureaucracy, role, alienation, anomie, class, functionalism, marginalization, mass communication, mass media, postmodernism, sex (gender), socialization, status, stereotypes.
2. What is meant by uses and gratifications? Which uses and gratifications do you think are the most important for people nowadays?
3. Do you think people today use the mass media differently compared with how people used media 10 or 20 years ago? Whatever your position, justify it.
4. What are the advantages and disadvantages of content analysis?
5. List and briefly describe any six uses and gratifications connected with the media discussed in this chapter and apply them to some well-known film or other text.
6. How should one define gender? Is gender natural, or is it socially constructed, and if it is socially constructed, does that mean gender is anything someone wants it to be?

7. What formulas do you find in new television shows? How do the writers adapt and modify traditional formulas in the more interesting and innovative shows? Are vampire shows formulaic? Explain your answer.

ANNOTATED BIBLIOGRAPHY

Arens, William, & Montague, Susan P. (Eds.). (1976). *The American dimension: Cultural myths and social realities.* Sherman Oaks, CA: Alfred. This collection of articles on food, films, football, fast foods, soap operas, and more is written from an anthropological perspective.

Berger, Arthur Asa. (1976). *The TV-guided American.* New York: Walker. This book analyzes a number of television shows (*All in the Family, Kung Fu, Mission Impossible,* and more) in terms of what they reflect about U.S. culture and society.

Berger, Arthur Asa. (Ed.). (1987). *Television in society.* New Brunswick, NJ: Transaction. This is a collection of essays originally published in *Society* magazine on television shows, media events, and various social aspects of television.

Berger, Arthur Asa. (1995). *Essentials of mass communication theory.* Thousand Oaks, CA: Sage. This book offers an overview of mass communication theory, using focal points to discuss works of art, artists, audiences, society, and media and the ways these relate to one another.

Berger, Arthur Asa. (1997). *Postmortem for a postmodernist.* Walnut Creek, CA: AltaMira. This is a comic murder mystery with an international cast of zany characters that explains the basic principles of postmodernism while spoofing the mystery genre and satirizing academia. It includes numerous comic-strip framelike drawings by the author.

Berger, Arthur Asa. (1998). *Media research techniques* (2nd ed.). Thousand Oaks, CA: Sage. This book assists readers in carrying out a number of research projects involving the media; it includes discussion of content analysis, focus groups, and the rhetorical analysis of magazine advertisements.

Berger, Arthur Asa. (Ed.). (1998). *The postmodern presence: Readings on postmodernism in American culture and society.* Walnut Creek, CA: AltaMira. This is a collection of essays, many never before published, that deal with the impacts of postmodernism on contemporary American culture and society. Topics addressed include MTV, film, fashion, *The X-Files, The Terminator, Wayne's World,* museums, and architecture.

Berger, Arthur Asa. (2003). *Durkheim is dead: Sherlock Holmes is introduced to sociological theory.* Walnut Creek, CA: AltaMira. This book is nominally a mystery, but it is actually an exposition of sociological theory. It deals, in particular, with the ideas of Max Weber, Émile Durkheim, Georg Simmel, Sigmund Freud, Vladimir Lenin, W. E. B. Du Bois, and Beatrice Webb.

Berger, Arthur Asa. (2003). *Media and society: A critical perspective.* Lanham, MD: Rowman & Littlefield. This book deals with the social impact of media and considers topics such as audiences, media effects, media and violence, and the mass culture–mass society hypothesis.

Berger, Peter L., & Berger, Brigitte. (1972). *Sociology: A biographical approach.* New York: Basic Books. This innovative textbook in sociology focuses on the great thinkers of the discipline and their basic ideas.

Burns, Elizabeth, & Burns, Tom. (Eds.). (1973). *Sociology of literature and drama.* New York: Penguin. This is a collection of essays by some of the most important thinkers of the contemporary period. The essays are written from a sociological point of view, although Marxist and structuralist thinkers are also included.

Butler, Judith. (1999). *Gender trouble: Feminism and the subversion of identity.* New York: Routledge. A pathbreaking book about the nature of gender that also played an important role in the development of queer theory.

Coser, Lewis. (1971). *Masters of sociological thought: Ideas in historical and social context.* New York: Harcourt Brace Jovanovich. This classic text deals with the theories of many important sociologists, such as Max Weber and Émile Durkheim.

Danesi, Marcel. (2009). *X-rated! The power of mythic symbolism in popular culture.* New York: Palgrave Macmillan. This book deals with topics such as branding and advertising, occultism in pop culture, pop culture and the feminine form, and other aspects of popular culture.

Danesi, Marcel. (2012). *Popular culture: Introductory perspectives* (2nd ed.). Lanham, MD: Rowman & Littlefield. Danesi defines popular culture and its role in media such as print, radio, television, cinema, and video.

hooks, bell. (1992). *Black looks: Race and representation.* Boston: South End. This book is an impassioned study of the way the media deal with Blackness by one of the foremost African American critics.

Jones, Steven G. (Ed.). (1997). *CyberSociety: Computer-mediated communication and community.* Thousand Oaks, CA: Sage. This stimulating collection of essays covers everything from virtual reality to Nintendo, computer games, and standards of conduct on the Internet.

Lyotard, Jean-François. (1984). *The postmodern condition: A report on knowledge* (Geoff Bennington & Brian Massumi, Trans.). Minneapolis: University of Minnesota Press. This slender volume by the French scholar Lyotard is an influential analysis of postmodernism. It includes an introduction by Fredric Jameson, a prominent postmodernist theorist.

McLuhan, Marshall. (1967). *The mechanical bride: Folklore of industrial man.* Boston: Beacon. McLuhan offers a brilliant study of the sociological significance of American advertisements and comics. This pioneering effort is still worth careful attention.

Rapaille, Clotaire. (2006). *The culture code: An ingenious way to understand why people around the world buy and live as they do.* New York: Broadway Books. Rapaille's book deals with the codes in societies that shape behavior in general and consumption in particular.

Real, Michael R. (1977). *Mass-mediated culture.* Englewood Cliffs, NJ: Prentice Hall. Real provides studies of Disney, the Super Bowl, Marcus Welby, and Billy Graham, along with material of theoretical importance.

Rosenberg, Bernard, & White, David Manning. (Eds.). (1957). *Mass culture: The popular arts in America.* New York: Free Press. This is one of the earliest and most important collections of articles on the subject of mass culture.

Tuchman, Gaye, Daniels, Arlene Kaplan, & Benét, James. (Eds.). (1978). *Hearth and home: Images of women in the mass media.* New York: Oxford University Press. This book contains articles on images of women in television and women's magazines and includes an extensive annotated bibliography on the subject.

Weibel, Kathryn. (1977). *Mirror-mirror: Images of women reflected in popular culture.* Garden City, NY: Anchor. This book deals with images of women found in fiction, television, the movies, women's magazines, print advertising, and fashion.

Wilson, Robert N. (Ed.). (1964). *The arts in society.* Englewood Cliffs, NJ: Prentice Hall. This book focuses on high culture, but it includes some excellent articles of interest to media analysts, including two by Ian Watt (on *Robinson Crusoe* and on literature and society).

PART II

Applications

This chapter examines *Murder on the Orient Express* and classic murder mysteries in general from semiotic and Marxist points of view. The chapter includes discussion of how Agatha Christie violates the "code" of the single murderer and how mysteries are, in fact, problems in applied semiotics that readers or viewers often cannot solve because they either neglect or misinterpret the signifiers (clues) provided. The elements of class conflict found in mysteries are also discussed, as well as the role these elements may play in diverting people's attention and mystifying them. Finally, it is suggested that, ironically, mysteries may have a revolutionary element implicit in their structure.

Murderers on the Orient Express

*M*urder on the Orient Express is generally considered to be one of Agatha Christie's best works and a classic in the analytic detective mystery genre. It was also made into a highly successful movie featuring major stars such as Albert Finney, Lauren Bacall, and Ingrid Bergman that was beautifully acted and wonderfully absorbing.

What is distinctive about this particular story is that, unlike in most mysteries, *all* of the suspects are the actual murderers. And once Hercule Poirot figures this out, everything else falls beautifully into place—as things must in a well-constructed mystery. A mystery story is, semiotically speaking, like a coded message. All kinds of signs and significations are observable, but the connections among them are not obvious. Once we see how they are related and "break the code," the mystery is solved. Clues, then, are signifiers with a number of different signifieds. We must assemble these clues and interpret them properly to make sense of things and find the killer(s).

In *Murder on the Orient Express*, Christie's decision to create a dozen suspects who are all guilty was a remarkable and ingenious structural innovation, a reversal of the conventional situation in which only one suspect is guilty. The fascination of watching the movie or reading the story lies in seeing how Poirot puts everything together. Many of the people who have seen the film probably had previously read the book; often readers want to see a book they have enjoyed actualized on film—to see it "come alive," reinterpreted—and in this case that is what the film's viewers get.

ORGANIZING A MYSTERY

If we forget (to the extent this is possible) about the actual plot and examine the story in terms of characters and relationships, we find that Christie's *Murder on the Orient Express* (1940) has a very symmetrical organization. There are three main characters—or, rather, two characters who are polar opposites and a group of a dozen other interrelated characters who form a third character and mediate between the first two. We find Poirot, the detective, on one side and Ratchett (an alias for a kidnapper, Cassetti) on the other. By chance, Poirot happens to board the Orient Express on his way back to France with Ratchett and a dozen other people. Ratchett recognizes Poirot and, because Ratchett has received some death threats, he offers Poirot $20,000 to protect him. But Poirot has taken an immediate and instinctive dislike to Ratchett and so refuses.

Ratchett looks "evil" and Poirot, Christie tells us, looks comic. He is described as "a ridiculous-looking little man. The sort of little man one could never take seriously" (p. 14). In addition to Ratchett and Poirot, a dozen assorted passengers of varying classes and nationalities are also traveling on the Orient Express.

At the very beginning of the book, on the first day of the trip, Poirot is speculating with a friend, Monsieur Bouc, over lunch. Bouc has been "studying" the people on board the train:

> "Ah!" he sighed. "If I had but the pen of a Balzac! I would depict this scene." He waved a hand.
>
> "It is an idea, that," said Poirot.
>
> "Ah, you agree? It has not been done. I think? And yet—it lends itself to romance, my friend. All around us are people, of all classes, of all nationalities, of all ages. For three days these people, these strangers to one another, are brought together. They sleep and eat under one roof, they cannot get away from each other. At the end of three days they part, they go their several ways, never perhaps to see each other again."
>
> "And yet," said Poirot, "suppose an accident—"
>
> "Ah, no, my friend—"
>
> "From your point of view it would be regrettable, I agree. But nevertheless let us just for one moment suppose it. Then, perhaps, all these here are linked together—by death." (pp. 29–30)

This leads Poirot to examine rather carefully the other persons on the train, all of whom are also in the dining car at the time, and to speculate about them. All of the characters are in fact linked together by death—by the various tragedies ensuing from Cassetti/Ratchett's kidnapping of a child, Daisy Armstrong, in the United States in the distant past. And this link, dangled before the reader several times in the story, is the key to solving the mystery.

Table 5.1 presents the characters' relationships and some of the interesting paradigmatic oppositions.

The puzzle in the story involves discovering how the 12 seemingly random characters on the train are connected. Had Ratchett discerned that they were connected, he might have lived. When Poirot discovers they are connected, he finds the murderers—although, curiously enough, he lets them go. He is able to do this because he is provided (by the murderers) with an acceptable explanation or counterexplanation of the murder, and he chooses to accept this alternative, which involves a mysterious stranger who supposedly left the train after Ratchett's murder.

Table 5.1 Charater Relationships in *Murder on the Orient Express*

Poirot	12 Murderers on the Train	Ratchett
Discovers killers	All kill (stab) Ratchett	Is killed
Refuses to work for Ratchett	All connected to Ratchett and become involved with Poirot	Asks Poirot to work for him
Looks ridiculous	All look different	Looks evil

Once Poirot recognizes that some of the occupants of the train were involved in the Armstrong case, he is able eventually to link all 12 characters together. Toward the end of the book, but before it is revealed that all 12 occupants of the train are connected, we find the following bit of dialogue:

"Nothing would surprise me now."

"Nothing! Even if everybody in the train proved to have been in the Armstrong household, I should not express surprise."

"This is a very profound remark," said Poirot. (p. 234)

We do not at the time recognize the significance of this remark, but Bouc has accidentally stumbled on the solution to the mystery, and Christie has him offer it to us, knowing we will not take it seriously. When we look back at the end of the story, we discover that Christie has given us all we needed to know to solve the mystery, but we have either neglected or misinterpreted all the clues. That is, we either neglected important signifiers or misinterpreted them and ended up with the wrong signifieds.

DETECTIVES AS SEMIOTICIANS

Murder mysteries fascinate us because they involve, ultimately, decoding a series of clues—signs and significations (actions, words, objects) that seem random, irrelevant, or both and that are meaningless until we find the code that ties everything together. The great detectives of analytic murder fiction are semioticians, whether they know it or not. And the pleasure we derive from reading mysteries stems in part from the semiotic problems they pose—the puzzles we all try to figure out. One reason Sherlock Holmes mysteries are so popular is that Holmes is such a marvelous semiotician, such a perceptive analyst of signs—signs readers of the stories do not recognize as important. One of the most common ways mystery writers hide clues is in long descriptions of characters, places, and events. Readers aren't aware the writer of the mystery has provided them with all the information they need to solve the problem because they don't recognize important clues (signs) when they encounter them. One of the unwritten rules of mystery writing is that the writer has to provide enough information for a discerning person to solve the crime.

The resolution to the story in *Murder on the Orient Express* comes when Poirot seizes on the tale of the fictitious murderer as a means of enabling the real murderers to escape punishment. This resolution is itself connected to certain moral codes we have, such as the notion that evildoers "deserve" to be punished for their crimes and that, in the right circumstances, a sufficiently evil character should be murdered. The dilemma faced by this unusual group of vigilantes (for that's what they are, although some of them are cloaked in European finery) is the dilemma faced by all such groups: How do you justify lawlessness—in this case murder—in the name of law and order? Poirot's response is emotional, which may suggest, as psychoanalytic literature so amply demonstrates, there are forces aside from "little gray cells" that influence the actions of men and women.

The classic murder mystery is a subcategory of the murder mystery genre in which rationality and logic are stressed and in which a primal confrontation takes place between the emotion, irrationality, and hatred of the murderer (who must also be extremely devious and calculating) and the mind of the detective. This genre is highly formulaic and includes many conventions that must be observed if the mystery is to be legitimate. A good classic mystery, then, involves a confrontation between two minds.

Some Freudian analysts have suggested that the fascination with murder mysteries is connected to children's frustrated desires to know what is going on in their parents' bedrooms; these analysts assert that adults transfer these desires to other locked doors and mysterious sounds in the night. Martin Grotjahn, a Freudian analyst, discusses mystery stories in his book *Beyond Laughter: Humor and the Subconscious* (1966). He offers many interesting observations about why people love mysteries and what they signify. He writes:

> The popularity of the murder mystery is only partially explained by the unconscious desire to murder. The plot is a variation of a few simple themes which are endlessly repeated. Some secret wrongdoing between two people is suddenly discovered when one of the participants is found dead. The secret of the deed, including its motivation, constitutes a baffling mystery. It must be uncovered, and the tedious search begins. During the course of events almost everybody is suspected of having committed the crime, including the reader. . . . The innocent readers are fascinated, curious, and eager to help in solving the mystery. They behave like children who begin to discover the mystery of the parental bedroom. (pp. 155–156)

Later Grotjahn (1966) adds that our interest in mysteries is a "reactivation of the long-suppressed interest in the bloody details of life and death, intercourse, menstruation, defloration, pregnancy, birth, delivery and all the rest of it" (p. 156). So our fascination with mysteries, in all their forms, is tied, to a considerable degree, to our childhood and our attempts to find out what happens in the parental bedroom and our interest in parental sex, which we repress as we get older. These suppressed interests are reactivated by mysteries.

SOCIAL AND POLITICAL DIMENSIONS

Murder on the Orient Express, both the book and the film, may also be examined in terms of social and political dimensions. The characters are all linked together, but not by what should join people together—love and a sense of community. Rather, they are linked by hatred and death. However, this escape from an alienated and estranged relationship is only momentary. When the Orient Express arrives in France, all the passengers go their separate ways, with only memories of a ritual murder to bind them together.

Ironically, however, the book does suggest the possibility of a society based not on class differences and estrangement but on a communality of interest—on common goals all men and women share. The inversion in *Murder on the Orient Express* is interesting because it demonstrates that members of different classes can work together when they see it is in their interest to do so. Class differences can be overcome.

Of course, we must always keep in mind that Cassetti/Ratchett kidnapped the child of a wealthy family, and it might be argued that the poor and working-class characters serve, ultimately, as instruments of the wealthy (and even royal) elements among the murderers. Cassetti/Ratchett had, we know, "touched" the lives of all involved, but it is the insistence, we may presume, of the upper-class people involved that has brought everyone together, remarkably, on the Orient Express. And it is the very social, national, and class differences everyone counts on to confuse anyone who might be suspicious. It might be argued that the mystification the murderers create parallels the social mystification the bourgeoisie finds so important to maintain.

A mystery, in its own way, is a kind of microcosm of the larger society. Perhaps it is no accident that so many mysteries—especially the classic English ones involving deduction—feature people from the wealthy and aristocratic levels of society as killers, rather than having "the butler do it." This would suggest class conflict too overtly. Many mysteries, of course, include class strife and conflict between the poor and the rich, but many also involve only intra–upper-class murder, a sign of the degeneracy of the bourgeoisie. Ironically, the murders in these stories are usually solved by detectives who come from working-class and middle-class backgrounds, so an element of class conflict is still visible in these works.

POIROT AS REVOLUTIONARY

In a strange way, then, characters such as Poirot may be said to have a revolutionary dimension, although their efforts are focused on the personal, not the societal, level, and they function most immediately as instruments of official bourgeois social morality.

Behind our fascination with the wealthy and their glamorous self-indulgent lifestyles, there is a germ of hostility and resentment and a sense of relative deprivation that has political (and even revolutionary) implications. At the same time, mysteries serve as diversions; they take our attention away from the real world and our problems and offer us characters, many of whom are vile and degenerate, who ultimately pay for their crimes. Thus they function as sacrificial victims, enabling us to purge ourselves (somewhat) of hostile feelings toward the rich and powerful.

Instead of a real revolution against the real bourgeoisie, we "kill off" the rich one by one in mystery stories. But these are the imaginary rich, and so our hostility (and its revolutionary potential) is dissipated. This might be the ultimate form of mystification, in which imaginary confrontations between a potentially revolutionary proletariat, symbolized by the detective and police, and the bourgeoisie are all acted out in fantasy.

We also learn one other thing from mysteries such as *Murder on the Orient Express*: We, the common people, lack the intelligence and wisdom to solve such mysteries; by implication, we may be unqualified to run our own social and political institutions. We are reduced, psychologically, to children who do not understand what really is going on. The implication of these stories is that we are better off entrusting the control of society to those wiser and more powerful than us, which is exactly what the bourgeoisie wants the masses to believe (that is, the status quo is functional).

Although the murder mystery is a commodity manufactured to be sold to the largest possible market, and although the mystery generally acts as an instrument of false consciousness (which distracts people from their real interests), it may also, ironically, have a revolutionary potential. This is because many of the murders found in this genre are committed by members of the upper classes and show the degeneracy of these people. Replacing them, then, seems quite reasonable. The murders also reveal the vulnerability of the upper classes; they cannot be protected from their fates despite their huge homes, servants, and so on. Thus every murder has political implications and dimensions in spite of itself, and every murderer, without knowing it, helps break the iron grip that the classes have on the consciousness of the masses.

Many of the murders that take place in classic mysteries suggest, even if vaguely, the possibility of revolutionary violence; they play a role, even if in an oblique manner, in the class struggle. (Actually, in the classic English murder mysteries, the upper class seems to be killing itself off in rapid fashion. Eventually, we may surmise, there will be nothing left but the working class, whose members will be surprised to discover that the upper class has, bit by bit, destroyed itself, so there is no need for a revolution.) Agatha Christie would be astonished at such notions. Poirot, of course, would not find them surprising at all.

STUDY QUESTIONS AND TOPICS FOR DISCUSSION

1. What oppositions are found in *Murder on the Orient Express*? How do they generate meaning in the text?
2. Which characterization of Poirot seems more reasonable—Poirot as semiotician or Poirot as revolutionary? Justify your answer.
3. Why are there so few classical detectives and so many police procedurals on television?
4. What gratifications do violent crime shows provide viewers that other kinds of shows don't provide? What functions do these police procedural programs have for viewers and for society?

In this chapter, football is described from a semiotic viewpoint, as a system of signs, with emphasis on sign subsystems (uniforms of the players, officials, and cheerleaders; sign sections in the stands; and so on). Special attention is paid to time and its manipulation by teams and by television broadcasters using the instant replay camera. The chapter then turns to the socializing function of football and its role in preparing people to work in a specialized and bureaucratic society—in particular, in the corporate world. Football is contrasted with baseball, which is described as a 19th-century pastoral game, no longer synchronous with Americans' "hopped-up" and time-bound sensibilities. Football is also described, sociologically speaking, as a functional alternative to organized religion. A Marxist interpretation of the game is also offered, focusing on football's role as a diversion, the treatment of players as commodities, and the business aspects of the game, especially in regard to television advertising.

CHAPTER 6

Seven Points on the Game of Football (and Some Interesting Statistics)

FOOTBALL IS A GAME OF SIGNS

Football is an interesting subject for the semiotician because the game is simultaneously full of signs and a signifier of some importance. The stadium is itself one huge sign—a sacred space where enthusiasts (and sometimes fanatics) gather to watch a highly organized, ritualized contest that many have suggested functions as an alternative to war. It is not unusual for 60,000 people or more to gather together for a game, and, including television coverage, millions of people watch a game, which means the entire country "becomes" a football stadium.

Where an individual sits in the stadium—on the 50-yard line or way up behind a goalpost—is a signifier of wealth, power, or status. The field itself is a huge grid, a 100-yard rectangle of white lines against brilliant green grass (or Astroturf). The intensity of the colors adds considerably to the excitement of the event and must not be underestimated. On and around the field are people in all kinds of different uniforms: the officials in their zebra stripes, the players with their helmets and pads, members of marching bands, cheerleaders and pom-pom girls in sweaters and miniskirts, coaches with earphones and other electronic paraphernalia, drum majors and majorettes, and many other people. The uniforms and trappings of these participants are signifiers of the wide variety of skills, activities, and functions taking place at a game: rule enforcement, athletic activity, musical diversion, sexual display, planning and rationality, and so on. Thus a football game is not merely an athletic event but is part of a much larger system of events that are connected to the game and enlarge its significance greatly. (I have not said anything about the people who attend games wearing the colors or emblems of their teams. Sometimes they carry signs. Frequently there are "sign sections" in stadiums, especially at college games, and they flash various messages during halftime, when the bands play and there are other entertainments.)

The game of football itself is based on signs. Signals are called in the huddles to announce offensive plays. These signals are analogous to what semioticians call codes (see Chapter 1); they indicate precise series of activities that are to be followed at given points in time. Defensive players learn to watch their opponents for indications that a pass is to be thrown or a certain play is to be run. And a good deal of the game is based on deception—that is, giving opponents false signifiers so they will make mistakes. It is the capacity of signs to lie, to give false information, that creates much of the complexity found in football.

The officials also use signs—a variety of gestures that indicate what rules have been violated and the penalties assessed. These signals are nonverbal visual metaphors that enable officials to indicate to everyone in the stadium the nature of a given transgression. The most important sign, the one in which an official stretches both hands over his head to indicate a score, is a signifier with two signifieds: triumph or success for the offensive team and failure for the defensive team. When this sign is given, thousands of people in the stadium (and in the television audience) cheer madly or groan.

While the game progresses, there is a great deal of activity taking place on the sidelines. During college games, bands play rousing songs at certain times to encourage their teams, and cheerleaders lead cheers, jump up and down (displaying their breasts and legs), and carry on, often in rather mechanical dancing and movement displays. Many professional football teams employ groups of attractive young women who "wiggle and jiggle" on the sidelines, indicating a sexual dimension to the game or, more precisely, to the spectacle in which the game is embedded.

INSTANT REPLAY AND THE MODERN SENSIBILITY

As the subsystems inherent in the spectacle of football work themselves out, one sign is crucial to the understanding of what football means—in its televised form, in particular—and that is the huge scoreboard clock. Time is of the essence in football, but, unlike in baseball and other sports, in football time can be manipulated. And it is this manipulation of time in tightly fought games that generates incredible tension in the sport.

In a one-sided game there is little tension, and the game often turns into an exhibition of power and competence for the winning team and a study in humiliation for the losing one. But in close games, time is everyone's enemy. The team that is ahead fights to hold on to its advantage, and the team that is behind tries to use what time is left to its best advantage and to score. Many football games are decided in the last minutes and often even in the last seconds of play. A minute of playing time, because of the rules of the game, can take many minutes of real time.

Further complicating matters, especially in televised games, is the use of instant replay, which can show a given play from a variety of perspectives and suggests, ultimately, that time doesn't pass in football the way it does in real life. We keep seeing the past (a given play) over and over again from different angles, so that our sense of continuity and perspective are rendered problematic. Time doesn't pass the way we thought it did, and we see that our perspective on the world isn't the only one.

Televised football has become an incredibly sophisticated art form. It now may be said to resemble avant-garde films, in that both often simulate stream-of-consciousness thought, which moves backward and forward in time, jumping around almost incoherently at times. Instant replay is vaguely equivalent to the flashback in film, and the invention of instant replay has dramatically altered the nature of televised football (and other sports as well) in particular and the modern American sensibility in general. In Super Bowl XLVII in 2013 between the Baltimore Ravens and San Francisco 49ers, CBS used a total of 62 cameras. Can anyone doubt that a new sensibility arises out of seeing such programming? Or at least that a new sensibility is made possible because of the development of such a remarkable kind of program?

FOOTBALL SOCIALIZES US

Football does more than just entertain us. The word *entertain* is like the word *interesting*, in that neither tells us very much. The questions we should ask about football include the following: Why do we find football so absorbing? What do we get out of the game? What does it do *for* us (that is, what gratifications does it offer)? What might it be doing *to* us? What does it tell us about American society?

One very important aspect of football is the way it socializes and enculturates us. It teaches us how to get along in society, what roles to play, what rules to follow, what life is all about, and so on. We are not aware that this is going on most of the time, which means we are all the more susceptible to the influence of what the game suggests, teaches, and implies. This section looks at the game as a signifier of values, attitudes, and beliefs and attempts to ascertain what these signifieds are and what effects they may have on people (admittedly, this is a speculative activity).

One thing we learn from examining football is that we live in a highly complex society in which time is critical and communication is important. A good deal of the game involves communication between coaching staff and players. Signals are called on both sides for every play. Nothing is done that has not been planned, rehearsed, and prepared over and over again in practice sessions. It is only because people make mistakes, or do things that cannot be anticipated, that coaches' plans are altered.

In addition, we learn that society is highly specialized and that this specialization functions within group situations. Teams are now made up of offensive and defensive specialists, each with particular talents and abilities. Football teams function as "models" for modern society, and we learn from watching football that we must be specialists working in highly structured organizations, controlled from above (the coaches), and that we must pursue our specializations for the good of the group, first and foremost, and then for ourselves. That's what it means to be a "team player." We learn from football, without being aware of it, that we must prepare ourselves to function in a highly bureaucratic society—most likely within a large corporate entity. Watching football is "training" for working in the corporate world, and the violence in football is transformed into sales campaigns aimed at "smashing" the public, one's competitors, or both.

We also learn that specialization and ability constitute a means of upward mobility, especially in professional football, where farm boys, Blacks from working-class families, and others who have never before been wealthy often earn huge salaries. Many youngsters identify very strongly with football stars, whose heroics on the football field are, at times, quite incredible.

In a sense, football is really about containment and breaking free, about order and randomness—although always within the context of the game (which is highly structured and rule dominated). These moments of freedom are exciting and highly exhilarating, but they are fleeting and quite unpredictable. It is not too much of an oversimplification to say that much of football is routine and boring and that what makes the game exciting are the moments when remarkable things happen. Because we can never know when one of these great plays will happen, we must pay attention all the time, lest we miss something.

STATISTICS ON TELEVISED FOOTBALL

An article by David Biderman (2010) in the *Wall Street Journal*, "11 Minutes of Action," breaks down the components of a typical game broadcast:

11 minutes in a 3-hour game involve actual playing time. Plays average 4 seconds.

17 minutes are devoted to replays.

67 minutes involve players "standing around," which means getting back to the huddle.

75 minutes are used for commercials.

3 seconds are devoted to cheerleaders.

10-to-1 ratio of inaction to action.

40 seconds allowed for the offensive team to snap the ball.

If a typical play lasts 4 seconds, that means there could be 15 plays in a minute of action—from the time the ball is snapped until the play ends. But this does not consider the 40 seconds teams have to decide on plays and snap the ball. If you add the 40 seconds to snap the ball and 4 seconds for a typical play, you get approximately one play a minute. These figures are affected by the amount of running plays offensive teams use, since the clock continues to move after a run has ended; so if a team were to use many more running plays than passes, the statistics would be affected. Also, some teams now use a "hurry-up offense" that speeds up the pace of games.

So why do so many people go to football games or watch them on television? One reason is that all games generate tension, since nobody can be certain who will win. Upsets in football create drama. In addition, in some cases the games are very close and are only resolved in the last minutes or seconds of the game, leading to a powerful catharsis for viewers. You can tell this by the collective groans or shrieks of joy coming from people at the game. In addition, many of the men who play the game are remarkable athletes, so sometimes you see incredible plays, analogous to acts of heroism in dramas. Football games are narratives with powerful dramatic qualities. We must also consider the historical rivalries that color the feelings of the fans, many of whom identify with teams in their cities or regions or with colleges they attended.

Using statistics to analyze football involves what we might call "the fallacy of reductionism" and doesn't consider the psychological and social gratifications gained by attending games or watching them on television. When we watch a football game on television, we are a member of an audience, but we are also, for a short period, part of an electronic virtual community.

WHY BASEBALL IS BORING

The reason we find football so exciting is that it closely approximates and reflects the contemporary social situation in the United States. Football is a 20th-century sport still relevant in the 21st century, a world in which time is precious (time is money), communication is important (we live in an "information" society), and bureaucratic entities are dominant (corporations, universities, and so on). Baseball, on the other hand, is a 19th-century pastoral sport in which time is irrelevant, specialization is not crucial most of the time, and there is relatively little reliance on set plays.

Table 6.1   Polar Oppositions of Football and Baseball

Football	Baseball
Urban	Pastoral
Educated players	Country boys
Time precious	Time not important
Specialized	General
Body contact important	Body contact minimal
Team effort	Individualistic
Upsets critical	No upsets
Vicarious excitement	Relaxation
Weekly	Daily
Spectacle	Austerity
Four quarters with intermission	Nine innings, uninterrupted flow
Calculation, planning	Little strategy
Body a weapon	Bat as a weapon
Small area	Large playing area
20th century	19th century
Territorial	Not territorial
Team on offense	One player at a time on offense

Table 6.1, taken from my book *The TV-Guided American* (Berger, 1976), displays some polar oppositions that reflect the differences between the two sports and their relationship to American character and culture. Baseball is essentially a 19th-century sport that is no longer congruent with contemporary American cultural dynamics and thus *seems* terribly slow and boring to many people. Baseball games are now events at which to drink beer and relax, and the ambience at baseball games is considerably different from what one finds at football games—especially crucial games, where ancient antagonisms or bowl bids hang in the balance.

Our boredom with baseball is a signifier that as a society we have become "hopped up," and so baseball seems much slower than it used to. Baseball doesn't offer the gratifications it once did, or, to put it somewhat differently, the gratifications baseball offers don't mean very much to most people anymore. Its heroes aren't as important to us as the heroes of football are, it doesn't provide models to imitate or help us gain appropriate identity the way football does, and it certainly doesn't have the sexual elements in the spectacle surrounding the game that football does.

Baseball still has its attractions, however, and it provides gratifications to many people. In part because it moves so slowly, the game can generate incredible tension—especially in situations where a hit or an out will lead to a team's winning the league pennant or the World Series. Baseball games are now televised as psychodramas, with cameras quickly switching back and forth between extreme close-ups of the pitcher to extreme close-ups of the batter and then to shots of the managers (who are often shown spitting out the shells of the sunflower seeds they munch to help them deal with their stress) and other players on both teams sitting in the dugouts.

During the 2003 World Series between the New York Yankees and the Florida Marlins, several games included moments of excruciating tension. This generally occurred when a pitcher was in trouble because men on the opposing team were on base, and the game—and maybe the outcome of the series—hung in the balance. For television viewers, cameras raced back and forth, cutting quickly from close-up shots of pitchers sweating profusely, shaking off their catchers' signaled pitches, and fidgeting endlessly to close-ups of batters staring at the pitchers intently, swinging their bats nervously. Then, when something happened, the cameras showed the reactions of the managers, coaches, and players in the two dugouts.

It was almost like watching a Greek tragedy, and the catharsis—the sense of relief from stress and anxiety—on the part of the Marlins' players and fans when the final game was over was palpable, as was the sense of tragic loss on the part of the Yankees and their fans. When the Marlins won the sixth game of the World Series and secured the world championship, the television cameras captured shots of some of the Yankees, emotionally drained and brokenhearted, crying in their dugout.

Some argue that baseball is a subtler game than football, which, if true, may be part of the reason many Americans find baseball boring. In any case, for a variety of reasons, baseball doesn't have the cultural force or resonance football does, and thus has taken on—inadvertently, I would argue—a different role from that of football.

FOOTBALL AS AN ALTERNATIVE TO RELIGION

I have suggested in my discussion of socialization in football that if football's manifest function is to entertain us, its latent function is to socialize us and offer us models to imitate and notions that will help us fit into the contemporary bureaucratic corporate world. I would like to turn now to another aspect of functionalist thought, namely, the notion that some phenomena function as alternatives for other phenomena. My thesis here is that football functions for many people as an alternative to religion, or, perhaps, that it has a religious or sacred dimension that generally goes unrecognized.

The passionate feelings many people have about football (and their teams) and the intensity of Americans' collective interest in the game leads me to think football has a dimension far beyond that of simply a sport. Indeed, Michael R. Real (1977) has written convincingly about the Super Bowl as a mythic spectacle; he suggests how, in secular societies, sports "fill the vacuum" left by people's noninvolvement in religion. I would like to suggest here that football—and I will focus on professional football—is in many ways analogous to religion. Table 6.2 reveals some interesting parallels between the two seemingly different phenomena: professional football and religion.

Curiously enough, as religions (especially liberal religions) have become more rational and have continued to demythologize themselves, football has become more arcane and mysterious, with incredibly complex plays and tactics that function much the way theology does for religion. People seem to have a need for myth, ritual, mystery, and heroism, and football, perhaps more than religion in contemporary societies, is helping people satisfy these needs.

Table 6.2   Correlation Between Professional Football and Religion

Professional Football	Religion
Superstars	Saints
Sunday game	Sunday service
Ticket	Offering
Great merger	Ecumenical movement
Complex plays	Theology
Players on the way to the Super Bowl	Knights in search of the Holy Grail
Coaches	Clergy
Stadium	Church
Fans	Congregation

Whether the messages we get from football are as valuable and positive as those we get from sermons and other aspects of religion is another matter and one that bears thinking about. Has football become "the opiate of the people"? There are some who hold that belief, and it is to their interpretation that we now turn.

THE MARXIST PERSPECTIVE

Football games, held in huge stadiums, with bands, cheerleaders, halftime shows, and so on, are spectacles par excellence. The function of these spectacles (that is, the latent function), it may be argued, is to divert people's attention from their real social situation, to drain them of their emotional energy (which might have been expended on political and social issues) and, ultimately, to convince them of the justness of the political order. A political system that can provide good football is worth keeping. And because football also trains us for our place in the modern, corporate, capitalist world, it is doubly valuable.

Great gatherings held in the United States are not generally held for political purposes, although at times this does happen. Instead, Americans gather together to watch spectacles—of which football is an important exemplar. It isn't hard to see a parallel between the old Roman principle of bread and circuses—to divert the mobs from their misery—and what goes on in the United States on Fridays (high school football games), Saturdays (college games), and Sundays (professional games, although these are now played on Thursday, Saturday, and Monday as well).

Is the intensity of our interest in football a measure of the alienation we feel in our everyday lives—lives in which we sense a radical separation from our possibilities, in which we feel hemmed in by huge bureaucratic structures that dominate our work lives and by the competitiveness that characterizes our social order? The less satisfying our lives, the more bothered we are by the "rat race," the more we turn to vicarious satisfactions like football, and, curiously, the less psychic nourishment we get from them. Ironically, football is itself essentially routine and boring, and it teaches us, although we generally are not aware of it, that we must learn how to accommodate ourselves to the society in which we live.

Football, especially professional football, is a huge business that exists for one purpose: to make money. It treats players as commodities—objects to be sold and traded, almost at whim (although unionization has modified this a good deal). Players also have little sense of loyalty. They see the huge profits the team owners make and they fight to be paid huge salaries—all that the market can bear. The ultimate irony is that it is television that benefits most from the existence of football, and television uses football for its main purpose—as filler between commercials. Television, as it exists in the United States, is a business that makes money by selling commercial time. Football attracts large audiences and costs relatively little to produce (compared with, say, crime shows or situation comedies), so it is very cost-effective.

Thus we have a situation in which everyone is exploiting or trying to exploit everyone else, and the result of all this are spectacles people use to obtain vicarious excitement and pleasure and that have the hidden function of teaching people to accept the status quo and to accommodate themselves to corporations and the political order. The potential for revolutionary violence in the masses is siphoned off as people watch linemen battle one another in the trenches and defensive players hit halfbacks and cornerbacks. After a weekend of football, the heavy viewer will have participated vicariously in enough violence to fuel a dozen revolutions.

A look at the rosters of football teams shows that Blacks are heavily and disproportionately represented. This is an indication of the fact that Black people suffer more under our economic system than Whites do and thus need football (as well as boxing and other sports) as an instrument of social mobility. For poor Black kids, football is a means of escaping from poverty and achieving middle-class status—at least for a while. To be a successful football player, however, one must learn to fit in—to adopt essentially bourgeois values, such as being a team player, not causing trouble, and respecting authority figures. A player, no matter how talented, who causes problems and doesn't follow the rules will not prosper in college or professional football. Thus football players must pay a price—namely, accommodation, which leads the way to co-optation.

FOOTBALL AND THE PSYCHE

I have suggested that football functions as a means of socializing people and of diverting their attention from their real concerns. I would also like to suggest that football is vitally connected with particular unconscious processes and that this explains, in part, the powerful hold football has on people. If large numbers of people do something, such as read the comics or watch football, quite likely it is because that thing provides them with important psychic gratifications, even though the people may not be aware of them.

Consider violence in football. The controlled violence of football may satisfy two contradictory desires: the desire to be violent and the desire to be under control, so that violence doesn't overwhelm us. Violence is integral to the game of football; every play involves blocks, hits, tackles, and the like. Our attraction to violence stems from a number of sources, such as the fact that we must restrain our impulsive behavior and the fact that we are all involved (unconsciously) in Oedipal problems, sibling rivalries, and so on. The matter of sexual repression is also probably important here; violence can become a kind of substitute gratification. (We must also keep in mind the connection between violence and eroticism. There is a sexual dimension to violence just as there is an aggressive and violent dimension to sexuality.)

The violence in football may also help men to form a masculine identity. We live in an information society, in which processing data and communicating account for a dominant part of the gross national product. In such a society, men find it hard to develop a male identity, especially given that American male identity has historically been connected to a 19th-century lifestyle—cutting wood, herding cattle, doing hard physical labor. Watching violence on the football field, even if that experience of violence is vicarious and potentially destructive, is one of the few remaining ways in which American men can form a masculine identity.

Football lends itself to a number of psychoanalytical interpretations. For example, Table 6.3 interprets the game as mirroring the battles among the id, ego, and superego forces in the human psyche.

In football, the offensive team wants to have long drives and score, the defensive team wants to stop these drives and get control of the ball, and the officials function as an ego, to keep the game going.

Arnold J. Mandell (1974), a psychiatrist who spent some time with the San Diego Chargers, categorized professional football players according to the athlete's place on the field, as shown in Table 6.4.

Mandell (1974) found that players need particular personality traits in order to function in their positions. For example, he discovered that offensive players on the Chargers kept their lockers neat and orderly, whereas the lockers of defensive players were invariably messy.

It became clear that offensive football players like structure and discipline. They want to maintain the status quo. They tend to be conservative as people, and as football players they take comfort in repetitious practice of well-planned and well-executed plays. The defensive players, just as clearly, can't stand structure; their attitudes, their behavior and their life-styles bear this out. (p. 12)

All of this is important because, more than anything else, according to Mandell, "the game is in the mind"; this is probably true of all games.

Table 6.3   Relating Football to Facets of the Human Psyche

Id	Ego	Superego
Offensive team	Officials	Defensive team
Drives	Rules	Prevention

Table 6.4   Arnold J. Mandell's Characterization of Football Player Personality Traits

Position	Personality Traits
Offensive linemen	Ambitious, tenacious, precise, attentive to detail
Wide receivers	Narcissistic, vain, loners
Quarterbacks	Self-confident, courageous
Defensive linemen	Restless, peevish, irritable, intolerant of detail, uninhibited, wild
Linebackers	Controlled, brutal, internally conflicted

CONCLUDING REMARKS

Although football might seem to be only a simple entertainment, it is actually a matter of some consequence from a number of points of view. We use language from football in our political discourse; the football season creates lamentable "football widows" every fall; the game is played by children, adolescents, college students, and grown men; it is an industry; it has a long history—I could go on endlessly. Football is a subject that attracts a great deal of attention from the general public and one that deserves attention from the media analyst. There are many problems involving football and universities. In some universities, the football coaches earn much more than university presidents (University of Alabama football coach Nick Saban earned more than $5.3 million in 2012) and often are more powerful than the presidents they work for. There is also the alarming fact that a large percentage of football players never graduate from the schools they play for. And now we find that many professional football players have serious neurological and other medical problems from all the hits they have taken while playing. Everyone recognizes that football is a violent sport, but until recently we never realized how much damage this violence was doing to the players.

But there is something else to be said here that every media analyst must remember. When examining programs carried by the media—whether the focus is football, soap operas, news, or any other genre—analysts must never forget that they are dealing with art forms, and art forms are extremely complicated phenomena. The media analyst must be careful not to reduce any program to nothing but a system of signs, nothing but a socializing agent, nothing but a means of manipulating people's consciousness, nothing but a subject in which drives, Oedipal problems, and the like are manifested. The analyst must somehow analyze each program from a number of points of view and still respect it as a creative effort (even if not a very successful one) and a work of art that has performance aspects, aesthetic elements, and more. To be a media analyst, an individual must know all kinds of things and, in a sense, know everything at the same time.

STUDY QUESTIONS AND TOPICS FOR DISCUSSION

1. Discuss football in terms of the following perspectives: a semiotic sign system, an avant-garde art form, a means of socializing people, a bourgeois capitalist enterprise, and a religion of sorts.
2. What do psychoanalytic investigations of football and football players reveal? (What significance may there be in football's obsession with penetrating end zones?)
3. Compare football with baseball and explain why many people find baseball boring.
4. What does the breakdown of the way time is spent on televised football reveal about American audiences? Why do people watch a 3-hour game that has less than 15 minutes of action in it?

5. Since soccer involves continuous action, are soccer fans getting more for their money? Why isn't soccer more popular in the United States?

6. Investigate research on the neurological and other medical problems caused by the violence in football on its players.

According to Russian semiotician Yuri (also spelled Jurij) Lotman, every aspect of a work of art is important. Taking this notion as a point of departure, this chapter analyzes in detail a print advertisement for Fidji perfume, considering 17 semiotic signs found in the ad. The advertisement is also analyzed paradigmatically; that is, the polar oppositions it suggests are discussed. In addition, a psychoanalytic interpretation of the advertisement and its symbols is offered. The advertisement is then analyzed using a "myth model" that shows how myths inform culture. Finally, an aside on moisturizers and women's fears is followed by a brief discussion of perfume and anxiety.

CHAPTER 7

The Maiden With the Snake

Interpretations of a Print Advertisement

Hamlet:	Do you see yonder cloud that's almost in shape of a camel?
Polonius:	By the mass, and 'tis like a camel, indeed.
Hamlet:	Methinks it is like a weasel.
Polonius:	It is backed like a weasel.
Hamlet:	Or like a whale?
Polonius:	Very like a whale.

William Shakespeare, *Hamlet*, act III, scene ii

In this chapter I offer interpretations of a remarkable print advertisement for Fidji perfume from the perspectives of semiotic analysis, paradigmatic analysis, and psychoanalytic theory.

SIGNS IN SIGNS: A PRIMER ON APPLIED SEMIOTICS

I would like to offer an analogy that might be useful here. When you are acting as a "practicing semiotician," think of yourself as being like Sherlock Holmes or some other detective investigating a crime. The detective is looking for clues, and everything is potentially significant. Remember what Peirce said: "The universe is perfused with signs, if not made up entirely of them" (qtd. in Zeman, 1977). And as Yuri (sometimes known as Jurij) Lotman (1977) has explained, everything in a work of art is important.

The difference between the detectives in crime novels and the readers of those novels is that the detectives don't miss important signs that readers gloss over. In novels, these important signs are frequently buried in descriptions, to which readers ordinarily pay little attention. So, let me ask, What might be important in a print advertisement or a radio or television commercial? What is important in any text? The answer—as Peirce would tell us—is everything!

It is possible to make a distinction between the sign or advertisement and the signs, semiotically speaking, found in the advertisement. For purposes of this discussion of advertisements from a semiotic perspective, it is useful to think of each signifier within an ad as an elemental sign, or *signeme*—a fundamental sign that cannot be broken down any further. For example, a bottle of champagne is in itself a sign, but within that sign are such signemes as bubbles, foil, the cork, and the way the champagne gushes out of the bottle when the cork is popped.

Following is a list of important nonverbal signemes. This list does not, of course, cover all possible signemes to be found in print advertisements, television commercials, or any other visual texts, but it suggests some of the most commonly found signemes. The level of importance these signemes have depends on the particular text:

Hair color

Hairstyle

Eye color

Facial structure

Body type

Age

Gender

Race

Facial expression

Body language

Makeup

Clothes

Style of eyeglasses

Earrings and other body adornments

Setting

Relationships implied

Spatiality

Occupations

Activities going on

Background

Lighting

Sound effects, music

Typefaces

Design

Color

Verbal signemes may include the following:

Words used

Questions asked

Metaphors and similes

Associations (metonymy)

Negations made

Affirmations offered

Arguments and appeals made

Slogans

Headlines

Paradoxes generated

Tone

Style

Keep in mind that a word is a kind of sign and that the definition of a word is based on convention and must be learned. This is, at least in part, why dictionaries are always being revised.

THE MAIDEN IN PARADISE: A CASE STUDY

Let's take an interesting print advertisement as a case study in applied semiotic analysis. An advertisement for Fidji perfume appeared a number of years ago in many fashion magazines (see Figure 7.1; although the ad is reproduced here in black and white, it appeared in magazines in color). The ad features a photograph that shows part of the face of an apparently Polynesian woman (from just below her nose) as she holds a bottle of Fidji perfume in her curiously intertwined fingers. Her fingernails are red. She has long, dark hair and full red lips (slightly parted), and a yellow orchid is tucked into her hair near her right ear (on the left in the photo). Around the woman's neck is a snake, part of whose body forms something that looks like an infinity symbol. The snake's head points downward, slightly covering the top of the perfume bottle. The lighting is rather dramatic, using chiaroscuro (which means, in essence, both clear and dark): Parts of the photograph are light, whereas other parts, particularly the upper right, are quite dark.

Figure 7.1	Advertisement for Fidji Perfume

Fidji: le parfum
des paradis retrouvés.

Available at Bloomingdales

Fidji de Guy Laroche.
De la Haute Couture à la Haute Parfumerie

What follows are some of the things a semiotician might address in interpreting this advertisement.

The formal design of the ad. In the minds of most Americans, formal design (approximating axial balance), simplicity, and spaciousness (a great deal of white or "empty" space) are associated with wealth and sophistication. Advertisements for expensive and "classy" products often are full of white space—that is, they are relatively empty.

The warm colors. The ad shows a yellow orchid in the woman's hair and full red lips and fingernails. Red is commonly used to suggest passion.

The partial obstruction of the woman's face. Because only the bottom part of the woman's face, from just above her lips, is visible, it is possible for women viewing the ad to identify with her more easily than if her complete face were shown. The woman's lips are partly open; open lips often are used to suggest sexual excitement or passion. Further, the lighting emphasizes her long and slender neck.

The woman's ethnicity. In the popular imagination, Polynesia is connected with fantasies of natural love and sexuality. The French painter Gauguin abandoned France for Polynesia, and many people are familiar with the story of his "escape" to paradise, where people are not burdened with rules and prohibitions (civilization and its discontents).

The woman's hair. Dark hair, in American culture, is often associated with warmth, heat, and sexual passion. Women with blonde hair, on the other hand, are often thought of as Nordic and cold or as innocent and sexually unresponsive. The woman's hair is long, also—something frequently connected in the popular mind with youth and sexual abandon. (This explains all those commercials showing young women, their long hair flying in the breeze, running through meadows toward—presumably—their lovers.) It is quite common for women to cut their hair short when they get older, so they don't have to bother with it as much.

The name of the perfume. The name *Fidji* makes the connection between the perfume and Polynesia (and all the connotations that go with it) explicit. The copy in the advertisement reinforces this notion.

The yellow orchid. Flowers are the sexual apparatus of a plant, so there is a hint of sexuality in the use of the orchid, which, due to the lighting, is prominently displayed. Also, *flowering* is a word often used to describe a woman's becoming physically developed and, with that, sexually receptive. Flowers are signs of love. Orchids are thought of as rare and delicate and are associated with the tropics.

The snake. According to Freudian theory, snakes are phallic symbols by virtue of their shape—an example of iconicity that is used in both semiotic and psychoanalytic interpretation. (I should note that in some countries, a similar advertisement appeared for this perfume without the snake.) This image, a woman with a snake around her neck (it has been suggested that the snake in the ad looks like a corn snake), is also found in Piero di Cosimo's portrait of Simonetta Vespucci and other works of art as well—an example of intertextuality (as discussed in Chapter 1), the conscious or unconscious borrowing from one work for another.

The relationship between women and snakes goes back a long way, to the Garden of Eden, and the outcome of that relationship, Adam's temptation, has been of considerable importance in Western history. One might argue that the snake in the story of the Garden of Eden is the prototypical advertising executive. According to the book of Genesis, "The serpent was more subtle than any beast in the field which the Lord God had made," and he convinced Eve that if she ate from the tree of knowledge of good and evil she wouldn't die but her eyes would be opened. After she ate from the tree and convinced Adam to do the same, they were both thrown out of the Garden of Eden, and all kinds of things followed from that expulsion. Eve's excuse was "The serpent beguiled me, and I did eat." Advertising executives have been beguiling the progeny of Adam and Eve ever since—although they have not been required to slide on their bellies and eat dust.

Another association with snakes is found in the Greek myth of Medusa, one of the Gorgons, whose hair was made of snakes. Any man who looked upon Medusa turned to stone. Hair, this myth suggests, has power. I will discuss this matter shortly.

The intertwined fingers. The woman's fingers are intertwined in a rather curious way, with a finger of one hand shown poking between two fingers of the other hand—giving the vague impression of a penis coming between two legs. We find intertwined fingers in some well-known works of art, such as Alessandro Botticelli's *Primavera*, so there is another intertextual relationship that might be considered.

The bottle. The perfume bottle has a large stopper and is shown with strong highlights that run across it. A vertical black line runs down the middle of the bottle and a horizontal black ribbon is wrapped around the neck of the bottle, below the stopper.

The woman's nakedness. The woman is not wearing any clothes, which reinforces the photo's paradisiacal image. Before Adam and Eve ate from the tree of knowledge, they were naked, and nakedness is associated in Western consciousness with innocence (and in the case of nudists, for example, with a desire to regain the innocence of paradise). Curiously enough, we do not see any indication of the woman's breasts—they seem to have been airbrushed out. Showing breasts might suggest maternity and related matters, which would not be conducive to fantasies of primordial sex with a natural (read "uninhibited") woman. Showing breasts is much different, I would argue, from showing cleavage and subtly indicating breasts—which is a sexual turn-on for men.

The use of French. The text of the ad is all in French, which is undoubtedly used because of its metonymic qualities—because Americans tend to associate the French with style, sophistication, and sexiness (whether any of these associations reflect reality is beside the point). The French language also acts as a means of separating those with refinement and "class," who know French (or at least can understand the French used in this advertisement—which is not very difficult), from the "masses."

The copy. In the upper right-hand corner of the advertisement, in relatively small type, we see "Fidji: le parfum des paradis retrouvés." I would translate this as "Fidji: the perfume of paradise regained (or rediscovered)." You really don't have to know French to understand most of the headline. The key French to understand is *retrouvés*. The phrase "paradise regained" is one that people with any degree of education are familiar with. So even if they don't know what *retrouvés* means, they can most likely figure it out. Thus a person doesn't really have to know French or be particularly "sophisticated" to be able to understand the headline.

On the bottle, the words "Parfums Guy Laroche Paris" appear, along with the Fidji logo. The only other verbiage is at the bottom of the ad, on a light band below the image of the woman and the snake, "Fidji de Guy Laroche," set in Roman typeface, and then in small italics, *De la Haute Couture à la Haute Parfumerie,*" which translates, roughly, as "from high fashion to high perfume."

There is, then, rather little in the way of copy in this ad. The image of the woman and the snake is used to sell Fidji, rather than any verbal arguments. This style is rather common in perfume ads, because they are selling, in one way or another, fantasies of sexual abandon, paradisiacal sex, and similar notions.

The "hidden word." The curves of the snake's body can be seen as forming the letter *S*; the highlights on the top of the bottle's stopper, on the top of the bottle itself, and on the bottom of the bottle can be seen as an *E*; and the woman's fingers clearly form an *X*. Thus the word *sex* is hidden, or embedded, in the image and, so some psychoanalytically inclined scholars argue, even though people who look at the advertisement may not consciously see the word hidden in the image, they pick it up unconsciously and are affected by it.

The crucifix. The vertical black line on the bottle and the horizontal ribbon at the bottle's neck may be seen as a highly stylized crucifix form, a bit of symbology that possibly links the passion of Christ with sexual passion in ordinary people. The way the *F* in the Fidji logo is designed also vaguely suggests a crucifix.

The infinity sign. Part of the snake's body, where it loops around on the woman's shoulder, appears to form the symbol for infinity—perhaps an indication of the infinite nature of the passion a woman will generate by wearing Fidji?

The painted fingernails. There is something incongruous, one might think, about a "natural" woman, in Polynesia, having brightly painted fingernails. Maybe the subtext of this advertisement is that you can have the best of both worlds—modernity, sophistication (the perfume is French and therefore, in the popular mind, sophisticated), and elegance as well as the kind of guilelessness and passion we associate with the innocent and natural woman. This duality is, in fact, at the core of the advertisement: a natural woman holding a bottle of French perfume. The bottle mediates between the primitive woman "within a woman" and the average woman's socialized, enculturated, everyday life.

A PARADIGMATIC ANALYSIS OF THE FIDJI ADVERTISEMENT

One of the most famous statements Saussure (1915/1966) ever made explains how people find meaning in their experiences: "Concepts are purely differential and defined not by their positive content but negatively by their relations with other terms of the system." He adds, "The most precise characteristic [of these concepts] is being what the others are not" (p. 117). In essence, language works by forcing us to see differences that explain how we make sense of things. Meaning is relational, not based on the essences of things themselves.

French anthropologist Claude Lévi-Strauss (1967) developed a method of analyzing myths by finding oppositions in them. In this section I adapt this method of analysis, paradigmatic analysis, to an examination of the Fidji advertisement. Let's look at some of the oppositions generated by the Fidji ad, which suggest what it is not (see Table 7.1). When people look at the ad, they go through the process of generating such oppositions—if they are to find meaning in it.

I am not suggesting that people consciously make a paradigmatic analysis when they see the Fidji ad (or any other advertisement), but if Saussure is correct, and concepts have meaning differentially, viewers of the ad must do something like this on an unconscious level if the advertisement is to make sense to them. The oppositions are, then, implicit in the advertisement.

There is also a good deal of redundancy in the Fidji advertisement, to help get the message across. We see the word *Fidji* three times—in the caption, on the bottle, and in the copy in the upper right-hand part of the ad. Further, the image of the woman with a flower in her hair (like the women in Gauguin's paintings) and the snake reinforce the Fidji-paradise theme. The perfume promises magic to transport women back to earlier times—before life was so complex and their lives were so full of everyday bothers—back to when, so we imagine, sexuality was natural and uninhibited. The fact that this primitive maiden is holding a bottle of very expensive French perfume is an irony that, no doubt, is lost on most of those to whom the advertisement is directed.

USING THE MYTH MODEL

In my discussion of the significance of the snake in the Fidji advertisement, I mentioned the mythic significance of snakes in Western culture. The snake plays a very important role in the Bible. Let me suggest, now, that we can find myths in many areas of culture. In *Understanding Media Semiotics*, Marcel Danesi (2002) offers a useful definition of myth:

Table 7.1 Polar Oppositions Drawn From the Fidji Advertisement

Woman of Color (Polynesian)	White Woman
Nature	Urban society
Escape	Imprisonment
Paradise	Hell
Dark hair	Light hair
Free sexuality	Inhibited sexuality
Magic	Rationality
Fidji perfume	Other perfumes

As Barthes argued [in *Mythologies*], the themes of humanities earliest stories, known as myths, continue to permeate and inform pop culture's story-telling efforts. As in the myths of Prometheus, Hercules, and other ancient heroes, Superman's exploits revolve around a universal mythic theme—the struggle of Good and Evil. This is what makes Superman, or any action hero for that matter, so intuitively appealing to modern audiences. . . . The word "myth" derives from the Greek *mythos:* "word," "speech," "tale of the gods." It can be defined as a narrative in which the characters are gods, heroes, and mystical beings, in which the plot is about the origin of things or about metaphysical events in human life, and in which the setting is a metaphysical world juxtaposed against the real world. In the beginning stages of human cultures, myths functioned as genuine "narrative theories" of the world. That is why all cultures have created them to explain their origins. . . . The use of mythic themes and elements in media representations has become so widespread that it is hardly noticed any longer, despite Barthes' cogent warnings in the late 1950s. Implicit myths about the struggle for Good, of the need for heroes to lead us forward, and so on and so forth, constitute the narrative underpinnings of TV programmes, blockbuster movies, advertisements and commercials, and virtually anything that gets "media air time." (pp. 47–48)

Myths play an important role in shaping social life and in validating, and in some cases creating, customs, beliefs, rituals, and other aspects of life, even though we may not be aware of them or their impact. They are, then, sacred stories about heroes and heroines and the creation of the world.

In my book, *Media, Myth, and Society* (2013), I offer what I describe as a "myth model" that shows how myths inform culture and society:

A myth from Greece or Rome or elsewhere

Psychoanalytical concepts that employ myths

Historical events that relate to myths

Texts from elite culture that are based on myths

Texts from popular culture that are tied to myths

Parts of everyday life that are based on myths

In the Western world, for people familiar with the biblical story, a woman with a snake evokes the myth of Adam and Eve. But there is another myth involving snakes, the myth of Medusa, which is more pertinent to Fidji's suggested "power" as a perfume. Let me suggest, then, that this advertisement is intertextually connected to a myth and that this myth informs certain aspects of our cultural past.

Medusa was a Gorgon whose hair was made of snakes, but she was originally a maiden who had beautiful hair. She incurred the displeasure of Athena, who turned Medusa into a monster. Anyone who gazed upon Medusa was turned to stone. From a psychoanalytical point of view, Medusa's hair of snakes was hyperphallic. From a historical perspective, we can use Cleopatra, who killed herself with an asp. Her story was told in an elite-culture text, Shakespeare's *Antony and Cleopatra*, and through paintings of Cleopatra and other books about her. In popular culture, we have the Fidji advertisement with the woman and the snake, and in everyday life, we have a woman who dabs on some Fidji perfume.

The following shows how the myth model relates to the Fidji advertisement:

Myth Medusa, the Gorgon with hair of snakes

Psychoanalytic theory Hyperphallic nature of Medusa

Historical aspects Cleopatra kills herself with a snake

Elite-culture text Shakespeare's *Antony and Cleopatra*

Pop-culture text Fidji perfume advertisement with snake

Everyday Life Woman puts on Fidji perfume

What we learn from the myth model here is that the meaning of a visual image is closely connected to the culture and society in which the image is found and, in many cases, to myths, fairy tales, and folklore found in that society. The culture in which an advertisement is found, including other texts in that culture, help supply some of the meaning of a visual image; we must recognize that an image's meaning is not exhausted in the signs and signemes found in it. What the myth model suggests is that many elite-culture and popular-culture texts, psychoanalytic theories (think, for example, of the Oedipus myth and the Oedipus complex), historical events, and aspects of everyday life are intertextually connected to myths and shaped by them.

PSYCHOANALYTIC ASPECTS OF THE FIDJI TEXT

In the previous semiotic analysis I have already covered a number of the psychoanalytic aspects of this text, such as the matter of the snake as a phallic symbol. As Freud notes in *The Interpretation of Dreams* (1900/1965), "Many of the beasts which are used as genital symbols in mythology and folklore play the same part in dreams: e.g. fishes, snails, cats, mice (on account of the pubic hair), and above all those most important symbols of the male organ, snakes" (p. 392). This symbolization, he adds, is found not only in dreams but in other areas as well:

> Symbolism is not peculiar to dreams, but is characteristic of unconscious ideation, in particular among the people, and it is to be found in folklore, and in popular myths, legends, linguistic idioms, proverbial wisdom and current jokes, to a more complete extent than in dreams. (p. 386)

So we are always being affected by symbols—in waking life as well as in dreams. These symbols are, from Freud's point of view, disguised manifestations of latent or unconscious thoughts and desires.

Erich Fromm (1957), as I have noted in Chapter 3, reminds us that for Freud these symbols represent either males or females by their shapes or functions. Flowers and bottles, according to Freud, obviously represent women, so the Fidji advertisement has very female symbols to go along with that preeminent phallic symbol, the snake. Thus it can be argued that the Fidji ad, through its basic symbolization—the snake, the bottle, and the flower—generates very strong sexual fantasies. Attached to these fantasies are the notions we have about paradise, the tropics, innocent passion, and so on, stemming from what we know about Gauguin's life and our exposure to books about life in Polynesia.

There is, for many people, an element of anxiety and fear connected with snakes. Among women, this may be tied to unconscious anxieties and ambivalent feelings they have about men's genitals "penetrating" them. Erik Erikson (1968) has suggested, based on his observations of children at play, that women represent an "incorporative" modality and men a "penetrating" modality. (To sum up Erikson's observations in a greatly abbreviated manner: The little girls he watched created enclosures, whereas the little boys built towers.) We also find this penetrating/incorporative polarity in electric plugs and outlets and in other tools and hardware. Finally, the presence of the snake around the woman's neck suggests that perfumes are powerful agents, similar to a snake's venom. Now that we call perfumes "fragrances," we can have a situation in which both men and women can wear dueling fragrances in an attempt to achieve whatever romantic or sexual goals they may have in mind with their dates, partners, or whomever. I will expand on this matter shortly.

AN ASIDE ON MOISTURIZERS AND ANXIETY

Moisturizers also mine the anxieties many women have about their sexuality and fecundity. A considerable amount of cosmetic advertising emphasizes wetness and moisture, generating anxiety in women that their bodies are continually in danger of becoming dry, arid, and desertlike—that is, devoid of life, infertile, and uninteresting. These ads work to generate anxiety in women about losing their body fluids, which is tied to anxieties they may have about being unable to reproduce or getting older. This, in turn, is connected to sexuality and desirability. Advertisements for moisturizers create fears that the body is continually "gushing water" and is in danger of becoming a kind of wasteland, a desert. Dehydration becomes a metaphor for loss of sexual attractiveness and capacity—that is, desexualization.

An advertisement that appeared in *Vogue* some years ago, for a product called Living Proof Cream Hydracel by Geminesse, explained the following:

Water keeps a rose fresh and beautiful. A peach juicy. All living things living. The millions of cells in your skin contain water. This water pillows and cushions your skin, making it soft and young-looking. But for a lot of reasons, cells become unable to hold enough water. And the water escapes from your skin. (If you'll forgive us, think of a prune drying up and you'll know the whole story.)

Thus a little drama is created and a very powerful metaphor is generated. Advertisements say to women, in effect, "You, who were once young and sweet and juicy, like a plum, face the danger of becoming old and drying up and ending up like a prune, if you don't use our product to moisturize and thus protect yourself."

FINAL COMMENTS ON PERFUME AND ANXIETY

The other side of the anxiety generated by the snake in the advertisement is that without some kind of magic, a woman will not be able to attract a man, and thus she really needs to use Fidji if she is to have a rich and satisfying sexual life. Perfume advertisements are, deep down, about magic and the fantasy that the power of a particular smell (made of flowers, let us remember) will excite a man and thus lead to some desired form of sexual consummation.

We know that perfumes have been used by women for thousands of years, but it is only recently that men have been convinced that they should wear perfume, now relabeled as a "fragrance." The word *fragrance* is now used for both perfumes for women and perfume-like products for men. Serge Lutens (n.d.), who creates perfumes, defines them in the following way: "Perfume, in and of itself, is not just an aroma. It is potentially a carrier for the imagination. Perfume is thick; it is poison and pure desire. It is Eros in prison." Lutens suggests that perfume has an erotic mission and can affect us in profound ways. Perfume, he explains, is not just an aroma. It is, he suggests, magical, like poison, except that it generates sexual excitement and passion, not death.

Magic, according to Freud, is based ultimately on the omnipotence of thought. And what is equally interesting is the way magical thinking switches from the motives or goals of a magical act to the means of carrying out the magic. Thinking makes it so, but having magic agents, such as perfume in this case, helps. We know that aromas do affect us in rather profound ways, so it is not too far-fetched to suggest that certain scents may have the ability to excite people sexually. What may add to the mix is the advertising that makes this argument, over and over again, and associates certain smells with mass-mediated fantasies.

Perfumes may work, to a considerable degree, on the basis of a placebo effect. Wearing perfume may convince a woman she is sexually alluring, and this confidence may be what is important, not the particular perfume (Fidji, Chanel No. 5, Target's best). Could it be that one thing perfume may do is either mask the "flop sweat" of women anxious about whether some man will find them attractive or prevent it by giving them enhanced confidence in themselves? (It is interesting that in most cases the bottle containing the perfume costs more to make than the perfume itself.)

There is something curiously peaceful about the Fidji maiden in paradise with the snake around her shoulders. The part of her face shown doesn't reflect any anxiety about the snake, and she holds the bottle of Fidji in her fingers, in a curious way, with a sense of security. Presumably she is wearing Fidji, and thus she need not fear she will lack companionship. Could it be that Fidji perfume (and every other perfume) is, in mysterious and magical ways, like snake venom—a powerful agent that has an incredible effect on those on whom it is used? But what does this say about women who use perfumes?

STUDY QUESTIONS AND TOPICS FOR DISCUSSION

1. What aesthetic considerations should you keep in mind when analyzing advertisements?
2. How is semiotics useful for interpretation of the Fidji advertisement featured in this chapter?
3. Discuss the signemes found in the Fidji advertisement.
4. What is the secret significance of moisturizers?
5. What role does figurative language play in advertising? Consider the role of metaphor in the Geminesse moisturizer ad mentioned in this chapter.
6. What brands of fragrances do you own? In what ways are they different?
7. Have your tastes changed as far as your fragrances are concerned? If so, how do you explain it? How much do you think is reasonable to pay for a fragrance?
8. Use the myth model to analyze advertisements, films, television shows, or other aspects of society and culture.

In this chapter, all-news radio stations are subjected to a Marxist interpretation. These stations are seen as signifiers of a malaise in American culture, and the dependency people have on these stations is linked to the American capitalist economic system, which generates anxiety and thus a need for constant surveillance. The information hunger many people feel is reinforced by the trivial, often commercial, news presented. A discussion of radio commercials is also offered; these commercials occupy approximately one-third of each broadcasting hour and often create anxiety and many other negative feelings. The chapter ends with an examination of the audiences of radio talk shows and all-news stations, with some speculation about what the demographics imply.

CHAPTER 8

All-News Radio and the American Bourgeoisie

What are we to make of the all-news radio stations operating throughout radio markets in the United States? How can we explain the existence of stations that broadcast news 24 hours a day? One might think all this news would result in incredible overkill or supersaturation, yet in many large cities, all-news stations are quite profitable.

The programming at all-news radio stations tends to be highly structured and formulaic: Sports news is broadcast at certain times, as are business news, weather reports, features, commentaries, local news, and network news—all have more or less regular time slots, so that listeners looking for certain kinds of news learn when to tune in to get whatever it is they are interested in.

NEWS AND ALIENATION

The existence of all-news radio stations, and all-news television stations, indicates a pervasive "information hunger" that this kind of programming helps to assuage. But why this voracity for news? Why this need to keep on top of everything? It is a sign (or, to be more precise, semiotically speaking, a signifier) of a widespread and powerful affliction in American culture—an overpowering sense of anxiety and fear (the signified) that tears at the psyches of many people. It also represents a desire to "participate" in history somehow, even if only vicariously.

Psychoanalysts would describe this news hunger as a neurosis, a compulsive form of behavior, even though it seems innocuous (and perhaps is even virtuous, given that citizens are supposed to be well informed), fueled by relentless and powerful urges quite likely to be harmful. In extreme cases we may even suggest that "newsaholics" are people who know everything but do nothing—except listen to (or watch) the news. There may even be something of a desire to be like God in these people—all-knowing, all-pervasive—except that the newsaholic is driven not by a sense of being all-powerful but by the reverse.

Ultimately, it would seem, the anxiety of the heavy news listener is the product of a sense of powerlessness and insignificance, which leads to a need for constant surveillance. From the Marxist perspective, this is quite understandable. Bourgeois capitalist societies generate alienation and a host of afflictions connected to it—a sense of powerlessness, insecurity, estrangement, rootlessness, and lack of identity. Because we have no coherent sense of history or ideology, and because we live in a society that may be described as dog-eat-dog, we must, if we are to survive, keep on top of things and never be caught napping.

Our capacity to absorb the enormous amounts of programming aired by all-news stations is tied to this anxiety and to something else (to continue the Marxist critique): What we are offered is not really news but essentially trivia—sensational "junk food for the mind" that does not deal seriously with our social and political problems but instead diverts and entertains us. Because this so-called news is insubstantial, we are able to devour huge quantities of it and never get full. We lack a well-defined and coherent political sensibility that enables us to make sense of events. All we get, for the most part, is "figure" divorced from "ground"—that is, a succession of reports on things (fires, crimes, political events, film reviews, food tips, the weather) that all occupy the foreground.

This "news" is all superficially interesting and satisfies our curiosity, but it doesn't help us to orient ourselves, because nothing fits together with anything else. The pressure within the news media to cover events as they happen, to get the news first, prevents them from providing useful background information and thoughtful analysis. "To the blind, all things are sudden," someone once said, and to those with no sense of history and social relations, with no understanding of the causes of events and their implications, all-news stations are literally sensational. What we get may be fascinating, but it is not particularly edifying or useful to listeners who wish to uncover the meanings of events.

Frequently, media scholars distinguish between "hard" and "soft" news. Hard news is supposedly serious; it deals with important events in the social, political, and economic arenas. But many of the stories classified as hard news are really products of the public relations mills of political leaders, government agencies, businesses, and other organizations. News reporters are, as a rule, highly moral and responsible professionals who do the best they can to avoid being manipulated, to offer accurate information, and so forth, but they have, without recognizing it, adopted the establishment's point of view. Thus their ideas are, as Marxists would put it, "the ideas of the ruling class."

NEWS AND RULING-CLASS IDEOLOGY

A study of televised news conducted in Great Britain reached some conclusions about the role of broadcasters in the presentation of ideology:

> News talk occurs within a cultural framework which stresses balance and impartiality. Yet despite this, detailed analysis reveals that it consistently maintains and supports a cultural framework within which viewpoints favourable to the status quo are given preferred and privileged readings.

> This representation of events as news is not governed by a conscious attempt to present ideology. The journalists and producers and those they allow to broadcast of course believe that their routines and codes merely serve to fashion the news into intelligible and meaningful bulletins. (Glasgow University Media Group, 1980, p. 122)

The ideological assumptions newscasters make are all the more insidious because neither the news-casters themselves nor their audiences generally recognize those assumptions for what they are. News professionals select the topics on which they focus their attention from a huge inventory of available information. Their selection of items for broadcast (along with their failure to provide audiences with background on those items) is crucial. What is neglected? What is not seen as worth dealing with? What is determined to have little news value? These are some questions we might ask as we consider the adequacy of the news diet available on all-news radio stations. It is possible that some stories of possible significance are neglected or mentioned only in passing because of the unconscious assumptions of the news editors and audiences of these news programs, who have been taught over a number of years what is important and what isn't. Some issues, by their nature, are harder than others to uncover or more complicated to analyze; editors and reporters who face the pressures of limited time and production budgets often pass over such issues.

In the case of soft news—features of various kinds—an insidious commercialization is present, for soft-news stories almost always contain, as an end result, the promotion of some product or service. We learn about "undiscovered" restaurants, interesting films, and the best boutiques in which to buy this or that kind of clothing. Ultimately, although these features may seem quite innocent, they serve as free advertisements for businesses. From a sociological perspective, the manifest functions of such features are to entertain and provide useful information; the latent function is to "sell" restaurants, movies, and all manner of other things. To the Marxist, hard news and soft news are more or less the same: Both help to support the ideological perspectives of the ruling classes and fuel the engines of consumption.

COMMERCIALS AND ANXIETY

The most important engines of consumption in radio broadcasting are the commercials; about 16 to 18 minutes of every hour—roughly one-third of broadcast time—is devoted to commercials. Thus one-third of the information broadcast on all-news stations is product news. When soft news is added to the mix, it is clear that a very large block of news airtime is actually given to commercial information. In addition, most of the imagination, intelligence, and creativity found on radio—and in popular culture in general—is lavished on commercials. This is because they are what is most important; they are the raison d'être for the stations, which, after all, are businesses that exist to make money through the use of the public airwaves.

We are bombarded with slogans, jingles, and announcements that use whatever subliminal or other persuasive techniques are available to make us feel anxious about ourselves, to generate feelings of relative deprivation, and to get us to *buy* something (see Chapter 7 for more on the power of advertising). Ironically, to assuage our bad feelings, to rid ourselves of these anxieties about ourselves and our situations, we turn to the mass media—movies, soap operas, music, even all-news radio stations—which reinforce the very problems we hope they will help us solve. Thus we become caught in a vicious cycle from which there is no escape. The more we listen to the news (and the ubiquitous commercials that are part of radio news programming), the unhappier we become, and the unhappier we become, the more we listen to the news.

When we listen to all-news radio stations, especially for long periods of time, we seldom can avoid ending up disturbed. We become anxious about the world and plagued by negative emotions. This may explain why, in certain circumstances, no news is good news. Small wonder that the average all-news radio station listener tunes in for only 20 or 30 minutes at a time.

CAUGHT IN THE MIDDLE

Demographic studies of the audiences of all-news programs indicate that listeners tend to be upscale—that is, professional types who are well educated and, it would seem, far removed from the pathetic figures I have described. Trendy affluents most certainly are not tense, anxiety-ridden souls endlessly searching for security and desperate about keeping abreast of things lest they be caught unawares. Or are they?

Do all of these upscale people have a real sense of security and a well-defined identity? Or is there, perhaps, a faint tinge of desperation showing in the way they follow the business news or listen to the features to be told the "right" movies, the "right" restaurants, and the "right" opinions to have?

News listeners tend to be upper-middle-class people. Those in the proletariat (who live in poverty) have relatively little interest in the news. The less well-off tend to be fatalists, believing they are unable to change the system that oppresses them; they are generally uninvolved in and unconcerned about events in the world, except in cases immediate to their personal interests. Those in the upper classes own the means of production—including the media—and need not worry too much about what is going on. They control the events. Older people also don't worry much about what is going on in the world (aside from issues dealing with social security and related matters), and, instead of listening to news radio, they listen to talk shows in large numbers. Approximately half of the audience of radio talk shows comprises people over age 65. Young people are busy listening to music stations and worrying about such age-related problems as acne, sex, fashion, cars, and love. When we shear off the relatively old, the very young, the poor, and the rich, we are left with the middle-aged (and postteenage and pre–middle-aged), middle-class people who make up the prime audience of all-news programs.

The members of this group have the most to gain or lose from the tide of events. They have no power to alter the system set up by the upper classes—nor do they have the desire to. They have been thoroughly indoctrinated by the ideology fed them day and night on their radios and through other media and hope only to improve their situation so that someday they may join the upper class they have tried so long to emulate. But this requires that they pay constant attention to the news if they are to maintain their current status and possibly someday get the edge on their competitors—other middle-class people much like themselves. These people, according to Marxist thinking, are the guilt-ridden victims of all-news radio.

NEWS AND CONVERSATION

There is a distinction between what can be called news shows, which we find on local and network news programs, and news analysis, which we find on many talk shows on both radio and television. Take, for example, a popular television talk show, the *Charlie Rose Show* on the Public Broadcasting Service. Rose often has important politicians, scholars, writers, and newsmakers on his show. His guests typically include Supreme Court justices, senators and Congress members, important government officials, kings of countries, and other high-level persons. They discuss with him (and sometimes he has a number of guests at the same time) economic and political matters of consequence, often involving events in the news. Rose asks many questions of his guests in an attempt to understand the significance of whatever it is they are discussing.

Some news-based talk shows involve interaction. Listeners can call the show and ask questions of the people being interviewed or can send e-mails with their comments. This means that news now is often a matter of conversation and dialogue rather than passive listening. On radio, conversation plays a large role in our media diet. The public television station in San Francisco, KQED, broadcasts *Forum* from 9:00 a.m. until 11:00 a.m. with a local talk show host. Then it has another hour-long talk show with Terry Gross that deals with popular culture but occasionally covers politics and news events.

So our attitude toward news has changed. People are no longer passive receivers of newscasts but now, with many talk shows, can actually participate in the discussions that take place on these shows. We no longer merely listen to the news but now can have a role in discussing news events and questioning people involved in making the news. And now that so many people have smartphones that can take photographs and create video, people help create news. They can make videos of important events, such as the terrible fire at a fertilizer plant near Waco, Texas, and the tragic events at the 2013 Boston Marathon.

NEWS FROM THE INTERNET AND SOCIAL MEDIA

Americans don't listen to the radio as much as they used to—it is estimated that the radio audience in the United States has shrunk by about 15% in the past 10 years. The growth of the Internet, including blogs and sites about news, politics, and related matters (such as Politico, the Huffington Post, and the Drudge Report), has led to a change in the way Americans get their news. Social media sites such as Facebook and Twitter are often used to spread reports about news events as they are happening, and many people use their smartphones to videotape newsworthy events and upload them to YouTube. As a result, newspapers, news magazines, television news shows, and all-news radio stations are declining in popularity. Even search engines such as Google and Yahoo now have services that aggregate news of all kinds, and most newspapers have Internet editions. And now some news organizations have created news publications specifically for iPads and other tablets. For example, on my tablet I access the following news apps frequently to keep up with what's happening: Google News, KQED News, CNN, News 360, NPR News, Pulse, and Zinio, as well as YouTube, Facebook, Twitter, and TuneinRadio. Many people have news apps on their smartphones as well. We now have many more sources for news, which we can access whenever we feel like it, so "all-news" radio is not as significant a player on the news front as it used to be. This means our passion for surveillance and for keeping up with events is now satisfied much differently from the way we obtained news a decade or so ago, when all-news radio stations were popular.

Let me conclude this discussion with a quote from the Podcaster (2010). It offers disquieting information about the impact of the Internet on radio listeners:

> The latest annual report (19th) by Arbitron and Edison into the impact of digital platforms on radio shows that whilst radio is still held in high regard it has now been eclipsed by the internet as the medium of choice by the public.
>
> The highlights from the report are:
>
> - Internet now exceeds radio and TV as the "most essential" medium when people are asked
> - Almost 50% believe that newspapers will cease to exist in their current form in the future
> - Internet now exceeds radio as the medium where 12–34 year olds learn about new music
> - Social Media is now a mainstream tool
> - 25% of people now consume audio content in cars via iPod/MP3 players
> - Texting is a daily activity for almost 50% of people
>
> This, and other research shows the increasing reach and impact of podcasting in people's lives. With increasing use of "smartphones" content is being consumed on the move allowing much more targeted and relevant messaging.
>
> Businesses can now use podcasts to create content targeting "communities of interest" relevant to their product and service. Rather than paying for radio adverts and sponsorship highly targeted edutainment programs can be developed that will attract and retain an audience.

Radio will continue to be an important source of news and entertainment for people, but its role will be considerably diminished in the future as people become used to getting news on their smartphones, tablets, and computers.

STUDY QUESTIONS AND TOPICS FOR DISCUSSION

1. What is the relationship between news (and information hunger) and alienation? How is sensationalism in the news related to this alienation?
2. How may news programs and the ideology they reflect be interpreted from a Marxist viewpoint?

3. Define *relative deprivation* and explain how it is related to a Marxist interpretation of radio programming.
4. Why are middle-class Americans so passionately involved with news?
5. How do you get your news? Which Internet sites do you use? What changes do you think the Internet will lead to as far as newspapers and other kinds of news are concerned?

In recent years, video games have become a major form of entertainment for millions of people, of all ages, throughout the world. This chapter considers whether video games are an art form or a medium and how the genres of video games might be classified. It also discusses the role of interactivity in video games and the many uses and gratifications these games provide their players. Particular attention is paid to the problem of addiction to video games and the ways in which the games foster addiction in players. Other topics addressed include the violent nature of many video games, the treatment of sexuality in many games, and the social and physical problems associated with video game playing.

Video Games

A New Art Form

Pong, an electronic game that simulates the action of Ping-Pong, is generally held to be the first important video game. Compared with today's video games, Pong is very primitive; players do nothing but hit a ball of light back and forth across a video screen. Video games have progressed with incredible speed since Pong appeared, and many are now complicated texts, in many cases similar to films in their aesthetic qualities. Unlike films, however, video games are interactive. The video game player becomes the "star," so to speak, of the game.

Video games have clearly evolved considerably, but what they have evolved into is a matter for discussion. The analysis of video games that follows deals with a number of aspects of this relatively recent popular culture phenomenon. First, I deal with the question of whether video games are an art form or a new medium, listing some of the more important genres found in video games and offering examples of each. I then offer some comments about how the development of new technologies has affected video games. This is followed by a brief discussion of some insights about video games provided by Janet Murray in her important analysis of narrative video games, *Hamlet on the Holodeck: The Future of Narrative in Cyberspace* (1997). I then address the psychological gratifications that video games provide and the ways they "hook" players. Finally, I discuss the social and cultural impacts of video games, including issues of violence and sexuality.

If we count all of the money spent on video game–playing equipment as well as the games themselves, the video game industry is currently larger than the film industry in the United States. It plays a major role in our daily media diet. Video gaming is no longer just for children, either—a considerable number of video game players are adults. In 2003, Americans spent $6.9 billion on game software and billions more on video game consoles such as Microsoft's Xbox, Sony's PlayStation 2, and Nintendo's GameCube as well as on powerful computers with special chips and audio systems designed for video gaming. In 2009, the total sales for video games and game consoles in the United States were $19.6 billion, according to the NPD Group (Wawro, 2010). For 2013, CNBC (2013) estimates the size of global video game market revenue, including mobile games on smartphones and tablets, at $66 billion, up from $63 billion in 2012. Sales are expected to grow to $78 billion in 2017.

The Entertainment Software Association (2013), an organization devoted to supporting and lobbying for the video game industry, offers the following information about the video game industry:

1. Fifty-eight percent of Americans play video games.
2. Consumers spent $20.77 billion on video games, hardware, and accessories in 2012.

3. Purchases of digital content, including games, add-on content, mobile apps, subscriptions, and social networking games, accounted for 40 percent of game sales in 2012.
4. The average game player is 30 years old and has been playing games for 13 years.
5. The average age of the most frequent game purchaser is 35 years old.
6. Forty-five percent of all game players are women. In fact, women over the age of 18 represent a significantly greater portion of the game-playing population (31 percent) than boys age 17 or younger (19 percent).
7. Fifty-one percent of U.S. households own a dedicated game console, and those that do own an average of two.
8. Thirty-six percent of gamers play games on their smartphone, and 25 percent play games on their wireless device.
9. Ninety-one percent of games rated by the Entertainment Software Rating Board (ESRB) in 2012 received a rating of "E" for Everyone, "E10+" for Everyone 10+, or "T" for Teen. For more information on game ratings, please see www.esrb.org.
10. Parents are present when games are purchased or rented 89 percent of the time.

So video games are a huge industry and play an important role in the lives of many people and the American economy. The *Wall Street Journal*'s Market Watch site (2013) lists the best-selling video games of 2012:

Call of Duty: Black Ops 2

Madden NFL '12

Halo 4

Assassin's Creed 3

Just Dance 4

NBA 2K13

Borderlands 2

Call of Duty: Modern Warfare 2

Lego Batman 2: DC Superheroes

FIFA '12

We can see that sports, warfare, fighting, and violence are common threads in many of the best-selling games of 2012. One of the more common criticisms made of the video game industry is that games are too violent and players may become desensitized to the impact of real violence on others.

In their book *Digital Play: The Interaction of Technology, Culture, and Marketing* (2003), Stephen Kline, Nick Dyer-Witheford, and Greig De Peuter explain why video games focus so much on the same themes. They write:

Software development is a risky business. Most products fail. There are fortunes to be made with pioneering games that break new cultural ground. But for each successful experiment, scores crash and burn, taking with them companies and careers. This creates a powerful incentive to stick with the tried and true and ride on the coattails of proven success. The repetitive pattern is reinforced by the fact that game developers are recruited from the ranks of game players. Such asexual reproduction gives game culture a strong tendency to simple self-replication, so that shooting, combat, and fighting schemes, once established, repeat and proliferate. (p. 251)

They add that the pressure to lower costs also leads to a focus on violence, since violence is a cheap and easy way to generate narratives everyone can understand.

ARE VIDEO GAMES AN ART FORM OR A MEDIUM?

There is some question as to whether video games should be categorized as an art form in which there are many different genres (as there are in novels) or as a medium. One can make a decent argument for either position. One of the main features of video games is that they are interactive, but so are some other kinds of texts (think, for example, of crossword puzzles), so their interactivity doesn't necessarily mean they should be considered a medium—unless you wish to argue that any form of text with interactivity is a medium.

The best way to think about video games, I would suggest, is to compare them with novels—especially given that many video games have a strong narrative thrust. Novels use the medium of print (in the case of graphic novels, print and drawings) to tell stories. Within the art form of the novel there are many genres—such as mysteries, romances, and science fiction stories—as well as nonformulaic, nongenre stories about individuals and their relationships. There are all kinds of novels, from tough-guy mysteries such as Dashiell Hammett's *The Maltese Falcon* to James Joyce's *Ulysses*. Video games are similar to novels in that they encompass many genres; thus, I think it best to think of the video game as an art form. (Of course, the distinctive medium of film contains many genres, too, but unlike film, video is a medium used for other things in addition to game playing.)

Jay David Bolter and Richard Grusin use the term *form* in a discussion of video games in their book *Remediation: Understanding New Media* (2000):

The term *computer game* covers a range of forms, including violent action games, role-playing and narrative games, erotic and frankly pornographic applications, card games, puzzles and skill-testing exercises, and educational software. Some of these forms are clear repurposings of early games. . . . Computer games are delivered on a variety of platforms. (p. 89)

These authors use the term *remediation* in describing the ways in which new media are refashioned from earlier media forms. This concept may help us understand how to categorize video games. It is difficult to classify some games as belonging to one genre or another because many blend two or more genres.

Table 9.2 lists important video game genres and examples of particular games within these genres. This table is based on information found in the December 2003 issue of *PSM: PlayStation 2 Magazine* as well as other sources. *PSM* lists other genres as well, such as music, horror, and extreme sports, but they don't seem to be as important as the genres listed here. Also, some games fall within more than one genre; Tomb Raider, for instance, is classified as an adventure game as well as a first-person shooter.

Table 9.1	Categorizing Video Games
Genre	**Examples**
Simulation	*The Sims: Bustin' Out*
Strategy	*Wrath Unleashed; Robin Hood*
First-person shooter	*Tomb Raider*
Action	*Mortal Kombat; Prince of Persia; Jak II*
Adventure	*Tomb Raider; Myst; Riven*
Racing	*R: Racing Evolution; Gran Turismo 4*
Fighting	*DragonBall Z: Budokai 2*
Role playing	*Final Fantasy X-2; Everquest* (online)
Sports	*ESPN Basketball; Madden NFL '12, FIFA '12*

NEW TECHNOLOGIES AND VIDEO GAMES

In recent years, with the development of new technologies and specialized playing consoles, the quality of the images and sound in video games has improved to a remarkable degree. The current playing consoles are actually very powerful dedicated mini-supercomputers with incredible sound- and image-generating capacities. Some have hard drives, which greatly increases their capacity to support complex game features. The manufacturers of these devices clearly hope to position these consoles as the center of home entertainment in the future.

As a result of improvements in technology, video games are now able to offer highly absorbing inter-active narrative texts that feature multidimensional characters. Some games approximate the techni-cal qualities of films and allow players to immerse themselves in these texts and determine, to varying degrees, what happens in them. There is always the problem, however—especially for narrative video games—of the story. A game can be supported by all the technology in the world, but if it doesn't tell a good story—or, more precisely, involve a player in a good story—it will not be successful.

JANET MURRAY ON INTERACTIVITY AND IMMERSION

In this section I draw upon Janet Murray's classic study of narrative video games, *Hamlet on the Holodeck: The Future of Narrative in Cyberspace* (1997). When we say that a video game is interac-tive, we mean it responds to our inputs and to our responses to events that take place in the game. This means we can participate in the events that take place in the game and our decisions affect the outcome of the game.

The stories in narrative video games usually have a branching structure. That is, the player is faced with choices to make at various stages of the game, and each choice made affects the course of the game and thus other choices that will need to be made. The possible choices and their outcomes all have to be programmed into the game, which means that although the player makes choices, the player's feeling that he or she is in control is only an illusion. Every choice, and its attendant consequences, has already been placed in the story by the programmers, writers, and artists who created the game.

Interactive video games have the effect of "immersing" players in simulated environments, surrounding them with alternative realities. When we play these games, we tend to experience the same thing we do when we become fully engrossed in novels or movies—that is, we become "lost" in the worlds they create. We experience what the English poet and critic Samuel Taylor Coleridge described as "the willing suspension of disbelief." When we suspend disbelief, we forget we are seeing a play, watching a film, or playing a game, and we start identifying with characters in the story we are being told.

It is interesting to note that reviewers of video games often mention the willing suspension of disbelief when they describe games that have the ability to capture players' attention and make them forget they are playing a game. When we play video games, however, we take a more active role than we do when we read novels or view films or television programs. Video games provide what Murray calls "agency," a sense of satisfaction that the player gains from making decisions and taking actions in playing the game.

Murray (1997) suggests that the creators of storytelling video games must deal with two opposing poles: One involves the narrative elements that generate pleasure in players, as, for example, when they solve some problem or succeed in a quest; the other involves the satisfaction derived from the contest-winning elements of a game. According to Murray, video games give players pleasure in three ways: immersion, agency, and transformation. Depending on the game, players can transform themselves into a variety of roles, such as fighters, car thieves, adventurers, football players, and space heroes. As Murray explains,

> Storytelling can be a powerful agent of personal transformation. The right stories can open our hearts and change who we are. Digital narratives add another powerful element to this potential by offering us the opportunity to enact stories rather than to merely witness them. Enacted events have a transformative power that exceeds both narrated and conventionally dramatized events because we assimilate them as personal experiences. (p. 170)

Experiencing an immersive environment in which one plays an active role, making decisions that matter—that is, having agency—is so powerful that certain video games have been found to be effective tools for psychotherapy.

There is, however, an element of danger here. It seems that the gratifications video game players derive from being immersed in different worlds (of their own choosing), from gaining a sense of agency and power to transforming themselves, if only for a short while, into whatever they want to be, are very powerful—so powerful, in fact, that playing video games can be addictive for many people.

VIDEO GAMES AND ADDICTION

Robert W. Kubey (1996), a communication scholar, explains why video games are addictive:

> As with television, the games offer the player a kind of escape, and as with television, players learn quickly that they momentarily feel better when playing computer games; hence, a kind of psychological reinforcement develops.

> But video and computer games also have particular characteristics that make children and adults especially likely to report that they are "addicted" to them. There is the general challenge posed by the game and the wish to overcome it and succeed, and there is the critical characteristic that the games are designed to minutely increase in challenge and difficulty along with the increasing ability of the player. (p. 242)

These games, Kubey suggests, are cleverly calibrated to generate increasing but manageable levels of difficulty for players, who derive satisfaction from solving the problems or overcoming the difficulties the games present. Thus there is a subtle kind of reinforcement going on.

In connection with the feelings aroused by playing video games, Kubey cites psychologist Mihaly Csikszentmihalyi's research on "flow" experiences:

> Many of us are never quite as exhilarated as when we have harnessed our abilities and set them against a difficult but surmountable challenge (Csikszentmihalyi, 1990). Video and computer games can offer children and adults such a challenge.

> Indeed . . . computer and video games offer all the essential features that we know are likely to result in a "flow" experience of intense and enjoyable involvement and a high level of concentration: closely matched skills and challenges in an activity and rapid feedback regarding one's performance. (pp. 242–243)

It is no wonder, then, that video games are so addictive; they do a superb job of generating flow experiences. Kubey admits that although he isn't certain that video games are addictive, he thinks they may be.

Another factor connected to the issue of video game addiction might be called the "escalation effect." An analogy to drug abuse comes to mind here. As their bodies become accustomed to the drugs they are taking, drug addicts have to keep increasing their intake to get the high they want. It may be that some video game players find themselves in the same kind of predicament: They have to increase the amount of time they spend playing to obtain the level of pleasure to which they have become accustomed. It is reasonable to suggest, then, that there is an addictive aspect to video games.

VIDEO GAMES AND THE PROBLEM OF VIOLENCE

Violence pervades the mass media. Before I discuss violence in video games, let me offer a definition of media violence from Nancy Signorielli and George Gerbner's introduction to *Violence and Terror in the Mass Media: An Annotated Bibliography* (1988), a compilation that offers brief descriptions of 784 studies of television violence. These authors observe that "most research studies have defined media violence as the depiction of overt physical action that hurts or kills or threatens to do so"; such portrayals of violence, they add, can "intimidate people; provoke resistance, aggression, or repression; and cultivate a sense of relative strength and vulnerability as they portray the social 'pecking order'" (p. xi).

This suggests that exposure to violence in the media can provoke aggression and other forms of anti-social behavior in some people. Some media scholars, I should point out, believe that mass-mediated violence is harmless or possibly even cathartic, purging viewers of violent feelings and making it less likely they will act out violently. Although this might seem reasonable in theory, in actuality it does not seem to be the case. Various studies, for example, have found a significant association between television viewing and violence.

The amount of violence in video games in general and the nature of the violence in certain video games and video game genres have been causes of alarm among many critics and researchers who believe such violence has negative effects on players. In terms of encouraging real-world violence, playing violent video games may, in fact, be worse than watching violence in films and television, because the players control the violent actions of the game characters who represent them (known as avatars). Some video games, such as wrestling and other fighting games, include little in the way of story lines; rather, they provide players with nothing but a series of fights and violent actions. Among the most notorious violent video games are those in the *Mortal Kombat* series; in these games, players kill their opponents on screen in numerous ways, including ripping out their hearts, electrocuting them, and tearing their heads off. Some 4 million copies of games in this very popular series were reportedly sold in 1999, and by 2007, *Mortal Kombat* creator Ed Boon said 26 million copies had been sold to date (Official Nintendo Magazine, 2007).

It seems quite likely that, as some observers argue, violent video games desensitize players to the consequences of violence, especially given that in many games characters who have been "killed" can be brought back to life. The danger is that players, having learned to use violence to solve problems in these games, may start acting violently in real life.

When children play video games, they become used to a heightened level of excitement and to receiving almost immediate responses to their commands. Some scholars have suggested that these elements may lead some young children to become "hopped up," and thus there may be a relationship between video game playing and hyperactivity.

A NOTE ON VIDEO GAMES AND SCHOOL MASSACRES

William Weir's (2013) article, "Experts Disagree on How Violent Video Games Affect Children" shows both sides of the argument on video games and violence, which has surfaced after recent terrible school massacres. He quotes Brad Bushman, a psychologist at Ohio State, who coauthored a study that examined 380 studies on video games: "The results show that violent videogames increase angry thoughts and aggressive behavior, and they decrease helping behavior and decrease empathy and compassion for others."

On the other hand, psychologist Chris Ferguson, who teaches at Texas A&M, argues that there is considerable disagreement among researchers about the impact of video games on young people. He suggests that "the field of video game study is plagued by confirmation bias, in which researchers ignore evidence that doesn't fit with preconceived notions. . . . With Adam Lanza, it would be weird if he didn't play video games because 80 to 90 percent of people in that age group play video games." (Lanza killed 20 children and 6 adults at Sandy Hook Elementary School on December 14, 2012.)

Weir concludes his article with a discussion of the amount and kinds of video games young people play:

> Common Sense Media, a nonprofit group that advocates for responsible use of media for children, released a report this month which found that children ages 8 to 18 spend an average of 90 minutes a day playing computer and video games. Of the 60 most popular games, according to the report, 68 percent contain violence. In a typical session of game-playing, a child will see an average of 138 "aggressive exchanges." The report found that it's common for children to play games rated as inappropriate for their age group—for instance, 65 percent of children 7 to 12 have played Grand Theft Auto, which the game maker says is for mature players. The report also states that there is a need for long-term studies to follow the behaviors of people over decades.

The relationship between video games and violence continues to perplex Americans. It would seem that these games do not have serious and long-lasting negative effects on well-adjusted children, but they can have very negative effects on disturbed children, who, in some cases, become mass murderers. As the number of these terrible school shootings increases, because of the easy access to guns in American society, our suspicions about the connection between violent video games and mass murders in our schools and other places grows.

SOCIAL AND PHYSICAL PROBLEMS CAUSED BY VIDEO GAMES

Although video game players sometimes play in groups with their friends or compete with others by playing on the Internet, for the most part, players play alone. Even when they compete with others online, they are still alone, sitting in front of their monitors. This isolation can lead to a sense of alienation on the part of serious players, who may become increasingly separated from their friends and family members.

The widespread popularity of video games may also be contributing to the development of obesity in the American public. Instead of getting exercise, video game players sit still and play, often snacking at the same time. Obesity has considerable social costs. Among other problems, the incidence of diabetes and heart disease is higher among obese people than among thinner people, and treating the increasing numbers of Americans with these conditions puts a strain on the health care system. Statistics suggest that American children are increasingly obese, and there may be a connection between video game playing and obesity.

We know there is a connection between video game playing and certain physical problems. Video game players suffer from mental stress, caused by the need to deal almost instantaneously with events in the games, and from a number of related physical ailments described generally as repetitive stress syndrome. Players who log more than 2 hours a day playing these games often develop blisters on their hands and have problems with muscles in their hands, wrists, and shoulders that can lead, in later years, to serious complications.

VIDEO GAMES AND SEXUALITY

The sexual content of some video games is a source of considerable anxiety among many parents of young video game players. Media—especially television programs, films, and music videos—are full of sexual material, and most viewers develop an ability to distance themselves from this content. The interactive nature of video games, however, means the impact of sexual material on players is more intense. In certain video games, women are portrayed as objects to be possessed—that is, as commodities available for the pleasure of the player. Provenzo (1997) describes one of the more infamous sexually explicit video games:

> CD-ROM games such as *Virtual Valerie*, for example, allow you to enter a voluptuous young woman's apartment. Once inside you can look through her things, including her purse, her books, and even her personal copy of the game *Virtual Valerie*. The point of the game is to eventually interact with Valerie herself. In one scene Valerie appears on the computer screen wearing a see-through brassiere, panties, and hose while lying on a couch. With her legs spread apart, she asks the player to remove her brassiere, which she finds "a little snug." The object of the program is to eventually remove all of Valerie's clothes and get her into bed with you. If you don't answer certain questions correctly, Valerie won't take her clothes off. Give her the right answers and she's yours. (pp. 104–105)

It must be said that *Virtual Valerie* is not a typical video game, but this example does show how closely some video games can resemble pornography. And although many video games feature heroines who aren't as titillating as Valerie, it is not uncommon for the female characters who play important roles in video games to be very attractive and scantily clad. Lara Croft, the heroine of the highly successful *Tomb Raider* series of games (as well as of two less successful films), has large pointy breasts, legs that are long and shapely, and a tiny wasp waist. Players control this voluptuous woman and decide what she does, where she goes, when she shoots her guns and uses other weapons, and how she interacts with others. As of 2006, more than 45 million copies of games in the *Tomb Raider* series have been sold worldwide.

Despite the presence of some sexy heroines, women are underrepresented in video games. When they do appear, the roles they have tend to be very stereotypical—as is true of portrayals of women in the mass media in general.

As a response to public concerns about the sexual content of video games as well as the amount of violence in many games, the companies that make these games have adopted a rating system to inform the parents of young players about the nature of each game. Along with a rating, each video game package now carries information on the game's sexual content, its language, and the nature of any violence it includes. Surveys have shown, however, that less than half of the adults who purchase video games, or whose children purchase the games, are aware of these ratings or pay any attention to them.

CONCLUSIONS

Video games have incredible potential to influence players. Their unique power can be used to teach and entertain people in new ways. Many games require players to heighten their powers of observation, infer rules from their observations, and glean information from a variety of sources, such as nonverbal cues. Some video games may be described as prosocial and as having positive effects on their players. Unfortunately, however, most video games are similar to the kinds of shows that make up the majority of the programming content on television, which has famously been described as a "vast wasteland." In this respect, video games are no different from other kinds of mass-mediated popular culture.

The function of the media analyst who examines video games is to apply to these texts the various methods of criticism described in this book, to understand how they achieve their effects and what their impacts are—both on those who play the games and on society. I have offered what might be described as an overview of some of the more interesting aspects of video games. A considerable literature on video games now exists, and an enormous number of Internet sites are devoted to video games in general and to particular video games. Some universities and a number of art schools are now offering degrees in creating video games. Some of the newer video games are so realistic and lifelike that players become disturbed when they play them. A reviewer of Sony's baseball video game *MLB 10* complained that he found it difficult to play and became mildly upset because of the astonishing visual elements found in it.

Video games have the devoted attention of their players—there's no doubt about that. But let me suggest that the video game phenomenon requires the attention of semioticians, psychologists, sociologists, and other critics and scholars, because it is an increasingly important part of the globalized media industry that plays such an important role in our lives.

STUDY QUESTIONS AND TOPICS FOR DISCUSSION

1. In what important ways do video games differ from films?
2. Would you categorize video games as an art form or a medium? Explain your answer.
3. What impact has the development of new technologies had on video games?
4. Define *interactivity* and *immersion* and explain the significance of each concept for video game playing.
5. How do video games foster addiction in players? Do you agree with the arguments made in this chapter about this issue?

6. Discuss the various social and physical problems that some people develop as a result of playing video games. How should society deal with such problems? Do you think there is a connection between playing video games and the mass murders at Sandy Hook Elementary School and other schools? Justify your answer with evidence from research by social scientists.

7. If you play video games, what games are your favorites? Why do you like them so much? Has your taste in video games changed over the years? If so, how do you explain the change?

8. What new developments do you think will take place in the video game industry?

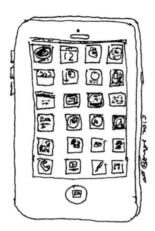

Social media and cell phones play an increasingly important role in the everyday lives of people in the United States and in countries all over the world. More than a billion people now belong to Facebook, and smartphones are being purchased at incredible rates. New and more powerful smartphones are being developed all the time. This chapter considers the social and psychoanalytic significance of social media and of the role mobile phones are playing in the way we see ourselves, in our understanding of our identities, and in our relationships with others.

Cell Phones, Social Media, and the Problem of Identity

Let me begin this discussion by offering two selections relevant to our interest in new technologies and their social and cultural impact. The first is from the abstract of Vincent Miller's "New Media, Networking, and Phatic Culture" (2008):

> Through a consideration of the new media objects of blogs, social networking profiles, and microblogs, along with their associated practices, I will argue that the social contexts of "individualization" and "network sociality," alongside the technological developments associated with pervasive communication and "connected presence," has led to an online media culture increasingly dominated by phatic communications. That is, communications which have purely social (networking) and not informational or dialogic intents. I conclude with a discussion of the potential nihilistic consequences of such a culture. (p. 388)

The second is from Peter Farb's *Word Play: What Happens When People Talk* (1974) and discusses Bronislaw Malinowski's ideas about phatic communication:

> Stereotyped phrases, which nevertheless offer important social benefits, are found in one form or another in speech communities around the world—as the anthropologist Bronislaw Malinowski pointed out half a century ago. He gave the name "phatic communication" (derived from Greek and Latin words that mean "verbal togetherness") to speech that is used as social cement. And he defined it as "a type of speech in which the ties of union are created by a mere exchange of words." (pp. 24–25)

The question I ask is this: If teenagers send each other 100 messages a day, can their messages be seen as anything other than phatic communication?

AN EPIPHANY

During a visit to Japan in 2000, futurologist Howard Rheingold noticed something curious in Tokyo. He described an epiphany he had in his book *Smart Mobs: The Next Social Revolution* (2002):

I began to notice people on the streets of Tokyo staring at their mobile phones instead of talking to them. The sight of this behavior, now commonplace in much of the world, triggered a sensation I had experienced a few times before—the instant recognition that technology was going to change my life in ways I can scarcely imagine. (p. xi)

What he was witnessing was texting, a phenomenon that has grown exponentially and now plays a major role in the everyday activities of people with smartphones, particularly, for reasons discussed shortly, teenagers.

During a trip I made to Japan in 2008, I noticed that on subway trains there, while some people read books and newspapers, large numbers of people were either reading or sending messages on their smartphones. Cell phones enable people to deal with awkward or uncomfortable situations when riding in elevators, traveling on subways and trains, or spending time in public places.

MEDIA USE BY 8- TO 18-YEAR-OLDS

A Kaiser Family Foundation (2010) study based on a large survey of media usage by 8- to 18-year-olds in 2009 provides us with the following statistics:

Time per Day	Activity
4.29 hours	Watching TV
2.31 hours	Music and other audio
1.29 hours	Computer use
1.13 hours	Playing video games
0.38 hours	Reading
0.25 hours	Movies
10.45 hours	Total

But since 8- to 18-year-olds multitask 29% of the time, the total time spent in these activities is reduced to 7.38 hours per day. The Kaiser Family Foundation survey didn't count cell phone use as media usage, though many 8- to 18-year-olds use their cell phones to watch television or listen to music. According to the report, they spend an average of 90 minutes a day on cell phones. The conclusion we reach from looking at these statistics is that young people in America lead media-saturated lives.

Young people are consuming something like 34 gigabytes of data each day from around 5 hours a day spent watching screens of one kind or another: computer monitors, smartphones, video game players, and television. Nick Bilton (2009), in an article in the *New York Times*, mentions a study by researchers at the University of California in San Diego that discovered the average American reads or hears something like 100,000 words a day from the web, radio, television, and other media and that consumption of media has increased around 350% in the last 30 years. We read less print media, but we do a great deal of reading from screens, of one kind or another, during a typical day, so we're reading more than ever.

From a sociological perspective, we have all kinds of demographic data on users of media in the United States and other countries. We can break users down along national, racial, sex, socioeconomic, age, and other classifications. And we know the use of media has increased over the past 10 years in most groups. The question we can't answer with any certainty is, What effects do all this media usage have on us as individuals and on the societies in which we live?

SOCIAL MEDIA

A considerable amount of the 90 minutes teens spend using their smartphones is devoted to texting—and now, for a small percentage of teens, a new wrinkle, sexting, in which they send seminude and sometimes nude images of themselves to their friends and other people. Of course, once an image is sent to someone, it can be forwarded on to other people or even uploaded to YouTube, where millions of people can see it.

The term *social media*, as I understand it, refers to sites such as Facebook, Twitter, LinkedIn, and YouTube that enable people to send messages, images, and video that can be read or seen by large numbers of people. These social media sites can be accessed on the Internet by computers, tablets, and smartphones. In the passage at the beginning of this chapter, Vincent Miller (2008) hypothesizes that much of the communication done through social media is "phatic." These messages, sometimes called "small talk," are not to communicate information as much as to indicate we are present.

| Table 10.1 | Top 10 Facebook Users by Country in 2012 |

Country	Number of Users
1. United States	167,554,700
2. Brazil	60,665,740
3. India	60,545,100
4. Indonesia	50,489,360
5. Mexico	39,388,040
6. United Kingdom	33,190,940
7. Turkey	31,415,080
8. Philippines	29,862,300
9. France	25,295,760
10. Germany	4,974,660

Source: www.socialbakers.com/facebook-statistics/?interval=last-6-months#chart-intervals

The huge numbers of text messages we send one another are caused more by the need to maintain our network of friends and consolidate our togetherness with one another than by the desire to convey information.

The mass media used to involve a small number of "senders" (writers, actors, directors, filmmakers, and so on) who made texts of various kinds and transmitted them through traditional media such as print, radio, and television to "receivers," that is, the potentially large number of people who formed the audience. Now, the old sender-receiver model has been obliterated since large numbers of people create texts of all kinds—whether texted and sexted messages, images, videos, or whatever. Everyone with a digital camera, a smartphone, or a video camera is now a potential video maker, and sites like YouTube provide people with the means of broadcasting their works. Marshall McLuhan wrote that the medium is the message. Let me play upon his famous dictum and suggest, in an era of social media, "The media are the message makers."

Members of all age groups are involved in social media, though the elderly do not participate to the extent younger and middle-aged people do. On a personal note, when I was in Japan a few years ago I made some short videos on different aspects of Japanese life that I uploaded to YouTube. One of my videos was in a Japanese *manga* (comic books) store. Remarkably, I continually get e-mail messages from manga fans that have seen that video telling me how they would love to be able to visit that store. I have many other videos from Japan on YouTube, but it is only the manga store video that gets much attention.

The fact that YouTube has millions of people accessing its videos, that people are sending billions of "tweets" a year, and that Facebook now has a billion members demands the attention of media and communication scholars. If the social media are that popular, they must be doing something important for all the people who use them.

A PSYCHOANALYTIC PERSPECTIVE ON YOUTH AND SOCIAL MEDIA

I have just suggested there is a strong relationship among computers, smartphones, and the social media. We might ask ourselves, why do people spend so much time with their computers and cell phones, texting one another and sending texts to social media sites? One reason, I believe, is that these devices enable people to connect with others and to ameliorate the alienation, loneliness, and sense of separation many people feel in modern society.

This is particularly the case with adolescents, who have powerful needs for affiliation, who suffer from anxiety about what they are to become, and who often feel alienated and estranged from their parents, other members of their families, and perhaps society itself. I asked one young woman I saw at my gym, who had both an iPhone and an iPod, about her texting. "I don't text as much as some of my friends," she said. "I only send around 40 text messages a day, mostly to four of my friends." It would seem that sending text messages allows her to maintain adequate contact with her friends. I can recall seeing articles that found some young people send and exchange a hundred text messages each day, or around 3,000 messages a month.

What is driving this behavior? For an answer, let us consider the ideas of two writers: one a novelist and one a leading psychoanalytic thinker.

We begin with the novelist.

Robert Musil deals with the anxieties of youth in his masterpiece *The Man Without Qualities* (1965). A celebrated passage in the book reads as follows:

By the time they have reached the middle of their life's journey, few people remember how they have managed to arrive at themselves, at their amusements, their point of view, their wife, character, occupation and successes, but they cannot help feeling that not much is likely to change any more. . . . For in youth life still lies before them as an inexhaustible morning, spread out all round them full of everything and nothing; and yet when noon comes there is all at once something there that may justly claim to be their life now. . . . Something has had its way with them like a fly-paper with a fly; it has caught them fast, here catching a little hair, there hampering their movements, and has gradually enveloped them, until they lie buried under a thick coating that has only the remotest resemblance to their original shape. And then they only dimly remember their youth when there was something like a force of resistance in them—this other force that tugs and whirrs and does not want to linger anywhere, releasing a storm of aimless attempts at flight. Youth's scorn and its revolt against the established order, youth's readiness for everything that is heroic, whether it is self-sacrifice or crime, its fiery seriousness and its unsteadiness—all this is nothing but its fluttering attempts to fly. Fundamentally it merely means that nothing of all that a young man undertakes appears to be the result of an unequivocal inner necessity, even if it expresses itself in such a manner as to suggest that everything he happens to dash at is exceedingly urgent and necessary. (pp. 151–152)

Erik Erikson

Musil is obsessed with the question of identity and the way in which our lives generally tend to "escape" from us; how we don't generally end up living the kind of lives we think we will when we are young. When we are young we are full of a sense of life's possibilities, Musil writes, and yet, when we are middle aged, we find that very seldom have we realized those possibilities as we become "stuck" on the fly-paper of life.

According to psychoanalyst and former Harvard professor Erik H. Erikson (1963), all adolescents have to deal with the rapid growth of their bodies and the problem of identity and role confusion they suddenly face. As he explains in his book *Childhood and Society*,

It is the inability to settle on an occupational identity which disturbs individual young people. To keep themselves together they temporarily overidentify, to the point of apparent complete loss of identity, with the heroes of cliques and crowds. This initiates the stage of "falling in love," which is by no means entirely, or even primarily, a sexual matter—except where the mores demand it. To a considerable extent adolescent love is an attempt to arrive at a definition of one's identity by projecting one's diffused ego image on another and by seeing it thus reflected and gradually clarified. This is why so much of young love is conversation. (p. 262)

Erikson published his book in 1963, well before the development of cell phones, but his comments about adolescent needs and the quest for identity ring true (to adopt a telephone metaphor) today as well. Table 10.2 outlines Erikson's eight crises of development, and I suggest that we can connect these crises to our cell phone usage. According to Erikson, human beings all face certain developmental crises at different stages of their lives. Table 10.2 lists Erikson's crises as polar oppositions and offers hypotheses about the role cell phones play in each of these crises. This material on our developmental crises is taken from his chapter "The Eight Ages of Man" in *Childhood and Society* (1963). I have left out infancy, when the first two stages take place, because infants don't use cell phones. According to Erikson, we all face these crises and must find a way to resolve them successfully as we move from infancy to old age. Thus, the countless text messages young people send one another have a deeper and more significant meaning than we might imagine, for they can be seen, among other things, as attempts at self-definition.

Table 10.2	The Role of the Cell Phone in Developmental Crises	
Stage	**Crisis**	**Cell Phone Functions**
Childhood	Initiative/guilt	Family integration, play
School	Industry/inferiority	Socialization, schoolwork skills
Adolescence	Identity/role confusion	Peer group bonding, schoolwork, romance
Young adult	Intimacy/isolation	Love, career, initiation
Adult	Generativity/stagnation	Career, community
Maturity	Ego integrity/despair	Contact, community

Young girls who become fans of Madonna or Lady Gaga or cute-guy vampire actors and young boys who idolize football and other sports stars or other kinds of heroic figures are, Erikson would say, going through a stage in which they are struggling to consolidate their identities and using their heroes as a means toward accomplishing this task.

But why texting rather than talking? Because texting is more private and less direct. If you talk on your cell phone around other people, they sometimes can hear what you are saying to the person you are talking to. In addition, texting enables people to send messages without needing to be concerned about where the recipients of these messages are or what they are doing. When you text a message, you don't face the problem of having to actually conduct a conversation. But the goal of texting is to have a kind of conversation, and conversation, Erikson has explained, plays a crucial role in the lives of adolescents.

Sherry Turkle, a professor at the Massachusetts Institute of Technology, was interviewed on PBS's *Fresh Air* and offered some insights into the texting phenomenon and its impact on young people. A summary of her discussion of text messaging follows (NPR Books, 2012):

When Turkle asked teens and adults why they preferred text messaging over face-to-face conversation, they responded that when you're face to face, "you can't control what you are going to say, and you don't know how long it's going to take or where it could go." But Turkle believes that these perceived weaknesses of conversation are actually conversation's strengths. Face-to-face interaction teaches "skills of negotiation, of reading each other's emotion, of having to face the complexity of confrontation, dealing with complex emotion," Turkle says. She thinks people who feel they are too busy to have conversations in person are not making the important emotional connections they otherwise would. All this leads to Turkle's theory that it is possible to be in constant digital communication and yet still feel very much alone. In Turkle's interviews with adults and teenagers, she found people of all ages are drawn to their devices for a similar reason: "What is so seductive about texting, about keeping that phone on, about that little red light on the BlackBerry, is you want to know who wants you," Turkle says.

If Turkle is correct, the cell phone negatively affects the development of young people, some of whom seem addicted to texting and who send around a hundred messages a day to their friends. They are not learning how to relate to others and have the conversations Erikson suggests are so important to their psychological development.

We can say that the social media create artificial or virtual communities of people. Thus, we have "friends" and "followers" on Facebook and Twitter. The same kind of thing applies to other sites. In addition, social media sites offer actual communities of people interested in subjects such as art or travel. I have more than 180 "friends" on Facebook—most of whom I don't know and never will meet. Some people on Facebook and other sites collect as many "friends" as they can get—the limit, for regular friend pages on Facebook is 5,000 friends. But are these "friends" really friends? Obviously not. Getting large numbers of friends on Facebook is a form of collecting, analogous to people who collect stamps or fountain pens or anything else. And this collecting is driven by psychological needs people have to excel in some way or to have mastery over something.

Sexting is different from texting. There is an element of narcissism in sexting, as young people send images of their bodies, in various stages of undress, to others. There may be an element of sublimation at work, as young women channel their sexual urges into exhibitionism as opposed to actual sexual relations, though research suggests that many young people are having sex now in their early teens. Sexting is a kind of electronic virtual sex. Many people worry whether sexting will lead to increased rates of actual sexual activity in young people, a decline in our collective morality, and a coarsening of our culture.

THE CELL PHONE AS SIGN: A SEMIOTIC PERSPECTIVE

From a semiotic perspective, the brand and kind of cell phone (and now smartphone) one purchases offers an opportunity to display one's socioeconomic status, technological savvy, and connoisseurship. The iPhone unleashed an avalanche of smartphones to compete with it. It isn't only the functionality of the iPhone that is important. We also have to consider the iPhone as a fashion statement and as a signifier that the user is a certain kind of person. Many reviews of cell phones take great pains to describe their aesthetics—as art objects and exemplars of great product design.

In addition, the number of text messages one receives and sends each day functions as a signifier of one's "popularity" and status in the circle of one's friends. Receiving large numbers of text messages from the right persons signifies a person has lots of friends who are worth "friending." When cell phone and Internet friends fall out, they then "unfriend" one another.

The iPhone has hundreds of thousands of "apps" (applications), each of which is identified with its own icon. The huge number of apps reflects the power of the iPhone and other smartphones. These apps are generally inexpensive and sometimes even free. What these apps mean, semiotically speaking, is that the smartphone now has defined itself as a device that can be used to do many thousands of different things. The smartphone has devastated the GPS device industry since smartphones now have apps that offer free GPS. Nobody knows what the next industry to be destroyed by smartphones will be. The Internet, the social media, smartphones, and tablets like the iPad are having a profound impact on the "old" print media such as newspapers, magazines, and books, many of which now find themselves in what might be described as a death spiral.

In their book *Moving Cultures: Mobile Communication in Everyday Life,* André H. Caron and Letezia Caronia (2007) point out how cell phones (they prefer to use the term *mobile*) function as status symbols. After discussing a number of advertising campaigns in Canada that equate youthfulness with cell phones, they write:

> The mobile's new status as an object of value, and thus as a means of increasing its user's social standing, can be seen in other advertising strategies, such as those around Christmas. At this time the mobile becomes a significant gift. Attributing the function of gift to the techno-object automatically makes it a desirable object, and consequently an object of value. (p. 97)

They point out that many cell phone advertisements portray cell phones as "cool," an important attitude held in esteem in most adolescent cultures. Having a cell phone, then, becomes a signifier of youth for adolescents—and has an identity-building function. Having the *right* cell phone confers status, as well.

MARXIST PERSPECTIVES ON CELL PHONES

Although many Marxists no doubt find the ways in which cell phone companies function in the United States and other capitalist countries objectionable, earning billions for large corporations for providing cell phones and cell phone networks on which to make calls and send text messages, Marxists are probably captivated by the revolutionary potential of the cell phone. During the riots in Iran in 2009, after the presidential elections widely regarded as "stolen," members of the Iranian opposition coordinated their campaigns against the government by using smartphones and social media like Twitter. The antigovernment parades were brutally suppressed by the government, but the ability of the opposition to mobilize itself was due, in large measure, to the power of the cell phone.

Rheingold offers a case study of the Philippines in the chapter "The Power of the Mobile Many" in his book *Smart Mobs* (2002):

> On January 20, 2001, President Joseph Estrada of the Philippines became the first head of state to lose power to a smart mob. More than 1 million Manila residents, mobilized and coordinated by waves of text messages, assembled at the site of the 1986 "People Power" peaceful demonstrations that had toppled the Marcos regime. Tens of thousands of Filipinos converged on Epifanio de los Santas Avenue, known as "Edsa," within an hour of the first text message volleys: "Go 2EDSA, Wear black." (pp. 157–158)

Rheingold discusses other "smart mobs" that show the power of texting to assemble large groups of people for political (and other) purposes.

The revolutions in 2011 in Tunisia, Egypt, and Libya were facilitated by youth using smartphones, Twitter, and Facebook. So the new information and communication technologies (ICTs) are actually realizing what contemporary Marxists would describe as their revolutionary potential.

One thing that bothers Marxists about cell phones is the way they are often marketed and sold in capitalist countries. In the United States, cell phones are generally sold along with 2-year service contracts from a provider, such as AT&T or Verizon, which enable people to make calls and send text messages. Service contracts vary in voice minutes, text messages, and data allowed, with many plans offering unlimited usage. In most other countries, people purchase unlocked cell phones, buy SIM cards, and aren't locked into contracts with cell phone service providers. Cell phone use is generally much less expensive than in the United States.

Another problem Marxists find with cell phones is that they provide yet another screen on which advertisements can be shown. To the extent that advertising helps capitalist societies maintain themselves, cell phones can play an important role in spreading false consciousness and generating the consumer cultures that help neutralize the revolutionary potential of the working classes.

So Marxists have to be ambivalent about the role of cell phones in society. Now that billions of people have cell phones, they present a dilemma for Marxists. They must figure out how to maximize their revolutionary potential and minimize their capacity to distract the masses from their "true" role as agents of revolution against capitalist oppression.

CONCLUSIONS

Cell phones and the social media represent a major transformation in the way societies function. The ubiquity of cell phones and the popularity of the social media are signifiers of a new social order in which almost anyone and everyone can make their presence known by sending messages, photos, and videos that potentially can be accessed by a huge number of people. This has broken the monopoly on sending messages in the mass media held by radio, television, magazines, and newspapers.

The popularity of cell phones and social media can also be seen as a signifier of the loneliness, alienation, and sense of separation modern societies generate. Our uses of cell phones and social media represent "escape attempts" in which we try to achieve a kind of electronic togetherness or virtual community. What the long-term consequences of the new media on American society and societies everywhere will be—for the new media are now global—is hard to say.

STUDY QUESTIONS AND TOPICS FOR DISCUSSION

1. What do the statistics about media and cell phone use suggest about changes in contemporary societies?
2. What are social media? What impact have they had on our everyday lives and on society? Do you accept the hypothesis about cell phones and social media essentially having a "phatic" role? Explain your answer.

3. What role do cell phones play in youth culture? How do they help young people deal with their problems with identity? What do you think about Erikson's theory of the eight developmental crises we face as we move from infancy to old age and the way these crises might relate to cell phone usage?

4. How do you feel about the Musil quotation from *The Man Without Qualities*? Is he right about your parents, others you know, and yourself?

5. Although there were no cell phones during Marx's days, his theories have implications for cell phone use. What points were made about how Marxists might regard cell phones?

6. Do a research project on the use of cell phones, Twitter, and Facebook by revolutionary movements in recent years.

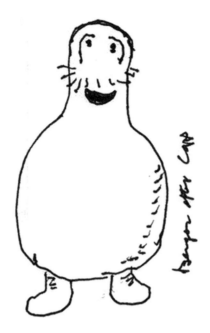

Shmoos and Analysis

In 1960, when I was about to enter graduate school to work on a doctorate in American studies, my brother Jason suggested I not bother. "American studies is like a Shmoo," he said. (For those who don't know what Shmoos are, let me explain. They are mythical creatures that love more than anything else to do things for people, including offering themselves as food. Fried, they taste like steak; baked, like ham; roasted, like roast beef. Their whiskers can be used for toothpicks and their skin for leather. And they multiply like crazy. They are the invention of Al Capp, and they appeared in *Li'l Abner*—one of the most important comic strips ever produced in the United States.) "American studies is like a Shmoo," Jason said. "If you bake it you're a historian, if you fry it you're a literary critic, if you boil it you're a sociologist, if you broil it you're a political scientist."

We can apply this insight to media analysis, for critics and media analysts don't just exist—every analyst has a point of view (or, in the case of eclectic analysts, several points of view). And analysts bring that point (or those points) of view, their sense of the world, and their understanding of people and society to whatever they analyze. Analysis, at least as I see things, doesn't just exist in and of itself.

For the discussion in this volume I have selected four techniques I consider to be of great importance, but I could have addressed other techniques as well. A room in which different critics watch an episode of a given television show, for example, could be crowded with different perspectives. There might be a literary critic, who would be concerned with such matters as plot, theme, point of view, motivation of characters, setting, and tone. There might be a "myth-ritual-symbol" critic, with an anthropological background, who has what might be described as "culturological" interests. An ethical critic might focus on moral problems raised in the episode and other philosophical concerns, whereas an aesthetically or technically oriented critic would be concerned with aspects of the production such as lighting, camera angles, kinds of shots, fades, cutting, and sound effects. A Jungian critic would look for archetypes, shadows, anima and animus figures, heroes, tricksters, and so on. An expert in nonverbal behavior might examine the program in terms of the facial expressions of the characters (especially in close-ups), their body language, and a host of similar concepts.

The goal of media analysis, as I see it, is to achieve the most comprehensive, interesting, and profound reading of a text possible. Some people think this kind of analysis is a waste of time or that it "destroys" a work. Those who take this "know-nothing" position assume that the more mindless we are in our responses to television programs, films, or other mass media, the better off we are.

I would argue that we need analysis if we are to appreciate and understand any work fully. Furthermore, creative artists of all kinds (and in all media) need to be self-critical—in the positive sense of the term—so they can understand how they have generated the effects they were after, what worked and what didn't. We need theory in order to be able to practice successfully and effectively; otherwise, the successes we have are just the results of accidents and luck. Just as creative people are generally also very analytic, analysts are often also very creative. I hope this volume has succeeded in encouraging you to combine analysis and creativity so that you look at the media—and yourselves—in new and more interesting ways.

STUDY QUESTIONS AND TOPICS FOR DISCUSSION

1. In what ways are media criticism, analysis, and interpretation like Shmoos?
2. What techniques for analysis other than those addressed in this book might be applied to works of art?
3. Is there an ideal way of analyzing works of art? If so, what is it?
4. When semioticians, psychoanalysts, Marxists, and sociologists analyze a given text and come up with different interpretations, which of them is right? Or is there no such thing as a "right" interpretation of a text?
5. Analyze a particular text (a film, television show, book, television commercial, video game, or something else) assigned by your instructor from the four points of view discussed in this volume. Which approach do you find most useful and interesting? Why?

Simulations, Activities, Games, and Exercises

I have developed a number of simulations, activities, games, and exercises (which I refer to collectively as *learning games*) that involve applying various aspects of media analysis techniques to the popular arts and mass media. These learning games require players to move from the level of theory, where the concepts may be vague (and their utility not terribly clear), to that of practice, where they can see how the concepts and theories associated with the four methodologies discussed in this book can help them make sense of works of popular culture as well as create them.

When I have students in my courses play such learning games, I usually divide them into groups of three or four; all students in each group are required to participate in the activities, but I ask each group to select one member to function as the designated scribe (to do the actual writing). Many of these learning games also make suitable homework assignments, for individuals or for teams of players. However, it should be kept in mind that the emphasis in these learning games is on *play*; my students have found these games both enjoyable and valuable. In games that involve scripts or stories, team members can present their results to the class by taking on the roles and acting out what they've written. In other kinds of games, the findings of the teams can serve as the basis of classroom discussion. Depending on the course, the students, and the context, variations on these learning games can be devised, and new games can be created. Several of the learning games presented here are adapted from my book *Narratives in Popular Culture, Media, and Everyday Life* (1997).

ANATOMY OF A TALE

In my discussion of Vladimir Propp's *Morphology of the Folktale* (1928/1968) in Chapter 1, I showed how Propp's functions can be used to analyze a story. In this exercise, you are to write a story based on the following set of Propp's functions. Use the descriptions of the functions listed in writing your story. Remember that you can modernize things—thus, at the end, the hero need not literally marry a princess and ascend the throne.

When you write your story, remember to use the past tense, include description and dialogue, and make sure there are action and conflict, to keep the reader's interest. (Do *not* write a fairy tale in this exercise.) Base your story on the following functions:

1. Initial situation: Members of the family and hero are introduced.
2. Absentation: One member of the family absents himself or herself.
3. Interdiction: Interdiction is addressed to hero (can be reversed).
4. Violation: Interdiction is violated.
5. Villainy: Villain causes harm to member of the family.
6. Mediation: Misfortune made known, hero is dispatched.
7. Receipt of agent: Hero acquires use of magical agent.
8. Spatial change: Hero led to object of his search.
9. Struggle: Hero and villain join in combat.
10. Branding: Hero is branded.
11. Victory: Villain is defeated.
12. Unfounded claims: False hero is exposed.
13. Wedding: Hero is married, ascends the throne.

After writing the stories, teams or individuals should share them with the larger group so that class members see the variety of stories that come from the same Proppian functions.

PARADIGMATIC ANALYSIS

Lévi-Strauss (1967) has argued that the paradigmatic analysis of a text tells us what it "really" means, in contrast to a syntagmatic (Proppian) analysis, which focuses on what happens in the text. In this modification of Lévi-Strauss's methods, you are looking for paired oppositions that give a text meaning. Saussure (1915/1966) has suggested that concepts are defined differentially; the same applies to characters in texts, their actions, and so on.

A Lévi-Straussian Analysis of *Upstairs, Downstairs*

Upstairs, Downstairs is a television series that deals with the lives of a wealthy English family, the Bellamys, and their servants. The title offers the basic opposition, but even if the series had been called something else, this opposition is still central.

Table A.1   Oppositions in *Upstairs, Downstairs* Television Series

Upstairs	Downstairs
Masters who command	Servants who obey
Wealthy	Poor
Leisure	Hard work
Marriage and infidelity	Bachelorhood/spinsterhood

The oppositions listed in Table A.1 apply to the series in general, but similar sets of oppositions could be generated for specific episodes in the series based on the events that take place within those episodes. From this very simple set of polar oppositions, the core of the series is clear.

Lévi-Strauss was interested in myth and not popular culture per se, but we can adapt his ideas to help us understand many kinds of texts, such as spy stories, detective stories, and science fiction tales.

Steps in Playing Lévi-Strauss

1. To take part in this activity, you need a narrative text, one that tells a story. You may choose a film or an episode from a television series to analyze, or your instructor may give you a story to work with, such as the following, taken from the beginning of Genesis:

   In the beginning God created the heaven and the earth. And the earth was without form, and void; and darkness was upon the face of the deep. And the Spirit of God moved upon the face of the waters. And God said, "Let there be light": and there was light. And God saw the light, that it was good: and God divided the light from the darkness. And God called the light Day, and the darkness he called Night. And the evening and the morning were the first day.

2. Determine the two opposing concepts central to the text you are analyzing, concepts that enable you to deal with the various characters and most important events in the text. Make sure you find real oppositions as opposed to simple negations (for example, *unhappy* is not the opposite of *happy*).

3. Create a list of oppositions based on your text like the one in Table A.1 for *Upstairs, Downstairs*. Remember that the oppositions should be linked to specific events in the story.

It should be noted that most people who read novels, see plays, or go to the movies do not consciously go through this process of finding oppositions. But, if Lévi-Strauss and Saussure are right, we have to elicit such oppositions in order to understand any story. We are so adept at doing this, and we do it so quickly, that we are not conscious of what we are doing.

DREAM ANALYSIS

According to psychoanalytic theory (and many psychologists would agree), dreams play a very significant role in our lives. Freud used his theories about symbolization, condensation, displacement, and so on to analyze dreams, as noted in Chapter 3. Now I offer a dream taken from Freud's *The Interpretation of Dreams* (1900/1965) and ask you to decode it, as best you can, using the concepts discussed in Chapter 3.

I went into a kitchen in search of some pudding. Three women were standing in it; one of them was the hostess of the inn and was twisting something about in her hands, as though she was making Knodel [dumplings]. She answered that I must wait until she was ready. I felt impatient and went off with a sense of injury. I put on an overcoat. But the first I tried on was too long for me. I took it off, rather surprised to find it was trimmed with fur. A second one that I put on had a long strip with a Turkish design set into it. A stranger with a long face and a short pointed beard came up and tried to prevent my putting it on, saying it was his. I showed him then that it was embroidered all over with a Turkish pattern. He asked: "What have the Turkish (designs, stripes) to do with you?" But we then became quite friendly with each other. (p. 237)

What sense can you make of the events that take place in this dream? In addition to analyzing this dream, you may wish to write down a dream you've had and try to analyze it.

WRITING A THERAPEUTIC FAIRY TALE

This exercise stems from the brief discussion in Chapter 3 concerning Bruno Bettelheim's book *The Uses of Enchantment: The Meaning and Importance of Fairy Tales* (1977). Bettelheim recounts how traditional Hindu healers often compose individualized fairy tales for their patients to help them deal with their problems. The patients study the fairy tales and learn, by identifying with the characters, something about their problems and how to solve them.

In this exercise, pretend you are a Hindu healer and are writing a fairy tale to help a person deal with an assortment of psychological afflictions. Please do the following:

- Write a traditional (not a modernized parody) fairy tale that starts with "Once upon a time, long, long ago" and concludes with "and so they all lived happily ever after." Use dialogue, description, conflict, and action.
- Write in the past tense and include typical characters from fairy tales: kings, queens, princes and princesses, dragons, animal helpers, heroes with names like Jack, Tom, or Jane.
- Have the actions of the characters reflect and provide resolutions for the numerous psychological problems of the person assigned to you from the following choices:
  - *Person 1:* Oedipus complex, castration anxiety, regression
  - *Person 2:* penis envy, narcissism, rationalization
  - *Person 3:* anal eroticism, ambivalence, fixation
  - *Person 4:* Oedipus complex, narcissism, fixation
  - *Person 5:* fixation, castration anxiety, narcissism
  - *Person 6:* Oedipus complex, ambivalence, sibling rivalry

ORIGIN TALES

Every comic book hero or heroine, or team of heroes and heroines, has an origin tale—a page or two in which the character is introduced to the audience. The most famous of these, no doubt, is Superman's, which tells of his origins on Krypton, his long travel in a spaceship to the planet Earth, his being found by the kindly couple who adopted him (the Kents), his great powers, and so on.

In this activity, draw an origin tale for a superhero or superheroine you have created. Draw your tale in 10 or 12 frames on a piece of paper or cardboard of a standard size agreed to by all teams or individuals participating in this activity. Remember to observe the following rules:

- Use 10 or 12 frames. Make real drawings and color them in. Do not use stick figures.
- Have the characters speak in balloons. You can also use parts of panels to give continuity information.
- Pay attention to facial expressions, characters' clothing, action depictions, sound effects, and dialogue.
- Consider what special abilities, powers, and so on your hero or heroine has.
- Tell a story. Even though you are introducing your character to an audience, you still have to include action, conflict, and so on.

When completed, the origin tales of all participants should be exhibited together so that everyone can observe the different kinds of heroes, heroines, villains, monsters, and so on created. Are there any similarities among the figures or themes addressed? What do the origin tales reflect about the age group of those creating the tales and about American culture and society?

RADIO SCRIPTS

Write a radio script that dramatizes and somehow explains semiotic analysis, psychoanalytic theory, Marxist criticism, or sociological analysis (or some combination of these techniques) to a person who has not studied these techniques. Use a well-known film or television show for your subject and follow these rules to create a script that appears in radio's traditional format.

- Divide the page into two columns. In the left-hand column, which should be about 1½ inches wide, use ALL CAPS for the names of the characters and indications for MUSIC or SFX (sound effects).
- Place instructions concerning music or sound effects, in ALL CAPS and underlined (or italicized), in the right-hand column.
- Use the right-hand column for the dialogue, set in normal sentence style to differentiate dialogue from other aspects of the script.
- Place instructions about how a character is to read his or her lines (or other action a character is to take) in ALL CAPS and in parentheses before or following the affected dialogue. Always double-space dialogue.

SFX: BAR SOUNDS: PEOPLE TALKING, LAUGHTER, ETC.

JOHN: (ANGRILY) You stood me up last night. And this wasn't the first time.

GWEN: (COYLY) Please forgive me, John. I was so involved learning about media criticism that I lost track of time.

MUSIC: JUKEBOX PLAYS FRANK SINATRA SINGING "MY WAY"

JOHN: I'm sorry, Gwen. But it's too late. We're finished.

GWEN: If that's the way you feel, it's fine with me. Besides, I was just in the middle of the section on dreams in the psychoanalytic chapter. Last night I dreamed you were a frog. What can that mean?

TELEVISION NARRATIVE ANALYSIS

Examine a television narrative in terms of some of the methods and concepts discussed in this book. After viewing the assigned television show, do the following.

- Apply Propp's morphology to the text. Try to find six or eight of Propp's functions reflected in the television program. List the functions and describe the events in the text that exemplify each.
- Make a paradigmatic analysis of the text; that is, list a series of paired oppositions you find in the text. The terms on the left side of your list should relate to one another and be opposite to the terms on the right side.
- Think of the text as being a kind of "public dream." Analyze the text in terms of the symbolic significance of the major events that take place within it. What might they reflect about the psyche, politics, society, culture?

You should be able to justify your choices and prepared to explain why you did what you did in all three cases. If there are widespread disagreements among members of the larger group about the application of Propp to the text, the oppositions found in the text, and/or the analysis of the symbolism in the text, what does that mean?

THE SIGNIFIER/SIGNIFIED GAME

The power of signs (in particular, signifiers) to generate meanings, feelings, attitudes, and so on is of great use to those who create the products of the mass media, for it is precisely the ability to stimulate particular feelings at specific moments that enables directors, actors, and others to reach people with their media texts.

The secret is to work backward—that is, start by deciding what effect you want and then figure out how to create it using the various aspects of the medium at your disposal. In television, for instance, certain effects are created through the use of color, camera angles and shots, sound effects, music, dialogue, and action. All television viewers learn how to interpret the signs they see and hear—they become "television literate," which means they know how to read the codes and conventions used in TV.

Figure A.1	Sample Chart for the Signifier/Signified Game		
Love	Hate	Horror	Terror
Los Angeles	Frenchness	Genius	The Future
Power	Alienation	Loneliness	Secret Agent
Wisdom	Stupidity	Happiness	Sadness

Start with an effect (or concept) and work backward to figure out how to create it, taking a simplified form. Here is how the game is played.

1. Choose (or your instructor will assign) a signified or—for our purposes—a concept or idea (good examples are *love, hate, genius*).
2. List a number of signifiers that can be used to signify the concept desired. All your signifiers must be images—objects, tangible things. No words are allowed.
3. List as many signifiers as you can. (In some cases the gestalt, or collection of objects, helps establish the precise meaning desired.)
4. Be certain that the objects and artifacts you use do not mislead people, making them think of the wrong signified.

An Example

Suppose your signified is "secret agent." You are a director and want to indicate to your viewers that secret agents are part of your story. Some of the signifiers you might use are trench coats, dark sunglasses, slouch hats, pistols with silencers, and fast sports cars. A six-gun would not be an appropriate signifier of a secret agent—it would be misleading.

METAPHORS

Metaphor is traditionally understood as a literary device in which one thing is seen in terms of another. That is, a metaphor suggests some kind of relationship between two things in the form of an analogy. For example, the statement "My love is a red rose" is a metaphor in which a person's love and a red rose are equated. (Simile is a relatively weak form of metaphor that uses *like* or *as*; for example, "My love is like a red rose.")

Metaphors are more than just literary devices, however; they actually affect our thought processes in profound ways. Linguists George Lakoff and Mark Johnson (1980) discuss the role of metaphor in our lives:

Metaphor is typically viewed as a characteristic of language alone, a matter of words rather than thought or action. For this reason, most people think they can get along perfectly well without metaphor. We have found, on the contrary, that metaphor is pervasive in everyday life, not just in language but in thought and action. Our ordinary conceptual system, in terms of which we both think and act, is fundamentally metaphoric in nature.

The concepts that govern our thought are not just matters of the intellect. They also govern our everyday functioning, down to the most mundane details. Our concepts structure what we perceive, how we get around in the world, and how we relate to other people. Our conceptual system thus plays a central role in defining our everyday realities. (p. 3)

They also point out that metaphors help shape our futures:

Metaphors may create realities for us, especially social realities. A metaphor may thus be a guide for future action. Such actions will, of course, fit the metaphor. This will, in turn, reinforce the power of the metaphor to make experience coherent. (p. 156)

As Lakoff and Johnson argue, the metaphors we employ have implications for the ways we live; they take on a kind of logical and coercive power.

How to Play the Metaphor Game

1. Write down a metaphor.
2. List the logical implications of your metaphor.
3. Consider whether your metaphor is likely to be beneficial or harmful to a person who accepts it—and its logical implications.
4. Try to improve on your metaphor.

Later, think about some of the metaphors you live by. What are your essential metaphors? What implications do these metaphors have for your life?

Things to Consider

After playing this game, what conclusions do you come to about the ways people find meaning in life?

1. Where do we pick up the metaphors that shape our lives? Be as specific as possible. Find a metaphor and see if you can find out where it comes from.
2. Is it possible that the problems of many unhappy people stem from their having unintentionally internalized destructive (or self-destructive) metaphors?
3. How can we deal with the problems caused by destructive metaphors? Is it also possible that people are illogical and that they don't live by the logical implications of the metaphors they accept? That is, is it possible that Lakoff and Johnson are incorrect in their assertion that people live by metaphors, given that people are so "illogical" or "complex"?

Figure A.2 presents two metaphors for analysis. Write down as many implications of each metaphor as you can think of. Each list has already been started for you with an example.

| Figure A.2 | Metaphors to Analyze |

Love is a game.	Love is a fever.
1. Games end.	1. You're all hot.
2.	2.
3.	3.
4.	4.
5.	5.
6.	6.
7.	7.
8.	8.
9.	9.
10.	10.
11.	11.

ADVERTISING ANALYSIS

Use one, several, or all the methodologies you have learned in this volume (semiotics, psychoana-lytic theory, sociological theory, Marxist theory) to analyze advertisements.

First, choose advertisements with material that lends itself to analysis—preferably ads with people, objects, interesting backgrounds, interesting copy, and so on. Next, apply the methodology or method-ologies your instructor assigns to analyze the ads you have collected. (Be sure to review Chapter 7 before undertaking your own analysis.) In analyzing your ads, consider the following:

- Signifiers and signifieds
- Icons, indexes, and symbols
- Sociological phenomena: demographics of people in the ads and of the people toward whom the ads are targeted, reflections of socioeconomic classes, lifestyles, and so on
- The nature of the appeals made to sell the products, through both the copy and the people used in the ads
- The designs of the advertisements, including typefaces, colors, and other aesthetic matters
- The publications in which you found the ads and the expected audiences of those publications

Be sure to turn in your advertisement(s) along with your analyses.

PLAYING AARON WILDAVSKY

The work of political scientist Aaron Wildavsky offers some ideas we can use to assess and analyze the media, popular culture, and related areas from an interesting perspective. Wildavsky (1989) and his colleagues (e.g., Thompson, Ellis, & Wildavsky, 1990) have drawn on the work of British anthropologist Mary Douglas to explain and describe four political cultures found in democratic societies, the members of which these scholars call hierarchical elitists, competitive individualists, egalitarians, and fatalists (see the discussion of political cultures in Chapter 2).

Figure A.3 shows some of the traits associated with the members of these four political cultures. In this game, look for reflections of the four political cultures in films, television programs, books, and so on. The connections you find will not necessarily be overt or recognized by many people who form the audiences for these works (but we know people seek reinforcement for their beliefs and want to avoid dissonance, so it is logical to assume that people choose texts congruent with their beliefs and values).

Figure A.3   The Four Political Cultures and Popular Culture

	Elitists	Individualists	Egalitarians	Fatalists
	Leadership from top	Individuals are own leaders	Charismatic leaders	No concern with leadership
	Inequality natural	Equality of opportunity	Equality of needs basic	Inequality natural
	Top helps bottom	Every person for him- or herself	Spread wealth to all	Hope for luck
	Keep order	Make money	Make everyone equal	Survive
Songs				
TV shows				
Films				
Magazines				
Books				
Heroes				
Heroines				
Games				
Sports				

Take the following steps:

1. Find one or more specific example of each of the topics listed in Figure A.3. Do not deal with genres; rather, select particular films, television programs, songs, and so on (for example, "God Bless America," not "patriotic song").
2. Make sure your example fits the category (to the extent this is possible). In some cases, you may have to do a bit of stretching, but try to be as precise as you can.
3. Be prepared to explain and justify your choices.
4. Consider matters such as trends and new developments in doing this exercise.

TEXTUAL ANALYSIS

Semiotic Analysis

1. Write a 1,000-word semiotic analysis of *Avatar*. Start your paper with an applications chart on a separate page, as shown in Figure A.4. To make the chart, list semiotic concepts on the left-hand side of the page and the applications of the concepts to events and dialogue in the film (or other text) on the right-hand side of the page. In your paper, amplify and explain your applications.

2. Using semiotic methods, write a 1,000-word analysis of the "Schizoid" episode of *The Prisoner*. Use the applications chart format described in Exercise 1. Note: Free videos of *The Prisoner* can be found at www.amctv.com/originals/the-prisoner.

Figure A.4   Sample of Applications Chart to Be Used in Analyses of All Texts

Arthur Asa Berger	
Sample Concepts/Applications Chart for "Arrival"	
Semiotic Concepts	**Applications to "Arrival"**
1. Signifier/signified	Filing cabinets Bureaucracy The Village Small town Numbers Prisoners Blonde housekeeper Innocence
2. Syntagmatic analysis	See chart in essay.
3. Paradigmatic analysis	See chart in essay.
4. Metaphor	One important metaphor in this text is that the Village is a prison.

(Continued)

Figure A.4 (Continued)	
5. Synecdoche	Rover stands for the authority of Number Two and the administration.
6. Icons	Some of the more important icons were the photographs of Number Six and the statues found in the Village.
7. Indexes	The smoke that poured into the agent's room while he was packing was a gas that knocked him out and enabled people to bring him to the Village.
8. Symbols	The helicopter was a symbol for escape and the pawns on the chessboard symbolized the Villagers.
9. Intertextuality	*The Prisoner* is related to a program that McGoohan was on earlier, *Danger Man*, and to spy and science fiction genres in general.
10. Codes	One important code is the smaller the number, the greater the power. Another is duplicity: Nobody can be trusted. Another is lack of privacy: Number Six and others are always being monitored.

Note: Use applications charts for all your analyses of texts.

Marxist/Ideological Criticism

1. You are appointed media critic for the Marxist journal *Arts Comrade*. Using the most important concepts from Marxist theory, write a 1,000-word Marxist interpretation of the film *Avatar* or any text your instructor assigns. Use the applications chart format described earlier. Which of the four political cultures does *Avatar* appeal to the most? Explain your answer.

2. Using Marxist concepts, write a 1,000-word analysis for *Arts Comrade* of "The General" episode of *The Prisoner*. Use the applications chart format described earlier.

Psychoanalytic Criticism

1. You are appointed media critic of *Psyche* magazine. Write a psychoanalytic interpretation of *Avatar* (or some other film or an episode from a television show or other text chosen by your instructor). Use an applications chart to make your analysis.

2. Write a 1,000-word psychoanalytic interpretation for *Psyche* magazine of the "A, B, and C" episode of *The Prisoner.* Use an applications chart for the first page of your paper.

Sociological Criticism

1. You are appointed media critic of *Media and Society.* Write a 1,000-word sociological analysis, using concepts learned in this book, of *Avatar* or any film, television program, or other text your instructor assigns. Use an applications chart for the first page of your paper.

2. Find a print advertisement that has interesting people in it, symbolic phenomena, and enough copy so you have something to write about and write a sociological analysis of the advertisement. Tie your analysis to specific things in the advertisement: the copy, the people and their facial expressions, the clothes they are wearing, and so forth. Use an applications chart for the first page of your paper.

3. Using sociological concepts discussed in this book, analyze a video game you like. Tie your analysis to research on the demographics and psychographics of video game players.

Note: Some of this material is adapted from exercises and activities found in my books *Media and Communication Research Methods* (2011, 2nd ed.) and *Games and Activities for Media, Communication, and Cultural Studies Students* (2004).

Glossary

Aberrant decoding: The decoding or interpretation of texts by audiences in ways that differ from those the creators of the texts expected. According to semiotician Umberto Eco (1972), aberrant decoding is the rule, rather than the exception, when it comes to the mass media.

Administrative research: Research that focuses on ways of making communication by organizations and other entities more efficient and effective. Compare with *critical research*, which has more interest in social justice and related considerations.

Aesthetics: In the context of this volume, elements that appeal to the senses; in the case of mass media, these include lighting, sound, music, kinds of camera shots and other camera work, and editing, all of which affect the ways members of audiences react.

Agenda-setting theory: The theory that institutions of mass communication determine not what we think but what we think about. They set the agenda for our decision making and thus influence our social and political lives.

Alienation: In the context of this volume, estrangement from the self (from *alien*, which means someone with no connections to others—*a* [no] and *lien* [ties]). According to Marx, alienation is the central problem of bourgeois societies and affects everyone in them; capitalism produces material things, but it also produces alienation.

Allegory: A metaphorical story that has symbolic significance, with implications beyond the story itself. An allegory employs themes and ideas of a broad philosophical nature and conveys some kind of a moral. For example, the television series *The Prisoner* (in which a man is imprisoned on a mysterious island, is deprived of his name and given a number instead, and has various adventures in which he fights with the administration of the island and tries to escape, eventually destroying the island and succeeding) can be seen as an allegory of the triumph of the human spirit and democratic individualism over the forces of a totalitarian bureaucracy and adversity in general.

Ambivalence: A defense mechanism involving a simultaneous feeling of love and hatred or attraction to and repulsion from the same person or thing.

Anomie: A condition in which people reject the norms of a given society (from the Greek *anomos*, meaning "no norms" or "no law"). The term was made popular by French sociologist Émile Durkheim.

Audience: In the context of this volume, a collection of individuals who receive a media text—watch a television program, listen to a radio program, attend a film or some kind of artistic performance, and so on. Members of an audience may be together in one room or scattered; in the case of television, each may be watching on his or her own set. In technical terms, members of an audience are addressees who receive mediated texts sent by some addresser.

Base: In Marxist thought, the economic system found in a given society. The base shapes (but does not determine) the superstructure—the institutions found in the society, such as art, religion, the legal system, and the educational system.

Blogs: Blogs are online journals individuals make available on the Internet. Some bloggers deal with daily events in their lives while others focus on some topic of interest to them or ones in which they have special knowledge.

Branding: A phenomenon in which people become emotionally attached to certain products and use these brands to construct their identities. People use their shopping choices to construct their identities.

Castration anxiety: In Freudian theory, the fear young males have that they will be castrated by their fathers. This anxiety leads young boys to renounce their love for their mothers and to identify with their fathers, thus overcoming their Oedipus complexes.

Cell phones: These devices play an important role in our business and social lives. More advanced cell phones are really small computers with multiple capabilities or functions: playing music, sending text messages, making phone calls, taking photographs, and making videos. See *smartphones.*

Characters: People whose actions constitute a story and lead to its resolution. Audience members (whether readers, viewers, or listeners) must find characters interesting and want to follow their adventures, so authors have to find ways of making their characters worth caring about. As a rule, characters in narratives are not representative of ordinary people. On television, for example, there are far greater percentages of police officers, private detectives, and killers than found in real life, and a far smaller proportion of blue-collar workers. Many narrative theorists argue that character is the basis of action in narratives, whereas others argue that action reveals character.

Class: A group of people or things that have something in common; in the context of this volume, the term refers primarily to social class or, more literally, socioeconomic class—groups of people who share the same income and lifestyle. Marxist theorists argue there is a ruling class that shapes the ideas of the proletariat, the working class, and generates "false consciousness" in order to prevent class conflict and revolution.

Class conflict: Conflict between the working class and the ruling class. According to Marxist theory, history is the record of class conflict. This conflict will end when capitalism is replaced by communism and classes are eliminated, because then everyone will own the means of production.

Climax or crisis: The turning point of a story, when the most important matter is somehow decided, setting the stage for the resolution. A story must have a climax so that it can lead to a resolution audience members find interesting and satisfying.

Codes: Systems of symbols, letters, words, sounds, and so on that generate meaning. Language, for example, is a code. It uses combinations of letters we call words to mean certain things. The relation between the word and the thing the word stands for is arbitrary and based on convention. In some cases, the term *code* is used to describe hidden meanings and disguised communications.

Cognitive dissonance: The psychological conflict that results within a person when he or she holds clashing beliefs or when his or her actions and beliefs are opposed to each other. According to psychologists, people wish to avoid ideas that challenge the ones they hold, because this creates conflict and other disagreeable feelings. (The term *dissonance* is also used to refer to sounds that clash with one another.)

Content analysis: A nonintrusive methodology in which the researcher examines particular elements in a text or collection of texts to quantify them and use them for statistical analysis.

Critical research: A kind of ideological approach to the study of media that focuses on the social and political dimensions of the mass media and the ways organizations and others allegedly use them to maintain the status quo rather than to enhance equality. Compare with *administrative research.*

Cultural homogenization: The destruction of cultures (such as Third World and certain regional cultures) other than the dominant culture, leading to cultural sameness and standardization.

Cultural imperialism or media imperialism: The alleged domination of Third World cultures through the transmission of certain values and beliefs through the flow of media products (such as songs, films, and television programs) and popular culture from the United States and a few Western European capitalist countries.

Culture: The specific ideas, arts, customary beliefs, ways of living, behavior patterns, institutions, and values of a group, transmitted from generation to generation. When applied to the arts, the term *culture* is generally used in reference to "elite" artwork, such as operas, poetry, classical music, and serious novels.

Culture codes: According to Clotaire Rapaille, children up to the age of 7 are "imprinted" with the particular codes dominant in their nation or some subculture in that nation. These codes then shape their behavior in many areas. As Rapaille writes in his book *The Culture Code* (2006), "If I could get to the source of these imprints—if I could somehow 'decode' elements of culture to discover the emotions and meanings attached to them—I would learn a great deal about human behavior and how it varies across the planet" (pp. 9–10).

Defense mechanisms: The methods used by the ego to defend itself against pressures from the id (or impulsive elements in the psyche) and superego elements such as conscience and guilt. Some of the more common defense mechanisms are repression (barring unconscious instinctual wishes, memories, and so on from consciousness), regression (returning to earlier stages in one's development), ambivalence (a simultaneous feeling of love and hate toward some person or thing), and rationalization (offering excuses to justify one's actions).

Demographics: Statistical characteristics of people, including race, religion, sex, social class, ethnicity, occupation, place of residence, and age. Compare with *psychographics.*

Deviance: Difference from the norm, whether in values and beliefs or in actions. Attitudes toward forms of deviance change over time. Many groups judged as deviant are marginalized—that is, pushed to the margins of society, where they can be ignored or persecuted (or both).

Dysfunctional: Contributing to the breakdown or destabilization of an entity.

Ego: According to Freudian theory, the executant of the id and a mediator between the id and the superego. The ego is involved with the perception of reality and the adaptation to reality.

Emotive function: The expression of feelings. According to Jakobson (1988), this is one of the functions of messages; the other functions are referential and poetic.

Ethical criticism: Criticism concerned with the moral aspects of what happens in texts and the texts' possible impacts. There is considerable debate about what is ethical in the production of texts and the role ethics should play in the arts and the media.

Facial expression: Paul Ekman and other semiotically informed psychologists and communication scholars have studied how facial expressions reveal our emotions. Ekman's research suggests that some facial expressions are universal.

False consciousness: In Marxist thought, the mistaken ideas people have about their class, status, and economic possibilities. These ideas help maintain the status quo and are of great use to the ruling class, which wants to avoid changes in the social structure. According to Marx, the ideas of the ruling class are always the ruling ideas in society.

Feminist criticism: Criticism that focuses on the roles of women and how women are portrayed in mass-mediated texts of all kinds. Feminist critics argue that women are typically depicted as sexual objects, as housewives, as weak or helpless or mindless, and so on, and this negatively affects the socialization of young women, young men, and society in general.

Formulaic texts: Highly conventional texts with stock characters and recognizable plot structures. Genre texts, such as westerns, science fiction stories, detective stories, and romances are often highly formulaic. They take place in certain locations and have specific kinds of characters who engage in predictable kinds of actions. On a continuum from highly conventional texts to highly inventive texts, formulaic texts are found very close to the conventional end. Some publishers of romance novels, for example, provide their authors with guidelines that specify such details as the ages heroes and heroines should be, what they should look like, whether or not they can be divorced (and, if so, when the divorce had to happen), and whether or not they can have sex before marriage.

Frame: In the context of this volume, a story that provides the means of telling other stories within it. For example, Kurosawa's classic film *Rashomon* employs the frame of a group of men taking shelter from the rain in a temple, where they discuss an incident that has occurred from several conflicting viewpoints; their individual stories are then told in flashback. Such frames are useful for serial plots or those that contain a number of stories, such as *1,001 Arabian Nights*.

Frankfurt School: This group of media critics, centered at the Institute of Social Research in Frankfurt, Germany, offered Marxist critiques of media and culture. Some of the more prominent members of the Frankfurt School were Theodor Adorno, Herbert Marcuse, and Walter Benjamin.

Functional: Contributing to the maintenance of a system. A functional institution, for example, contributes to the maintenance of society. Compare with *dysfunctional*.

Functional alternative: Something that takes the place of something else. For example, professional football can be seen as a functional alternative to religion.

Gatekeepers: Those with the power to determine who or what passes through a certain point. In the context of this volume, gatekeepers include the editors who determine which stories are used in newspapers and on television and radio news programs. In a broad sense, gatekeepers determine what programs and films we see, what songs we hear, and so on.

Gender: The sexual category of an individual—masculine or feminine—and the behavioral traits connected with each category. Many theorists argue now that gender is socially constructed rather than wholly natural.

Genre: A type of text characterized by a particular style or formula, such as soap opera, news show, sports program, horror show, or detective story. In French, *genre* means "kind" or "class." (For in-depth discussion of genre texts, see Berger, 1992.)

Horror. According to psychoanalyst Martin Grotjahn, horror in adults involves long-repressed childhood fears appearing to come true.

Humor: Humor is one of the more enigmatic aspects of communication. Humor scholars have suggested four competing theories to explain humor and mirthful laughter: Humor is based on incongruity, feelings of superiority, masked aggression, and paradoxical aspects of communication. Jokes are one of the more popular forms of humor, but many other forms exist.

Hypodermic needle theory: The theory, generally discredited now, holding that all members of an audience "read" a text the same way and get the same things out of it. The metaphor of a hypodermic needle is a reference to how media are assumed to be injecting all audience members with the same message. This model has been replaced, generally speaking, by the reader response theory.

Hypothesis: An assumption that something is true for the purposes of discussion or argument or further investigation. In a sense, a hypothesis is a guess or supposition made as a basis from which to explain some phenomenon.

Id: The element of the psyche representative of a person's drives, according to Freud's theory of the psyche (his "structural hypothesis"). It is also the source of energy, but it lacks direction, and so the superego must harness and control it. In popular thought, the id is connected with impulse and lust—with the "I want it all now" kind of behavior.

Ideology: A logically coherent, integrated explanation of social, economic, and political matters that helps establish the goals and direct the actions of some group or political entity. People act (and vote or don't vote) on the basis of their ideologies, even those who have never articulated or given any thought to them. Marxist critics typically seek to expose what they would describe as the ideology hidden in works of popular culture.

Image: In the context of this volume, "a collection of signs and symbols—what we find when we look at a photograph, a film still, a shot of a television screen, a print advertisement, or just about anything" (Berger, 1989, p. 38). An image may be a mental or a physical representation. Images can have powerful emotional effects on people, and some images have historical significance. (For in-depth discussions of image, see Adatto, 1993; Messaris, 1994.)

Intentional fallacy: The idea that it is an error to consider the intention of the artist as an important element in the analysis of the artist's work. In literary and aesthetic theory, this has been the subject of considerable debate; some critics believe the artist's intention is significant and should be considered, to some degree at least, in the analysis of a text.

Jokes: Humor scholars generally define a joke as a short narrative, meant to evoke mirthful laughter, that ends in a punch line. In my discussion of humor, I point out that humor scholars disagree on why we laugh at jokes—or anything else. In recent years, comedians have moved away from telling jokes to relying on observational humor.

Latent functions: Hidden, unrecognized, and unintended functions of some activity, entity, or institution. Social scientists contrast these with manifest functions, which are recognized and intended.

Lifestyle: The way people live, including the decisions they make about how to decorate their homes (and where their homes are located), the kinds of cars they drive, the styles of clothes they wear, the kinds of foods they eat and the restaurants they frequent, where they go for vacations, and so on.

Limited effects (of media): Minor effects of media on society. Some mass communication theorists argue that the influence of the mass media is relatively small in the larger scheme of things. They cite research that shows, for example, that effects from media do not tend to be long lasting.

Manifest functions: Obvious and intended functions of some activity, entity, or institution. Social scientists contrast these with latent functions, which are hidden and unintended. For example, the manifest function of a person's going to a political rally is to show support for a candidate; the latent function might be for the person to meet others with similar political views.

Mass: In the context of this volume, a large number of people who form the audience for some communication. There is considerable disagreement about how to understand the mass of people reached by mass communication. Some theorists believe the mass is made up of individuals who are heterogeneous, do not know one another, are alienated, and do not have a leader. Others attack these notions, asserting that they are based not on fact or evidence but on incorrect theories.

Mass communication: The transfer of messages, information, texts, and the like from a sender of some kind to a large number of people, a mass audience. This transfer is done through the technologies of the mass media—newspapers, magazines, television programs, films, records, computer networks, and so on. The sender is often a person in some large media organization, the messages are public, and the audience tends to be large and varied.

Medium: In the context of this volume, a means of delivering messages, information, and texts to audiences—that is, a communication medium. There are different ways of classifying media, one of the most common of which is to divide them into print (newspapers, magazines, books, billboards), electronic (radio, television, computers), and photographic (still photography, film, video).

Metaphor: A figure of speech that conveys meaning by analogy. Metaphors are not confined to poetry and literary works; according to some linguists, the fundamental way we make sense of things and find meaning in the world is through metaphors. A simile is a weak form of metaphor that uses either *like* or *as* in making an analogy.

Metonymy: A figure of speech that conveys information by association (for example, using the name *Rolls-Royce* to convey something expensive or of high quality). Along with metaphor, one of the most important ways people convey information to one another is through metonymy, although we tend not to be aware of how much we use association to get our ideas across. A form of metonymy in which the whole represents a part or vice versa is called *synecdoche* (for example, using *the White House* to mean the presidency).

Mimetic desire: Rene Girard's theory that mimesis or imitation is a powerful force in human behavior that both draws people together and pulls them apart.

Mimetic theories of art: Theories, dating from Aristotle's time, based on the notion that art imitates reality.

Model: In the context of this volume, an abstract representation that shows how some phenomenon functions. Theories are typically expressed in language, but models tend to be represented graphically or through statistics or mathematics. McQuail and Windahl (1993) define a model as "a consciously simplified description in graphic form of a piece of reality. A model seeks to show the main elements of any structure or process and the relationships between these elements" (p. 2).

Modern/modernist: Falling within the period approximately from the beginning of the 20th century to the 1960s. Modernist artists rejected narrative structure for simultaneity and montage and explored the paradoxical nature of reality. Important modernists include T. S. Eliot, Franz Kafka, James Joyce, Pablo Picasso, Henri Matisse, and Eugene Ionesco. Modernism was superseded, according to many critics, by postmodernism.

Myth model: It argues that myths can be found in psychoanalytic theory, historical experience, elite culture, popular culture, and everyday life. This suggests that myths play a role in shaping our thinking and behavior, though we may not be aware of them.

Myths: Ancient stories, believed to be true, involving gods and goddesses and heroes that validate our beliefs, customs, and institutions.

Narrowcasting: The dissemination of a media text narrowly, by focusing on discrete groups. For example, the medium of radio has many stations that tend to focus on, or narrowcast to, particular kinds of groups. This contrasts with broadcasting, which tries to reach as many people as possible.

Nonfunctional: Neither functional nor dysfunctional. Something that is nonfunctional plays no role in the maintenance or breakdown of the entity in which it is found.

Nonverbal communication: Communication that does not involve words, carried out through body language, facial expressions, styles of dress, hairstyles, and so on. Semiotics can shed light on how nonverbal communication works.

Objective theories of art: Theories based on the notion that art functions to project reality (that of the artist), like a lamp, as opposed to reflecting reality, like a mirror.

Opinion leader: A person whose opinions influence those of others. Opinion leaders play an important role in the two-step flow theory of communication, and the existence of opinion leaders is one of the arguments used to counter the mass-society hypothesis.

Phallic symbol: An object that resembles the penis, either in shape or function. Symbolism is a defense mechanism of the ego that permits hidden or repressed sexual or aggressive thoughts to be expressed in disguised form. (For further discussion of this topic, see Freud, 1900/1965.)

Phallocentric: Dominated by the masculine point of view. Some critics assert that the ultimate source of this domination, which shapes our institutions and cultures, is the male phallus. In this theory, which many feminist critics accept, a link is made between male sexuality and male power.

Poetic function: The function of expression through poetic language. According to Jakobson (1988), one of the functions of messages is the use of such literary devices as metaphor and metonymy. Messages also have emotive and referential functions.

Political cultures: Cultures comprising people with similar political values and beliefs in relation to the group boundaries and rules and prescriptions they observe. Wildavsky (1989) and his colleagues (e.g., Thompson, Ellis, & Wildavsky, 1990) assert that all democratic societies have four political cultures and that all four are needed to balance one another. They call the members of these four cultures individualists, hierarchical elitists, egalitarians, and fatalists. For an example of how Wildavsky's theories can be applied to mass media and popular culture, see Berger (1990).

Popular: Literally, "of the people" (from the Latin *popularis*). This term can be defined in many ways, but for the purposes of this volume, it generally is used in the sense of appealing to large numbers of people.

Popular culture: The culture of the people, usually understood to include texts that appeal to large numbers of people. Mass communication theorists often identify (or confuse) *popular* with *mass* and suggest that if something is popular, it must be of poor quality, appealing to the mythical "lowest common denominator." Popular culture is generally held to be the opposite of "elite" culture, which includes arts that require a certain level of sophistication and refinement to appreciate, such as ballet, opera, poetry, and classical music. Many critics now question this popular culture–elite culture polarity.

Postmodern/postmodernist: Falling within the period after the modern era, or from approximately the 1960s to the present. According to a leading theorist on the subject, Jean-François Lyotard (1984), postmodernism is characterized by "incredulity toward metanarratives" (p. xxiv). In other words, the old philosophical belief systems that had helped people order their lives and societies are no longer accepted. This has led to a period in which, more or less, anything goes. Postmodern texts may include irony, parody, and the mixing of genres or styles.

Power: The ability to implement one's wishes as far as policy in some entity is concerned. In the discussion of texts, *power* is often used to describe their ability to emotionally affect audience members—readers, viewers, or listeners. Critics of recent developments in the mass media have noted that smaller and smaller groups are controlling more and more media outlets; they fear this concentration of media power in the hands of a few will translate into political power.

Pragmatic theories of art: Theories based on the notion that art must do something, must have certain consequences held to be desirable. Thus art should teach, indoctrinate, or perform some other function. Marxist theorists generally hold to pragmatic theories of art; they believe art should help indoctrinate people, generate class solidarity, and be used to fight against capitalist bourgeois societies.

Psychoanalytic theory: A theory based on the notion that the human psyche includes an element Freud calls the "unconscious" that is ordinarily inaccessible to us (unlike consciousness and the preconscious) and continually shapes and affects our mental functioning and behavior. Freud also emphasizes matters profoundly affected by unconscious imperatives, such as sexuality and the role of the Oedipus complex in people's lives.

Psychographics: A marketing term used to describe the psychological characteristics of groups of people. Compare with *demographics.*

Public: A group of people, a community. Terms such as *public arts* and *public communication* are sometimes substituted for *popular culture* and *mass communication* to avoid the negative connotations of the words *mass* and *popular. Public* is also used in opposition to *private*, as in public acts (those meant to be known to the community) contrasted with private acts (which are not meant to be known to others).

Rationalization: In Freudian thought, a defense mechanism of the ego that creates a justification for some action (or for inaction when an action is expected). Ernest Jones, who introduced the term, used it to describe logical and rational reasons people give to justify behavior really caused by unconscious and irrational determinants.

Reader response theory or reception theory: The theory that readers (individuals who read books, watch television programs, go to films, listen to texts on the radio, and so on) play an important role in the realization of texts. Texts, then, function as sites for the creation of meaning by readers, and different readers interpret given texts differently. Compare with the *hypodermic needle theory* of media.

Referential function: The function of the expression of relationships between people and/or things. According to Jakobson (1988), the referential function of speech is to help speakers relate to their surroundings. He contrasts this with emotive and poetic functions of speech.

Reinforcement: A psychological process in which people seek out information that sustains their beliefs and actions and enables them to avoid cognitive dissonance.

Relativism: In philosophical thought, the belief that truth is relative and not absolute; that there are no objective standards. In ethical thought, relativism suggests there are no moral or ethical absolutes. Thus different cultures have different ways of living and practices that are as valid as those of any other culture. That is, morality and ethical behavior are relative to particular groups and cannot be generalized to all human beings. This contrasts with the notion that there are ethical absolutes or universals that can and should be applied to everyone.

Role: A socialized way of behaving appropriate to a particular situation. A person generally plays many roles with people during a given day: parent, student, worker, and so on.

Sapir-Whorf hypothesis: The hypothesis that language is not something transparent that merely conveys information from one person to another but rather something that affects the ways people think and act. According to this hypothesis, language is not like a windowpane but more like a prism. This argument is pushed to its extreme by Marshall McLuhan's assertion that the medium is the message.

Secondary modeling system: The system beyond that of language, our primary modeling system (Lotman, 1977), through which we use language to create art. For example, works of art that use such phenomena as myths and legends function as secondary modeling systems (that is, they are secondary to language).

Selective attention or selective inattention: Attention paid only to what we choose. We have a tendency to avoid messages that conflict with our beliefs and values (i.e., that would create cognitive dissonance), and we do this through selective attention. Thus people who belong to a particular political culture (as described by Wildavsky, 1989) tend to search for entertainments that reinforce their values and avoid those that would generate dissonance.

Semiotics: Literally, the science of signs (from the Greek *sēmeîon*, meaning "sign"). A sign is anything that can be used to stand for anything else. According to C. S. Peirce, one of the founders of the science, a sign "is something which stands to somebody for something in some respect or capacity" (qtd. in Zeman, 1977, p. 24).

Serial texts: Texts that continue over long periods of time. Examples include comic strips, soap operas, and other television genres in which story lines are continued for extended periods. Serial texts pose problems for critics, who must decide what to consider when analyzing them—the whole of a series or individual episodes?

Shadow: In Jungian thought, the dark side of the psyche, which we attempt to keep hidden. The shadow contains repressed and unfavorable aspects of our personalities as well as normal instincts and creative impulses. Thus in all of us there is a continual battle between shadow aspects of our personalities and our egos, which also contain some negative features.

Smartphones: Phones such as the Apple iPhone and numerous others, essentially small computers that allow people to talk with others, send text messages, check their e-mail, make and see videos, play games, and do many other things. There are now thousands of "apps" (as in "applications") for these phones that enable users to do an incredible number of things.

Social controls: Ideas, beliefs, values, and mores of a society that shape people's beliefs and behaviors. People are both individuals, with certain distinctive physical and emotional characteristics and desires, and members of societies. They are shaped, to a certain degree, by the institutions—especially education and the media—found in their societies.

Social media: Internet sites such as Facebook, Twitter, and YouTube that allow individuals to post words, images, and videos that can potentially be seen by large numbers of people. Social media have revolutionized the way people communicate with one another and are global in scope. They played an important role in the revolutions in Tunisia and Egypt and other countries in North Africa.

Socialization: The processes by which societies teach individuals how to behave: what rules to obey, roles to assume, and values to hold. Socialization has traditionally been a function of the family, educators, clergy, and peers, but the mass media seem to have usurped this function to a considerable degree nowadays, with consequences that are not always positive.

Socioeconomic class: A group categorized according to income and related social status and lifestyle. In Marxist thought, the ruling class shapes the consciousness of the working class, and history is, in essence, a record of class conflict.

Stereotypes: Commonly held, simplistic, and often inaccurate group-held portraits of categories of people. Stereotypes can be positive, negative, or mixed but are generally negative. Stereotyping always involves gross overgeneralization.

Subculture: A subgroup within the dominant culture that differs in religion, ethnicity, sexual orientation, beliefs, values, behaviors, lifestyles, or some other way from the dominant culture. Any complex society is likely to have a considerable number of subcultures, and the people in subcultures are often marginalized by those in the dominant culture.

Superego: The agency in the psyche related to conscience and morality. According to Freud, the superego is involved with the approval and disapproval of wishes on the basis of whether or not they are moral; critical self-observation; and a sense of guilt over wrongdoing. The functions of the superego are largely unconscious and opposed to the id element in the psyche. Mediating between the two, and trying to balance them, is the ego.

Symbol: Something that stands for something else (from the Greek *symballein*, which means "to put together"). A symbol brings two things together—for example, a particular object and an act by a character that has some higher meaning. In narratives, certain objects, events, and actions by characters have symbolic significance when they refer to things outside of themselves. Thus in *The Maltese Falcon*, the falcon has a symbolic significance, representing the villain's greed and obsessiveness and, by implication, the greed of a number of others—who are willing to lie, cheat, and kill to get their hands on it. The falcon turns out, ironically, to be made of lead and thus also symbolizes the futility of much human action and the genius individuals have for acting in self-destructive ways. In order to understand symbolism, we have to learn (through socialization and enculturation, for example) what various symbols mean. Critics often distinguish between *allegory* and *symbolism*, using the latter term for something that has a fixed, transcendental significance and the former for something whose meaning becomes evident as the action progresses.

Taste cultures: According to sociologist Herbert Gans, taste cultures are appropriate to the socioeconomic and cultural levels of different segments of American society.

Text: In the context of this volume, any work of art in any medium. Critics use the term *text* as a convenience, to avoid the need to specify particular kinds of works.

Theory: A systematic and logical attempt, expressed in language, to explain and predict phenomena. Theories differ from concepts, which define phenomena being studied, and from models, which are abstract, usually graphic, and explicit about what is being studied.

Trickster figure: In Jungian thought, a figure who represents the earliest period in a hero's development. Characteristics of the trickster include mischievousness, physical appetites that dominate behavior, desire for the gratification of primary needs, and actions that are often cynical, cruel, and unfeeling.

Two-step flow theory: The theory that mass communication reaches and affects people in a two-step process: First, the media influence opinion leaders; second, the opinion leaders influence others.

Uses-and-gratifications theory: A sociological theory that audiences use the mass media (or certain texts or genres of texts) for certain purposes and gain certain gratifications from the use of those media. Researchers who subscribe to this theory focus on how audiences use the media, rather than on how the media affect audiences.

Values: Abstract and general beliefs or judgments about what is right and wrong, or good and bad, that have implications for individuals' behavior and for social, cultural, and political entities. From a philosophical point of view, values are the source of several problems. For example, how does one determine which values are correct or good and which are wrong or bad? That is, how do we justify our values? Are values objective or subjective? What happens when groups that hold different central values come into conflict?

Youth culture: A subculture formed by young people around some area of interest, usually connected with leisure and entertainment, such as rock music or some aspect of computers—games, hacking, and so on. Typically, youth cultures adopt distinctive ways of dressing and develop institutions that cater to their needs. (Frith, 1981, discusses this topic at length.)

References

Adatto, K. (1993). *Picture perfect: The art and artifice of public image making.* New York: Basic Books.

Adorno, T. W. (1957). *The culture industry: Selected essays on mass culture.* London: Routledge.

Allen, W. (1978). *Getting even.* New York: Vintage Books.

Bagdikian, B. H. (1987, June). The 50, 26, 20 . . . corporations that own our media. *Extra!* (magazine published by FAIR). Retrieved from www .fair.org/extra/best-of-extra/corporate-ownership.html

Bakhtin, M. M. (1981). *The dialogic imagination: Four essays* (M. Holquist, Ed.; C. Emerson & M. Holquist, Trans.). Austin: University of Texas Press.

Barthes, R. (1972). *Mythologies.* New York: Hill & Wang.

Baudrillard, J. (1995). *Simulacra and Simulation.* (Transl. Sheila Faria Glaser). Ann Arbor: University of Michigan Press.

Bennett, T., & Woollacott, J. (1987). *Bond and beyond: The political career of a popular hero.* New York: Methuen.

Berger, A. A. (1976). *The TV-guided American.* New York: Walker.

Berger, A. A. (1989). *Seeing is believing: An introduction to visual communication.* Mountain View, CA: Mayfield.

Berger, A. A. (1990). *Agitpop: Political culture and communication theory.* New Brunswick, NJ: Transaction.

Berger, A. A. (1992). *Popular culture genres: Theories and texts.* Newbury Park, CA: Sage.

Berger, A. A. (1997). *Narratives in popular culture, media, and everyday life.* Thousand Oaks, CA: Sage.

Berger, A. A. (2004). *Games and activities for media, communication, and cultural studies students.* Lanham, MD: Rowman & Littlefield.

Berger, A. A. (2011a). The branded self. *American Sociologist, 42*(2–3), 232–237.

Berger, A. A. (2011b). *Media and communication research methods: An introduction to qualitative and quantitative approaches* (2nd ed.). Thousand Oaks, CA: Sage.

Berger, A. A. (2012). *Culture codes.* Mill Valley, CA: Marin Arts Press.

Berger, A. A. (2013). *Media, myth, and society.* New York: Palgrave Macmillan.

Berger, J. (1972). *Ways of seeing.* London: British Broadcasting Corporation.

Bernstein, B. (1977). *Class, codes and control.* London: Routledge & Kegan Paul.

Bettelheim, B. (1977). *The uses of enchantment: The meaning and importance of fairy tales.* New York: Vintage.

Biderman, D. (2010, January 15). 11 minutes of action. *Wall Street Journal.*

Bilton, N. (2009, December 10). The American diet: 34 gigabytes a day. *New York Times,* p. B6. Retrieved from http://bits.blogs.nytimes.com/2009/12/09/the-american- diet-34-gigabytes-a-day

Bolter, J. D., & Grusin, R. (2000). *Remediation: Understanding new media.* Cambridge: MIT Press.

Bourdieu, P. (1993). *Sociology in question.* London: Sage.

Brenner, C. (1974). *An elementary textbook of psychoanalysis.* Garden City, NY: Doubleday.

Brooker, P. (1999). *Cultural theory: A glossary.* London: Arnold.

Butler, J. (1990). *Gender trouble: Feminism and the subversion of identity.* New York: Routledge.

Caron, A. H., & Caronia, L. (2007). *Moving cultures: Mobile communication in everyday life.* Montreal: McGill–Queen's University Press.

Cashmore, E., & Rojek, C. (Eds.). (1999). *Dictionary of cultural theorists.* New York: Oxford University Press.

Caudwell, C. (1971). *Studies and further studies in a dying culture.* New York: Monthly Review Press.

Christie, A. (1940). *Murder on the Orient Express.* New York: Pocket Books.

CNBC. (2013). *Factbox: A look at the $66 billion video-games industry.* Retrieved from www.cnbc.com/id/100803611

Coser, L. A. (1971). *Masters of sociological thought: Ideas in historical and social context.* New York: Harcourt Brace Jovanovich.

Csikszentmihalyi, M. (1990). *Flow: The psychology of optimal experience.* New York: Harper & Row.

Culler, J. (1976). *Structuralist poetics: Structuralism, linguistics and the study of literature.* Ithaca, NY: Cornell University Press.

Culler, J. (1986). *Ferdinand de Saussure* (Rev. ed.). Ithaca, NY: Cornell University Press.

Danesi, M. (2002). *Understanding media semiotics.* London: Arnold.

Dichter, E. (1960). *The strategy of desire.* London: Boardman.

Dichter, E. (1964). *Handbook of consumer motivations: The psychology of the world of objects.* New York: McGraw-Hill.

Douglas, M. (1997). In defence of shopping. In P. Falk & C. Campbell (Eds.), *The shopping experience* (pp. 15–30). London: Sage.

Durham, M. G., & Kellner, D. M. (Eds.). (2001). *Media and cultural studies: Key works.* Malden, MA: Blackwell.

Durkheim, É. (1965). *The elementary forms of the religious life* (J. W. Swain, Trans.). New York: Free Press. (Original work published 1915)

Eco, U. (1972, Autumn). Towards a semiotic inquiry into the television message. *Working Papers in Cultural Studies, 3,* 103–121.

Eco, U. (1976). *A theory of semiotics.* Bloomington: Indiana University Press.

Eidelberg, L. (1968). *The encyclopedia of psychoanalysis.* New York: Macmillan.

Ekman, P., & Sejnowski, T. J. (1992). *Executive summary to final report to NSF of the planning workshop on facial expression understanding.* Retrieved from http://face-and-emotion.com/dataface/nsfrept/exec_summary.html

Eliade, M. (1961). *The sacred and the profane: The nature of religion* (W. R. Trask, Trans.). New York: Harper & Row. (Original work published 1957)

Engels, F. (1972). Socialism: Utopian and scientific. In R. C. Tucker (Ed.), *The Marx-Engels reader.* New York: W. W. Norton.

Entertainment Software Association. (2013). *Industry facts.* Retrieved from www.theesa.com/facts/index.asp

Enzenberger, H. M. (1974). *The consciousness industry: On literature, politics and the media.* New York: Seabury.

Erikson, E. H. (1963). *Childhood and society* (2nd ed., Revised and enlarged). New York: W. W. Norton.

Erikson, E. H. (1968). *Identity, youth, and crisis.* New York: W. W. Norton.

European Graduate School. (n.d.). *Jean Baudrillard—Simulacra and simulations—I. The precession of simulacra.* Retrieved from www.egs.edu/faculty/jean-baudrillard/articles/simulacra-and-simulations-i-the-precession-of-simulacra

Farb, P. (1974). *Word play: What happens when people talk.* New York: Vintage.

Freud, S. (1960). *Jokes and their relation to the unconscious.* New York: W. W. Norton.

Freud, S. (1962). *Civilization and its discontents.* New York: W. W. Norton.

Freud, S. (1963). *Character and culture* (P. Rieff, Ed.). New York: Collier.

Freud, S. (1965). *The interpretation of dreams* (J. Strachey, Trans.). New York: Avon. (Original work published 1900)

Friedson, E. (1953). Communication research and the concept of the mass. *American Sociological Review, 18*(3), 313–314.

Frith, S. (1981). *Sound effects: Youth, leisure, and the politics of rock 'n' roll.* New York: Pantheon.

Fromm, E. (1957). *The forgotten language: An introduction to the understanding of dreams, fairy tales and myths.* New York: Grove.

Fromm, E. (1962). *Beyond the chains of illusion: My encounter with Marx and Freud.* New York: Simon & Schuster.

Gans, H. (1974). *Popular culture and high culture: An analysis and evaluation of taste.* New York: Basic Books.

Gitlin, T. (1989, July–August). Postmodernism defined, at last! *Utne Reader,* 52–58, 61.

Glasgow University Media Group. (1980). *More bad news.* London: Routledge Kegan Paul.

Grotjahn, M. (1966). *Beyond laughter: Humor and the subconscious.* New York: McGraw-Hill.

Grotjahn, M. (1971). *The voice of the symbol.* New York: Delta Books.

Hall, S. (1997). Introduction. In S. Hall (Ed.), *Representation: Cultural representations and signifying practices.* London: Sage.

Haug, W. F. (1986). *Critique of commodity aesthetics: Appearance, sexuality, and advertising in capitalist society.* Minneapolis: University of Minnesota Press.

Haug, W. F. (1987). *Commodity aesthetics, ideology, and culture.* New York: International General.

Henderson, J. L. (1964). Ancient myths and modern man. In C. G. Jung with M.-L. von Franz, J. L. Henderson, J. Jacobi, & A. Jaffé, *Man and his symbols* (pp. 104–157). Garden City, NY: Doubleday.

Hinsie, L. E., & Campbell, R. J. (1970). *Psychiatric dictionary.* New York: Oxford University Press.

Hollitscher, W. (2002). *Sigmund Freud: An introduction.* New York: Routledge.

hooks, b. (1992). *Black looks: Race and representation.* Boston: South End.

Jakobson, R. (1988). Linguistics and poetics. In D. Lodge (Ed.), *Modern criticism and theory: A reader* (pp. 32–57). New York: Longman.

Jameson, F. (1991). *Postmodernism; or, The cultural logic of late capitalism.* Durham, NC: Duke University Press.

Jones, E. (1949). *Hamlet and Oedipus.* New York: W. W. Norton.

Jung, C. G. (1964). Approaching the unconscious. In C. G. Jung with M.-L. von Franz, J. L. Henderson, J. Jacobi, & A. Jaffé, *Man and his symbols* (pp. 18–103). Garden City, NY: Doubleday.

Kaiser Family Foundation. (2010, January). *Generation M2: Media in the lives of 8-to 18-year-olds.* Retrieved from www.kff.org.entmedia/upload/8010.e-pdf

Katz, E., Blumler, J. G., & Gurevitch, M. (1979). Utilization of mass communication by the individual. In G. Gumpert & R. Cathcart (Eds.), *Inter/media.* New York: Oxford University Press.

Kellner, Douglas. (1995). *Media culture: Cultural studies, identity, and politics between the modern and the postmodern.* London: Routledge.

Kline, S., Dyer-Witheford, N., & De Peuter, G. (2003). *Digital play: The interaction of technology, culture, and marketing.* Montreal: McGill–Queen's University Press.

Kubey, R. W. (1996). Television dependence, diagnosis, and prevention: With commentary on video games, pornography, and media education. In T. M. MacBeth (Ed.), *Tuning in to young viewers: Social science perspectives on television* (pp. 221–259). Thousand Oaks, CA: Sage.

Lacan, J. (1966). *Écrits: A selection* (A. Sheridan, Trans.). New York: W. W. Norton.

Lakoff, G., & Johnson, M. (1980). *Metaphors we live by.* Chicago: University of Chicago Press.

Lazere, D. (1977). Mass culture, political consciousness, and English studies. *College English, 38,* 751–767.

Lefebvre, H. (1984). *Everyday life in the modern world.* New Brunswick, NJ: Transaction. (Original work published 1968)

Lesser, S. O. (1957). *Fiction and the unconscious.* Boston: Beacon.

Lévi-Strauss, C. (1967). *Structural anthropology.* Garden City, NY: Doubleday.

Lotman, J. M. (1977). *The structure of the artistic text* (G. Lenhoff & R. Vroon, Trans.). Ann Arbor: Michigan Slavic Contributions.

Lowenthal, L. (1944). Biographies in popular magazines. In P. F. Lazarsfeld & F. Stanton (Eds.), *Radio research 1942–43.* New York: Duell, Sloan & Pearce.

Lutens, S. (n.d.). *Q&A with Serge Lutens: Around the launch of Jeux de Peau.* Retrieved from www.mimifroufrou.com/scentedsalamander/perfume_q_a

Lyotard, J.-F. (1984). *The postmodern condition: A report on knowledge* (G. Bennington & B. Massumi, Trans.). Minneapolis: University of Minnesota Press.

Mandell, A. J. (1974, October). A psychiatric study of professional football. *Saturday Review/World,* 12–16.

Mannheim, K. (1936). *Ideology and utopia: An introduction to the sociology of knowledge* (L. Wirth & E. Shils, Trans.) New York: Harcourt Brace.

Market Watch. (2013). 10 best selling video games in 2012. *Wall Street Journal.* Retrieved from www.marketwatch.com/story/10-best-selling-videogames-in-2012-2013-01-10

Marx, K. (1964). *Selected writings in sociology and social philosophy* (T. B. Bottomore & M. Rubel, Eds.; T. B. Bottomore, Trans.). New York: McGraw-Hill.

McLuhan, M. (1967). *The mechanical bride: Folklore of industrial man.* Boston: Beacon. (Original work published 1951)

McQuail, D., & Windahl, S. (1993). *Communication models for the study of mass communication* (2nd ed.). New York: Longman.

Messaris, P. (1994). *Visual literacy: Image, mind, and reality.* Boulder, CO: Westview.

Miller, V. (2008). New media, networking, and phatic culture. *Convergence: The International Journal of Research Into New Media, 14,* 387.

Mitchell, S. A., & Black, M. J. (1996). *Freud and beyond: A history of modern psychoanalytic thought.* New York: Basic Books.

Monaco, J. (1977). *How to read a film.* New York: Oxford University Press.

Murray, J. (1997). *Hamlet on the holodeck: The future of narrative in cyberspace.* Cambridge: MIT Press.

Musil, R. (1965). *The man without qualities* (E. Wilkins & E. Kaiser, Trans.). New York: Capricorn Books.

Mysterynet.com. (n.d.). *The adventure of the blue carbuncle.* Retrieved from www.mysterynet.com/Christmas/classics/blue/blue02.shtml

NPR Books. (2012). *In constant digital contact, we feel "alone together."* Retrieved from www.npr.org/2012/10/18/163098594/in-constant-digital-contact-we-feel-alone-together

Official Nintendo Magazine. (2007, June 7). *Mortal Kombat: Ed Boon interview.* Retrieved from collider.com/ed-boon-interview-mortal-kombat

O'Sullivan, T., Hartley, J., Saunders, D., Montgomery, M., & Fiske, J. (1994). *Key concepts in communication and cultural studies* (2nd ed.). London: Routledge.

Patai, R. (1972). *Myth and modern man.* Englewood Cliffs, NJ: Prentice-Hall.

Pines, M. (1982, October 13). How they know what you really mean. *San Francisco Chronicle.*

Podcaster. (2010). *Impact of Internet on radio audiences—latest US research.* Retrieved from www.adrianjmoss.com/?p=151

Propp, V. (1968). *Morphology of the folktale.* Austin: University of Texas Press. (Original work published 1928)

Provenzo, E. F., Jr. (1997). Video games and the emergence of interactive media. In S. R. Steinberg & J. L. Kincheloe (Eds.), *Kinder-culture: The corporate construction of childhood* (pp. 103–113). Boulder, CO: Westview.

Radway, J. A. (1991). *Reading the romance: Women, patriarchy, and popular literature.* Chapel Hill: University of North Carolina Press.

Rapaille, C. (2006). *The culture code: An ingenious way to understand why people around the world buy and live as they do.* New York: Broadway Books.

Real, M. R. (1977). *Mass-mediated culture.* Englewood Cliffs, NJ: Prentice Hall.

Rheingold, H. (2002). *Smart mobs: The next social revolution.* Cambridge, MA: Perseus.

Rieff, P. (Ed.). (1963). *Freud: Character and culture.* New York: Collier Books.

Rossi, W. A. (1976). *The sex life of the foot and shoe.* New York: Saturday Review Press/E. P. Dutton & Co.

Saussure, F. de. (1966). *A course in general linguistics* (W. Baskin, Trans.). New York: McGraw-Hill. (Original work published 1915)

Sebeok, T. A. (Ed.). (1977). *A perfusion of signs.* Bloomington: Indiana University Press.

Signorielli, N., & Gerbner, G. (1988). Introduction. In N. Signorielli & G. Gerbner (Comps.), *Violence and terror in the mass media: An annotated bibliography.* Westport, CT: Greenwood.

Thompson, M., Ellis, R., & Wildavsky, A. (1990). *Cultural theory.* Boulder, CO: Westview.

von Franz, M.-L. (1964). The process of individuation. In C. G. Jung with M.-L. von Franz, J. L. Henderson, J. Jacobi, & A. Jaffé, *Man and his symbols* (pp. 158–229). Garden City, NY: Doubleday.

Walker, R. (2008). *Buying in: What we buy and who we are.* New York: Random House.

Warner, W. L. (1953). *American life: Dream and reality.* Chicago: University of Chicago Press.

Wawro, A. (2010, January 14). *NPD reports poor 2009 software sales despite record-setting holiday.* Retrieved from www.gamepro.com/article/news/213596/npd-reports-poor-2009-software-sales-despite-record-setting-holiday/

Weir, W. (2013, February 25). Experts disagree on how violent video games affect children. *The Hartford Courant.*

Wildavsky, A. (1982). *Conditions for a pluralist democracy, or cultural pluralism means more than one political culture in a country.* Unpublished manuscript.

Wildavsky, A. (1989). Choosing preferences by constructing institutions: A cultural theory of preference formation. In A. A. Berger (Ed.), *Political culture and public opinion* (pp. 21–46). New Brunswick, NJ: Transaction.

Williams, R. (1977). *Marxism and literature.* Oxford, UK: Oxford University Press.

Zeman, J. J. (1977). Peirce's theory of signs. In T. A. Sebeok (Ed.), *A perfusion of signs.* Bloomington: Indiana University Press.

Author Index

Subject Index

About the Author

Arthur Asa Berger is professor emeritus of broadcast and electronic communication arts at San Francisco State University, where he taught from 1965 to 2003. He graduated in 1954 from the University of Massachusetts, where he majored in literature and philosophy. He received an MA in journalism and creative writing from the University of Iowa in 1956. He was drafted shortly after he graduated from the University of Iowa and served in the U.S. Army in the military district of Washington in Washington, D.C., where he was a feature writer and speechwriter in the district's Public Information Office. He also covered high school sports for the *Washington Post* on weekend evenings.

After he got out of the army, he spent a year touring Europe before undertaking graduate work at the University of Minnesota, where he received a PhD in American studies in 1965. He wrote his dissertation on the comic strip *Li'l Abner*. In 1963–1964, he was a Fulbright scholar and taught at the University of Milan in Italy. He also spent a year as visiting professor at the Annenberg School for Communication at the University of Southern California in Los Angeles in 1984.

Dr. Berger has authored more than 100 articles and countless book reviews in publications such as the *Journal of Communication*, *Society*, *Rolling Stone*, *Semiotica*, the *San Francisco Chronicle*, and the *Los Angeles Times* and has written more than 60 books on media, popular culture, humor, and tourism. Among his books are *Media and Communication Research Methods* (Sage), *What Objects Mean* (Left Coast Press), *Bloom's Morning* (Westview Press), *An Anatomy of Humor* (Transaction), *Ads, Fads, and Consumer Culture* (Rowman & Littlefield), and *Shop 'Til You Drop* (Rowman & Littlefield). He has also written a number of darkly comic academic murder mysteries: *Postmortem for a Postmodernist*, *The Mass Comm Murders: Five Media Theorists Self-Destruct*, *Durkheim Is Dead: Sherlock Holmes Is Introduced to Social Theory*, and *Mistake in Identity: A Cultural Studies Murder Mystery*. His books have been translated into eight languages, and he has lectured in more than a dozen countries over the course of his career. Thirteen of his books have been translated into Chinese.

Dr. Berger is married and has two children and four grandchildren. He lives in Mill Valley, California, and enjoys travel and dining in ethnic restaurants. He can be reached by e-mail at either arthurasaberger@gmail.com or arthurasaberger@yahoo.com.